al Readers

The Communist States
at the Crossroads

The Communist States at the Crossroads

Between Moscow and Peking

Edited by
ADAM BROMKE

With an Introduction by
PHILIP E. MOSELY

FREDERICK A. PRAEGER, *Publishers*
New York • Washington • London

FREDERICK A. PRAEGER, *Publishers*
111 Fourth Avenue, New York 3, N.Y., U.S.A.
77-79 Charlotte Street, London W.1, England

Published in the United States of America in 1965
by Frederick A. Praeger, Inc., Publishers

© 1965 by Frederick A. Praeger, Inc.
Library of Congress Catalog Card Number: 65-12191

This book is Number 154 in the series of
Praeger Publications in Russian History and World Communism

Printed in the United States of America

Preface

THIS VOLUME stems from a series of public lectures given in January–March, 1964, at the invitation of the Department of Political Science, Carleton University, in Ottawa. Eight of the chapters originated as lectures delivered in the series; these, however, have been substantially revised for purposes of publication in book form. The remaining papers were solicited especially for the volume, to round out our coverage of the subject.

The basic theme of the volume is the impact of the Sino-Soviet schism upon the Communist world and the resulting spread of "polycentrism." The period covered is the early 1960's—essentially from the public outbreak of the Sino-Soviet dispute in the spring of 1960 until what seemed to be an irreparable split in the Communist ranks in the spring of 1964 and the overthrow of Nikita Khrushchev in October, 1964. Whenever necessary, however, the relevant historical material is included. Also, special effort is made to analyze the significance of the events under discussion for future developments in the different Communist states.

My task would not be complete if I did not take the opportunity here to acknowledge the assistance in carrying out this project extended to me by many people at Carleton. I am particularly grateful to President A. D. Dunton, Dean D. M. L. Farr, Professors J. A. Porter, D. C. Rowat, R. A. MacKay, W. I. Illman, M. S. Hornyansky, Miss H. Gifford, and Miss A. Baird—all of whom in one way or another contributed to the completion of the undertaking. I also appreciate greatly the encouragement offered by the Department of External Affairs. Professor J. W. Strong and Mr. P. E. Uren assisted me in editing the various chapters; Mrs. D. Ryan and Mrs. D. Wright, of the office of the Department of Political Science, typed the manuscripts and otherwise assisted in collecting the materials for the present volume.

Finally, I am indebted to Mr. L. Barron of Frederick A. Praeger, Inc., whose expert editorial advice as well as enduring patience in updating the manuscript has been an invaluable asset.

A. B.

Contents

Preface   v

Introduction: Power and Ideology in the Communist
  States   3
    PHILIP E. MOSELY

1. Sino-Soviet Relations in Historical Perspective   21
    JOHN W. STRONG

2. The Sino-Soviet Split: A Reconstructed History,
   1956–64   43
    WILLIAM E. GRIFFITH

3. Poland   56
    M. K. DZIEWANOWSKI

4. Hungary   71
    FERENC A. VALI

5. Czechoslovakia   87
    H. GORDON SKILLING

6. Romania and Bulgaria   106
    J. F. BROWN

7. East Germany 126
   MELVIN CROAN

8. Outer Mongolia, North Korea, North Viet-Nam 140
   PAUL F. LANGER

9. Cuba 164
   C. IAN LUMSDEN

10. Yugoslavia 179
    MILORAD M. DRACHKOVITCH

11. Economic Relations Among the Communist States 199
    PHILIP E. UREN

12. The Communist States and the West 219
    ADAM BROMKE

Notes 241

Notes on the Contributors 261

Index 263

The Communist States
at the Crossroads

Introduction:
Power and Ideology in the
Communist States

PHILIP E. MOSELY

THE PUZZLEMENT with which people of the West, with their long attachment to liberal and individualist ways of thinking, view Soviet doctrine and action constantly gives rise to one central question, though it may be phrased in varying ways. One way this question can be put is: Are the leaders of Soviet Russia in fact pursuing an ideological goal? Or do they use ideological doctrines and slogans simply as an instrument to enhance their power at home and abroad? Another way of stating the quandary is to ask whether the Kremlin is more interested in spreading "world revolution" or in expanding the power and the writ of the Soviet state. Or, to state it in still another context, are the Soviet leaders nationalists who use inter-

3

nationalist doctrines and slogans to enhance the might of the Soviet state? Or are they basically internationalist doctrinaires who use the material and human resources of the peoples of the Soviet Union to promote the proclaimed world-wide goal of Communism?

The answers that students and practitioners of policy give to these questions, which are at bottom variants on a single question, often predetermine their predictions about future Communist actions and reactions. If a Soviet leader is basically acting as a nationalist, then he or his successors will presumably come some day to adopt the view that Russia in its Soviet form is merely one national state among many and that the international society of states will, into an indefinite future, embrace many different states with widely differing ideologies and goals. It would be logical, then, for the Soviet regime to abandon its claim to represent the sole valid system of the future and, instead of pursuing its messianic goal at varying levels of risk and tension, to seek to adjust its differences with other nations in a spirit of give-and-take or live-and-let-live. If, on the other hand, the answer given is that the ambitions and emotions of the Soviet leaders cannot be satisfied within the limits of a national or less than universal goal and that they will vary their tactics but not abandon their purpose, then the rest of the world must conclude that each period of limited cooperation or partial relaxation of tension will be followed sooner or later by a new straining of the revolutionary and expansionist will.

Since 1917, public opinion in the West has repeatedly searched eagerly for signs that the revolutionary volcano had burned itself out. When the New Economic Policy of the 1920's brought a partial restoration of capitalism in agriculture and retail trade and a more relaxed attitude toward scientific and literary activity, Western opinion was quick to assume that Russia, like the United States of Warren G. Harding, was returning to what the West regarded as "normalcy." In the 1930's, Stalin's call to "build socialism in one country" was widely interpreted as a renunciation of Communism's world-wide ambitions. In the years of the victorious alliance with Great Britain and the United States, many Western leaders became convinced that they could "do business with Stalin" in reaching a stable postwar settlement.

Today many commentators insist that Soviet policy in recent years—at least in the period that has followed the adventurous forward thrust of Soviet strategic power in the Cuban crisis of October, 1962—can follow only one path, that of reducing tensions, solving inherited conflicts, and eventually accepting the *status quo* of the world as it is today. To them, Soviet policy seems at last to have chosen the path of limited aims and limited risks, and for them it is only a question of time before the East-West conflict becomes as obsolete as the Wars of the Roses.

When the present-day champions of Marxism-Leninism look at the changes that have taken place since 1939 in the ideological geography of the globe, they find strong reassurance for their political and ideological arrogance. The Soviet Union emerged from the near-fatal trials of World War II with its territorial possessions greatly expanded in the West, though not in the South and East, and with an imposing array of dependent Communist regimes stretching beyond its western boundary. Shortly thereafter, a prolonged civil war brought all mainland China under Communist rule, flanked by Communist regimes in North Korea and North Viet-Nam. Communist parties have remained strong or become powerful in several major countries, including France and Italy, India and Indonesia. Clearly, in the classical Leninist fusion of "theory" and "practice," the fruits of practice have been rich. Whatever the political and doctrinal quarrels that now divide the various Communist leaderships, their spokesmen never tire of reminding their followers that "one-third of mankind now lives under socialism."

The theory of Marxism is in a much less satisfactory condition. The advanced industrial countries have simply not followed the path marked out for them by Karl Marx more than one hundred years ago. Instead of the inevitable concentration of wealth and grinding poverty at the poles of society, the advanced countries have seen the spread of middle-class standards of life to ever wider segments of their people. Instead of class warfare being the only driving wheel of history, class and group rivalries usually hinge on questions of "more of this" or "less of that." Instead of "the broad masses" rejecting the "bourgeois dictatorship," the institutions and practices of Western representative democracy are enjoyed and imitated more widely than ever in the past, and even the traditional slogans of "freedom" and "democracy" are usurped by those who deny or suppress them. And nationalism, which Marx denounced as a tool of the bourgeoisie in its exploitation of the workers, remains a powerful emotion within Communist countries and in quarrels among Communist states.

The fact that Communism was first victorious in Russia was not easy for Marxists to explain. Yet, for many reasons—the late survival of landlord-peasant antagonism, the uneven intrusion of capitalist enterprise, the inability or unwillingness of the bourgeoisie to complete the reshaping of Russian society and polity—Marxist ways of thought had a powerful impact on the militant wing of Russia's intelligentsia. And with the victory of Bolshevism, the revolutionary strain, which was gradually being drained out of the supposedly Marxist parties of Western Europe, was tremendously revived and concentrated in its Leninist version. Instead of waiting for proletarian revolution to come first in the older capitalist societies, Lenin called for the seizure of power in the "weakest link of imperialism," Russia. Instead of disdaining the revolutionary potential of the peasantry, he rallied the more discontented and land-hungry rural classes to his side. Instead of regarding the oppressed peoples of the colonies as a passive and negligible factor in the balance of political forces, Lenin sought actively to recruit them as allies of the new Soviet state.

To make history move in his way, Lenin stressed the central role of power, to be exercised by a disciplined and ideologically monolithic party, the self-appointed agent of world revolution. Finally, by denying that the Soviet revolution was a peculiarly Russian phenomenon and proclaiming it as only the first stage in a world-wide transformation, Lenin and his successors tapped a latent strain of Russian messianism. Russia, which had been the least advanced of major European nations, was suddenly endowed by Lenin with a universal mission, ordained by Marxist-Leninist ideology, of bringing salvation to mankind whether it liked the prospect or not.

The ideology and practice of present-day Communism have been strongly shaped by the fact that a Communist party came to power first in Russia. As the numerically and culturally preponderant national element in Soviet life, millions of Russians, whether active agents, resisters, or passive subjects, have helped shape the Soviet system in innumerable ways. Of course, no people is altogether uniform in its traditions, its psychological make-up, and its actions and reactions, and yet no political power and no ideological program can operate except through or on great masses of people.

There were many strands of Russian tradition, especially among the intelligentsia, that were not compatible with totalitarian dictatorship. The new rulers recognized this and undertook to form a new intelligentsia, loyal to the ruling party, and to destroy the influence of the small educated class it had inherited from the prewar period of intellectual variety and moral fervor. As the regime succeeded in this transformation, what was left by the early 1930's was a vast undifferentiated mass under the control of a highly centralized, secretive, and ruthless apparatus of rule.

Once the leaven of the prerevolutionary intelligentsia had been expelled from the body politic, the people generally reverted to simpler and older concepts of the nature of "authority" or "power" (*vlast'*). The age-old sense of living under a vast, arbitrary, and unknowable "power" returned in full force. The "little people" again studied the mysterious omens of "power" anxiously, hoping to divine its intentions toward them. They did not believe that they could influence that power, yet they felt a need for identifying it with a person. And so Stalin, in himself a most unlikely candidate for that role, had to become an all-powerful, all-seeing demigod, whose stern and sometimes cruel and arbitrary acts must somehow be accepted by the masses as a part of an incomprehensible but necessary design for achieving the highest good, not of men, but of *man*. Even today Soviet Communists explain how they "believed" in Stalin deeply and how hard it was for them to admit to themselves that the "all-wise teacher" had been less than wise. Russians have traditionally (that is, in the traditional, less Westernized way of thinking) hoped that "power" would act for their good, but they did not believe that they could control it except possibly by extravagant outpourings of loyalty and devotion which would then be rewarded by its benevolence.

In traditional Russian culture, "power," it is assumed, includes the power to decide everything, to determine what work people shall do, where they shall live, and what they shall think. And so Russians have often, in past and present, found it difficult to understand the cacophony of opinions in Western societies. If this paper or that radio or this commentator expresses an opinion contrary to that of the President of the United States, this must, they readily believe, be part of some subtle plot, for a real "power" would not tolerate dissent or divergence from the "truth" of which it is the guardian. Similarly, since the role of history, Communist-style, is to prove the rightness of the present policies of the ruler, it is both natural and indispensable to reweave the canvas of history almost continuously, for the edification of the people, to spur them to join in the battle of light against darkness. Mere historical facts are inevitably the first casualty of a starkly utilitarian view of the role of historiography, reduced to a morality play.

The feelings of impotence with which the individual awaits the next action by the "power" are reinforced by the secrecy with which the rulers prepare and carry out their decisions. Important laws and policies, even those favorable to the welfare of the ordinary subject, are often left unannounced and unpublished. One consequence, which often cuts across the immediate purposes of the leadership, is to place a premium on rumor as a means of guessing what "they" are going to do next.

Some of these same traditional Russian attitudes have greatly assisted the Soviet leaders in pursuing the goals of their ideology in their dealings with the outside world. Popular ignorance of what their own rulers may do next is easily translated into a similar distrust of the policies of other countries. This fear of the unknown outside world has naturally been reinforced by the painful memories of foreign invasions, which have made it easy to persuade the people that Soviet policy is purely defensive in purpose and that the only dangers that threaten their meager prosperity arise from the malevolence of ideologically alien systems. Thus the network of Western alliances and bases is widely viewed as an offensive threat of destruction, not as a reaction to Soviet conquests, pressures, and threats. With the logic of a nation of chess players, Russians easily regard a refusal to engage in trade or to recognize Communist China as proof of a carefully laid and threatening plot to destroy their homeland. Soviet policy at home and abroad is strongly influenced by this deep layer of suspicion; at the same time it profits by it at home to justify all its actions, no matter how offensive and threatening they may seem to people in the outside world.

Since Stalin's death many important changes have taken place in Soviet life, and nearly all of these must be welcomed. Substantial improvements have been effected in the supply of consumer goods, household appliances, and housing. The people now have much concrete evidence that the new leadership is genuinely interested in providing them with "goulash" and with many other good things that can be used and enjoyed. True, advance has not always been in a straight line. The supply of food remains monotonous, expensive, and sometimes, as in the winters of 1962 and 1963, irregular. Improvements in the quantity of consumer goods have not been matched by advances in variety, attractiveness, and quality. Yet the "long-suffering" Russian people, which has recently been both praised and blamed for this quality of patient endurance, has now granted a new extension of credibility to the benevolent purposes of their rulers.

It does not matter very much that many of the precise promises of an "American standard of living," as set forth in the Program of the CPSU of October, 1961, may never be carried out. People will measure what they have tomorrow by what they lacked yesterday. One of Khrushchev's great merits was to have recognized, unlike Stalin, that the Soviet system must come to terms with the revolution of rising expectations of its own people. Under Khrushchev, the Soviet leadership recognized that a great industrial country—the second biggest in the world—requires the willing services and the active initiatives of vastly enlarged numbers of managers and experts. In turn, this new intelligentsia, however well indoctrinated and patriotic it undoubtedly is, also needs the incentives of a more rewarding and varied standard of living if it is to help run a complex system more effectively and thus enable the country and the regime to reap the benefits of its lavish sacrifices and vast investment of effort. On the whole, despite a good deal of grumbling over shortages and poor quality of foodstuffs, consumer goods, and housing, the rapidly expanding middle class of managers, technicians, officials, and skilled workers believed firmly that the Khrushchev leadership really intended to devote a substantial share of the expanding national production to raising the standard of living, at least of the more skilled and more productive segments of the population.

A parallel, though more nebulous, change from compulsion to incentives is foreshadowed in the discussions, which have been widespread and continuous since the Party Congress of 1961, over the nature of the evolution of the "dictatorship of the proletariat" into an "all-people's state" of the future. What this involves basically is the gradual transfer of numerous welfare, educational, and other everyday functions from direct control by the state to management by "voluntary associations." Thus a beginning has been made in some cities, through a new kind of parent-teacher associations, in enlisting the active participation of fathers and mothers in improving the work and life of the schools. Similarly, city and town soviets are being urged to form groups of voluntary inspectors, often staffed from among the growing numbers of pensioners, to check on housing, sanitary, educational, marketing, and other services.

How far these efforts will succeed in improving the sluggish and indifferent bureaucratic apparatus remains unclear. But they are important psychologically in giving significant numbers of educated citizens a sense of participation in improving the way of life of the people. Thus, the proposed changes are designed to promote a partial "withering away" of the state apparatus. There is no indication, however, of any notion of the withering away of the all-po ful, all-directing role of the Communist Party. Apparently it is mainly expected to operate in a more flexible and direct manner through a variety of "citizens' organizations" rather than to rely solely on the rigid and formal controls of bureaucracy.

The post-Stalinist changes have been felt more deeply in the field of state security. Here improvement has been marked. The functions of investigation, prosecution, trial, and punishment, long gathered in the hands of the political police, have now been separated to a considerable extent into separate jurisdictions. Fear of arbitrary arrest and punishment has declined, though the regime retains and on occasion exercises wide powers of coercion against dissenters and critics who overstep the bounds laid down by it. In any case, the atmosphere of pervasive fear has been changed markedly, in contrast to the situation in Stalin's last years. Indeed, some officials and commentators publicly express regret and some uneasiness that people no longer seem afraid to circulate hostile rumors and critical jokes about the regime.

The Khrushchev adaptation has also brought with it a greater variety of themes and their more realistic treatment in Soviet literature and cinema. Much of this greater leeway—it is not "freedom" in the true sense of the word—serves the prestige and popularity of the new dispensation by stressing the cruelties of the period of the "cult of personality" and contrasting them to the more humane and rational methods of the Khrushchevian management of Soviet society. The decision to authorize the publication of Solzhenitsyn's *One Day in the Life of Ivan Denisovich,* and thus to acknowledge at last the grim realities of the widespread system of forced-labor camps, was fought over for several months within the *apparat* and was finally settled by Khrushchev's personal intervention.

The difficulties of the new-style leaders in drawing the line between what is advantageous to its policies and can therefore be licensed, and other actions and expressions that overstep those bounds, are illustrated by the ups and downs of Yevtushenko's relations with the top ranks of the Party. His bitter poem "Stalin's Heirs" received the supreme accolade of publication in *Pravda,* in October, 1962, and this was decided directly by Khrushchev. Only a few weeks later, Yevtushenko published his *Precocious Autobiography* in Paris without first submitting it to the customary review by Party authorities in Moscow. This breach of discipline was serious enough. But in addition, although this personal account of his life expressed a strong spirit of Soviet patriotism, it also asserted the right to exercise a personal and universally human right of moral judgment, in contrast to the Party's claimed monopoly to determine "the truth."

Khrushchev's reaction was doubtless fanned by Yevtushenko's literary rivals and by the fears of those who, having endured or welcomed the controls of the Stalinist period, saw an opportunity to justify their own criticisms and suspicions of the younger generation. In any case, Khrushchev's reaction was immediate and fierce. For a time, it seemed as if the Stalinist custom of "excluding" dissenters and critics from literature and "life" might be reinstated. In the end, however, Khrushchev settled for milder measures. Yevtushenko withdrew to his native town in Siberia for a period of "creative communication with the masses," and then resumed publication of his poems, albeit in a somewhat subdued mood.

Meanwhile the tug-of-war continues between those who want literature and the cinema to "speak" directly to the people and those who fear the regime will suffer from too outspoken and unvarnished presentations of Soviet life and its problems. On both sides of these controversies no challenge has been raised to the basic assumption that the Party has the right and the duty to regulate the arts and literature in its own judgment of what is best for the people. The question is how rigidly or how flexibly this right will be exercised.

All these changes, which can be highlighted only briefly here, are to be welcomed, for they are bringing new satisfactions and new energies to many segments of the Soviet people after several decades of extreme hardship and suffering. The question remains unanswered and presently unanswerable whether the domestic relaxation of strains within the Soviet system and of tensions between the regime and the people at large will proceed in a continuous line, leading inevitably into a happier future, or whether it will be broken from time to time by clashes between the desire of the people for a better and quieter life and the determination of the Communist leadership to enforce new transformations of Soviet life. Similarly, the question remains open whether the domestic evolution of the system will have a direct impact on the Kremlin's role in world politics.

In one respect, the gradual humanizing of the system at home is having an important if diffuse effect on the attitude of uncommitted countries toward the Soviet regime, for the steady if uneven improvement of the quality of Soviet life is bound gradually to strengthen the Soviet image among the leaders and intellectuals of developing countries. As they observe a fairly constant rise in the standard of living, a strengthening of the sense of personal security, and a broadening of the still narrow range of intellectual and literary expression, they will find it easier than in the past to overlook the continuing monopoly of power by the Party, and they will notice less and less the contrast between the attractive diversity of Western culture and the monotony of Soviet life. The Khrushchevian changes will, over time, make it easier to offer Soviet institutions and programs as a model to poor but ambitious countries. This impact will be the stronger if the Soviet leadership continues to provide support in Asia and Africa, not to Communist-oriented regimes alone, but even more to non-Communist and sometimes anti-Communist regimes, which it now calls "national democracies."

Any such subsidiary gain in Soviet influence abroad will be secondary, however, to the impact of the major instruments of Soviet policy: nuclear strength, political and economic support for developing nations, and the Communist model of political power.

Even if Soviet Russia should decide to devote more of its energies to improving the life of its people, it will still remain one of the two major nuclear powers. It will, as Khrushchev so often asserted, insist on having its say in any new conflicts anywhere in the world. It is easy to forget that the current limited *détente* in Soviet policy dates only from the Cuban missile crisis of October, 1962, and that there is no guarantee that the Kremlin will not make some new attempt, perhaps in the Arab world or Africa, to utilize the Soviet nuclear arsenal in order to effect a drastic change in the balance of power.

Between the demonstration of the first sputniks and intercontinental missiles in 1957 and the Cuban crisis of 1962, Khrushchev seemed to be seeking some way to "cash in" on his claimed strategic advantage. In the "agonizing reappraisal" that followed the first head-on nuclear confrontation, Khrushchev adopted a more sober view of the nature of the present strategic balance and a temporarily more realistic estimate of the American and Western political will. But does this represent a lasting change of heart?

The Kremlin's revised estimate of the balance of power has had important implications for its policy both within the Communist grouping of states and in the outside world. One of its first effects has been to deepen the conflict with Communist China and to strengthen the forces of division within an increasingly loose and pluralistic grouping of Communist states. The leadership in Communist China rejects the Kremlin's revised appraisal of the nuclear balance and insists that Khrushchev should have pressed the Cuban missile adventure to a showdown. By failing to do so, he had, Peking insists, become an "accomplice of the imperialists," a "backer of the *status quo*," and a "traitor to the cause of revolution."

Instead of drawing the reasonable conclusion that even the possession of a very large nuclear missile force is no guarantee of revolutionary expansion or even national survival, Peking redoubled the violence of its attacks on Khrushchev for his decision in 1959 not to proceed with the program, which he had agreed to in 1957, to back China's ambition to become a nuclear power in its own right. Thus, as so often, ideology and power are inextricably mingled, and the Kremlin's decision to maintain its nuclear monopoly within the Communist grouping of states has added fuel to the flames of its political rivalry with Peking.

The bitter clash over strategy and the use of force to "roll back imperialism" lends a sharper drama to the other conflicts, which are both ideological and political, between Moscow and Peking. Moscow ridicules Peking's "Great Leap Forward" of 1958 and taunts it for its attempt to go directly to "Communism" by sheer fiat and without first creating the indispensable "objective conditions." Peking attacked Khrushchev for allegedly fostering the "bourgeois degeneration" of the Soviet system. Moscow attacks Mao Tse-tung for attempting to exclude Russia from the circle of "Afro-Asian" peoples and for claiming the sole leadership of revolution among the developing countries. Peking accuses Moscow of seeking to restore a position of monopolistic control over all Communist regimes and parties. The confusion of power ambitions with ideological claims in this conflict makes clear the primacy of the power struggle over ideology.

The direct clash between the two major Communist powers has entailed far-reaching consequences for both. Khrushchev showed great sensitivity to the Chinese charges of Soviet hegemony, and after 1957 he repeatedly renounced the Stalinist insistence on the ideological sovereignty of the Kremlin over the forces of international Communism. At the same time, he made clear the Kremlin's hope of reasserting its primacy with the voluntary support of a majority of Communist parties, even at the cost of expelling Peking from the ranks of orthodoxy. In this ambition he was thwarted, at times, by the fears of weaker parties—for example, those of Poland and Italy—that a Moscow-organized international conference would in fact result in re-establishing that hegemony and would thereby narrow greatly their newly won freedom of maneuver at home and abroad.

The mounting tempo and fervor of the Sino-Soviet dispute have re-enforced the trend toward the assertion of varying degrees of autonomy among the East European satellites, a trend that has persisted and grown since the Polish and Hungarian experiences of October, 1956, persuaded Khrushchev that it was less risky to tolerate some recognition of "national paths" to socialism than to hold down the lid by Stalinist methods of domination. In this respect, again, ideological doctrines have been adjusted rather slowly to take account of new political realities.

Moscow's third and most recent reconciliation with the League of Yugoslav Communists, in defiance of Chinese Communist attacks on Tito's "revisionism" and "bourgeois degeneration," has similarly allowed Belgrade to broaden its ties and strengthen its influence in several of the satellites, notably in Romania. Unlike the first and abortive reconciliation of 1955, the new and more comprehensive *rapprochement* has brought with it the Kremlin's partial approval and tolerance for Yugoslavia's "separate path" to socialism. And, in turn, this new stance has emboldened some of the satellite leaders in their search for methods of rule designed to win broader support among their own people.

The re-emergence of a spirit of national autonomy within the satellites has brought to light striking variations in the situations of different parties. In Czechoslovakia the Party, which tried long and hard to ignore Moscow's summons to de-Stalinize its rule, has been timid about reducing the limits of its literary and intellectual controls. Its leaders are aware of the deep tradition of personal and political freedom among its people and fear its revival. On the other hand, in Slovakia the Communists, many of whom fought hard in 1943 and 1944 for the liberation of their country from Nazi rule, have been bolder than their Party comrades in the Czech lands, where the Party received power as a "gift" from the Red Army.

In Poland, where Gomulka has been concerned at the upsurge of pro-Western intellectual and artistic sympathies since 1956, the Party's controls have been markedly tightened in recent years. The Romanian Party, long considered abjectly subservient to Moscow's whims, has been pressing its own economic ambitions, in defiance of Soviet and CEMA (or COMECON) admonitions to put the interests of the bloc ahead of national development programs. It has also actively expanded its economic ties with the West and with China and has pursued a policy of cautious re-westernization in its cultural life.

In Hungary, the Kadar regime, though it remains for many a symbol of submission to Moscow's hegemony, has striven to remove many grievances through promoting better economic conditions and permitting increased personal and intellectual contacts with the West. Only East Germany has remained stridently Stalinist in its rule. Ulbricht is well aware that, so long as his regime exists side by side with the economic and intellectual vigor of West Germany and West Berlin, any attempt to follow the Polish or even the Hungarian pattern would be fatal to its survival.

The growing divergences within Stalin's formerly silent satrapies in Eastern Europe do not constitute a political challenge to the Kremlin's policies. But they do underline the new political necessity for Moscow to accept a poorly defined and fuzzy range of ideological variation instead of the old clear-cut dogmas. And they provide daily illustrations of the Kremlin's inability to lay down any single pattern of Communist doctrine except in broad and loose terms.

So far, the leadership of the Communist Party of the Soviet Union has come to terms more or less awkwardly with the political polycentrism that has been spreading even within the pro-Moscow majority of foreign Communist regimes and parties. It has not yet succeeded, however, in working out a doctrinal justification of ideological polycentrism, and it is probably extremely reluctant to do so. In this instance again, Communist ideology limps far behind political practice.

The Stalinist pattern was simple and clear-cut, even primitive. Its driving force was the monopoly of the Party—in practice, of an omnipotent and omniscient leader—both in deciding all matters of policy and in defining a sacrosanct standard of ideology. The Kremlin pressed its demands outward, as with a single will, on its own people and, so far as possible, on all other Communist regimes and parties. At times its policies were confused and often they were counterproductive, but under Stalin's rule the existence of a single center of political will and ideological orthodoxy was not in doubt.

The Stalinist straining of national will and endurance was too great to be pressed forever. It created and concealed vast areas of fear, apathy, evasion, and inefficiency. The Khrushchevian response to the changing needs of the Soviet system at home centered on the attempt to enlist the active participation of the by now more abundant intellectual and managerial resources in order to build a more efficient and more satisfying pattern. To do this, Khrushchev broadened substantially the bounds of permitted initiative and criticism. He sought in a groping way to re-establish two-way com-

munication between the rulers and the upper and middle ranks of
the Soviet people, whose cooperation he needed in moving the
Soviet system forward to the stage of "Communism."

Khrushchev knew his people well, and he believed that the
nearly two generations of Communist shaping of men's minds and
habits made it possible to reach a consensus of purpose between
the ruling Party and the ruled on a new basis. To make the consensus work, Khrushchev insisted, however, there can be no non-
sense about the "coexistence of ideologies," no slackening of the
ideological dogmatism to which the "activists" of Soviet society have
been trained to respond like Pavlov's dogs. He insisted that Communist leadership must continue in perpetuity to shape the thinking
and the responses of Soviet society through an active and monopolistic molding of men's minds.

Whether the peculiarly Khrushchevian blending of greater flexibility in practical policy with unyielding rigidity in dogma will
actually shape the future of Soviet society remains unanswerable at
this time. In calling to his assistance a genuine if limited spirit of
initiative and criticism, Khrushchev may have released a powerful
genie from its Stalinist bottle. Can the limits of freedom to think
remain forever confined to the narrow bounds that Khrushchev had
set for his own convenience? Perhaps they can, at least until another
generation or two have matured and taken over the responsibility
for charting the course of Soviet development.

A number of factors in Soviet thinking help make the Khrushchevian blend a workable one for today. For one thing, several
generations of Soviet activists have been rigorously drilled in the
spirit and assumptions of Marxism-Leninism. The Soviet regime
has been in power for over forty-five years, and that means that all
people under the age of sixty have lived their adult lives primarily
under the pressure of an all-intruding, all-shaping set of dogmas.
The results are evident in the high degree of uniformity that per-
vades discussions with most Soviet people.

The methods by which the Party selects the more intelligent and
promising elements of each new generation for promotion to greater
opportunities and responsibilities are designed to make sure, at each
stage of advancement, that they are fully indoctrinated in and loyal
to the purposes of the leaders. True, criticisms, rumors, snide jokes,
and forbidden information have some role in daily life, but this is a
politically unimportant factor. The pursuit of a moderately successful and rewarding career demands of each Soviet activist both
technical efficiency in performance and unquestioned loyalty to the

Party and its purposes. The Party's supervision of staffing and promotion in all parts of the system—industry, secret police, armed forces, education, and the Party machine itself—is designed to assure a maximum of ideological conformity. On the whole, it succeeds in this very well. In Soviet lives the path of dissent leads downward, if no longer to physical oblivion, at least to insignificant status and low rewards.

A second factor operating to stabilize the new system of rule is the growing Soviet optimism about the future achievements of the system and the improved prospects for a relatively high level of well-being. Soviet people are deeply impressed also by the "firsts" of Soviet science and technology, by sputniks and missiles, by astronauts and outsize nuclear warheads. They are impressed by the active policies Khrushchev launched in several continents, even if some people are unhappy over the diversion of scarce Soviet resources to the benefit of distant countries such as India and Indonesia, Egypt and Cuba. Even the grumblers recognized, however, the contrast between a dour Stalin immured within the Kremlin and an ebullient Khrushchev receiving triumphal welcomes in far-flung countries they would never see.

Few Soviet citizens give any thought to the potential risks with which the Kremlin's world-wide activist policy is fraught. Mostly they respond to each demonstration of Soviet might and prestige with a surge of pride and even chauvinism. This factor is reinforced by the Kremlin's constant reassurances that Russia, which has suffered so much in past wars, is now so strong that it can defy the might of the world's most powerful country and can, as it reminds the people frequently, "guarantee the maintenance of peace." The spread of a modest abundance at home, combined with unprecedented military and political prestige in the outer world, is a powerful stimulant of patriotic fervor, optimism, and loyalty.

In Soviet society, ordinary people believe that Khrushchev intended and expected to enlarge the Soviet role in world affairs while managing at the same time to avoid actual war. This popular confidence in his shrewdness was, it is true, somewhat less than complete after October, 1962, when many Soviet people came to understand the adventurous and risk-laden character of his Cuban missile gambit. On the other hand, by the time the basic facts had become clear even to better informed people accustomed to reading between the lines of the Soviet press, the crisis was already over. Thus, whatever residual misgivings the Kremlin's attempt to project its strategic power into the Western Hemisphere may have engendered in retrospect, they were largely offset by a feeling of profound relief on realizing that Khrushchev had chosen to withdraw from an overexposed salient rather than face a nuclear war. Few people in Soviet society would even have raised in their own minds the cutting question: If withdrawing the Soviet missiles from Cuba was such a great "contribution to peaceful coexistence," then how much of a contribution had it been to put them there in the first place?

The *détente* that has followed the near-spasm of October, 1962, has, unfortunately, been a superficial one. No progress has been made in resolving any basic issues, such as Cuba, Berlin, national self-determination in Eastern Europe, or effective and inspected measures of arms control. Yet even the partial steps toward relaxation, adopted since the crisis, have been useful if they do even a little to persuade the Soviet leaders that genuine and prolonged coexistence on the basis of the *status quo* is a useful and desirable policy for them as much as for the West. In the ever-present menace of nuclear war, a prolonged period of lessened tension and freer communication may make it somewhat more difficult for the Kremlin, at the next zig or zag of its policy, to mobilize the fears and suspicions of its people in support of new adventures.

The Kremlin draws a sharp line between "peaceful coexistence" of different economic and social systems, which it advocates unflaggingly, and "coexistence of ideologies," which it abjures as a mortal sin for any Marxist-Leninist. It is hard to understand how any historically minded person, Marxist or not, can arbitrarily draw a sharp line between a society's institutions and policies and the ideological framework and moral values that shape that society's being and actions. What the Kremlin really means, as a practical matter, is that it wants the rest of the world to accept at face value its claim to practice a policy of live-and-let-live with alien and hostile systems. But at the same time, in order to take advantage of spontaneous and created opportunities to expand the Communist system, it wants to protect the minds and feelings of its subjects at home and its followers abroad from any infection by non-Communist ideas and values, so as to keep their wills and ranks steeled to new advances toward the messianic and world-wide goals of Communism.

Can the successors of Khrushchev maintain indefinitely this imaginary barrier between theory and action, between policy and

ideology? Or will prolonged coexistence, even in an uneasy stalemate, eventually erode the Communist will to universal dominion?

For Khrushchev the decision was an easy one. He was the ruler of
an "ideocracy." He and his Party governed by virtue of their claim
to possess, interpret, and apply the sole "correct" view of history,
past and future. If he relaxed or renounced that claim, how would he
be able to legitimize his absolute power? To have admitted the possibility of the indefinite coexistence of competing ideologies in the
same world with Communism would have undermined his right to
rule the Soviet Union and his claim to "guide" all other Communist
regimes and parties to the predetermined goal. It was this arrogant
ideological stance that permitted Khrushchev, like Stalin before him,
to regard all other political systems as ill-begotten and temporary,
zombie-like obstacles to the triumph of the one true and everlasting
faith.

If the Leninist dogma should come to be viewed by Communists
as useful and probably true, but not absolutely inevitable and infallible, how could the Soviet rulers justify the mountains of suffering and the sledge hammer blows of force they have used to shape a
society according to the imperatives of that ideology? The idea of
relative truth and relative fallibility is too painful for Communists to
accept readily. If Soviet Communists accepted this idea, they would
be taking the first step toward transforming their present system
into a very different one, based on some new legitimation of its
authority.

In the minds of Communist leaders, power and ideology are inter-
related and interacting in many intimate and complex ways. Sometimes ideology far outruns the power base, as in the early years of
the Soviet regime; at other times theory lags behind practice, as in
the Kremlin's present difficulties in coming to terms with polycentrism. At all times, however, the Communist leadership has
drawn great political strength from its claim to possess the sole correct ideology of history. Today that claim is being diluted by contradictions and conflicts at home, by conflicts with other Communist
states, and by uncertainties regarding the safest and most profitable
policy to follow toward the non-Communist countries of the world.

Perhaps Communists will someday lose the arrogant certainty of
"knowing" the future. Perhaps the spread of pluralism, diversity,
and conflict among opposing views of Communist policy and dogma
will eventually weaken the drive to reshape the world and may thus
open the way to more stable relationships of ideological as well as

political coexistence. It would be rash, however, to assume that this evolution has already taken place in Soviet thinking; indeed, the Kremlin rejects indignantly the assumption that it can ever happen. Nevertheless, the course of history may well prove less predetermined, more open-ended, and less predictable by the dicta of dogma than either Stalin or Khrushchev could have imagined.

1. Sino-Soviet Relations in Historical Perspective

JOHN W. STRONG

THE DISAGREEMENT between China and the Soviet Union, which was made public in the early 1960's, has been given various names: polycentrism, Communist orthodoxy vs. Communist revisionism, the "new Cold War," Mao vs. Khrushchev, and so on. Regardless of its title, citizens of the West have reacted to the Sino-Soviet clash mainly with surprise and a smug feeling of satisfaction. To that mythical being, the "average man," the clash came as a totally unexpected development. Conditioned by the bipolar nature of the Cold War, he viewed the Communist world as a solid, monolithic political bloc. This view has suddenly been shattered, and because of the resulting surprise and shock, many people even today have been unable to adjust their thinking to the realities of Sino-Soviet relations. Consequently, they tend to regard the dispute as a minor family squabble at best, and at worst as a diabolic Communist plot to lull the West into a false sense of security and confidence.

The dispute also came as a surprise to students of Soviet and Chinese affairs. For them, the element of surprise was not that disagreements existed between the Russians and Chinese, but that these disagreements had been allowed to develop so rapidly and so bitterly. The real surprise lay in the timing of the conflict and the ugly vehemence with which the dispute was publicly aired by both sides. Even in the late 1950's, few experts would have predicted that the economically backward Chinese, beset by internal problems and dependent on the aid and good will of the Soviet Union, would, in the 1960's, break with their Russian comrades and challenge Moscow for the leadership of the world Communist movement. A prediction that could be made was that, owing to the historical relationship between the two countries, a Chinese-Soviet dispute would develop in time. It is the purpose of this chapter to explore the bases for such a prediction and to indicate why it would have been a reasonable assumption. This will be done by examining the Sino-Soviet dispute from the historical perspective of relations between the Communist Party of the Soviet Union and the Communist Party of China. Emphasis will be placed primarily on the political and power relations of the two Communist parties prior to 1956, leaving the more contemporary ideological factor in the dispute for other writers in this volume.

At first glance, the logical starting point for a history of Sino-Soviet relations would seem to be the Bolshevik Revolution of 1917. Immediately, however, doubts begin to creep in as to whether or not 1917 is really a suitable date from which to develop a clear perspective of the dispute. Finding the true beginning of any historical event is an agonizing problem which different people will solve in different ways. The People's Republic of China and the U.S.S.R. have many serious differences transcending their own existence as governments and even preceding the existence of Communism as an economic and political philosophy.

By stretching the historian's prerogative, one could claim that Sino-Soviet troubles originated in 1237–40, when the Mongol armies of Batu Khan overran the lands of Kievan Russia and began subjugating the Russian people to two hundred years of barbaric overlordship. For Russia, these were the "dark ages," characterized by stagnation and backwardness, while the rest of Europe was progressing from the Middle Ages to the reawakening of the Renaissance. Having been ruled for two centuries by Asian hordes left a deep scar on the Russian mind—a scar that has done nothing to increase Russian trust or friendship for the peoples of the Far East. It has even been said that the Soviet Union's firm control of

Outer Mongolia is Russia's final revenge against Genghis Khan's empire, as well as insurance that a "Tatar yoke" will never again be imposed on Russia.

More within the range of plausibility, one could say that Sino-Soviet problems really began in 1689, when Russia, under Peter the Great, signed its first agreement with the Chinese Empire. The Treaty of Nerchinsk was a diplomatic victory for China, in that it officially limited Russian imperial expansion in the areas of the Amur Valley and the maritime provinces of Siberia, where the interests of the two states had already collided. Understanding between the Russians and Chinese was already difficult at this time. Neither of the delegations at Nerchinsk could speak or read the other's language. Consequently, this first treaty between China and a European nation was negotiated and interpreted by a group of Jesuit fathers stationed at the court of the K'ang-hsi, Emperor in Peking, and the language of the treaty was Latin.[1]

By the nineteenth century, Russia's position vis-à-vis China had undergone a fundamental change. In the past, relations had taken place between a strong China and a relatively weak Russia. But Russia had now become a powerful Eurasian empire facing a backward China—a China torn by internal problems, foreign exploitation, and crumbling prestige. The Ch'ing (or Manchu) Dynasty was gradually losing its "mandate of heaven" to rule. The policies adopted by the Russian Government toward this weakening China in turn left a scar on the Chinese mind. The fact that China became a Communist nation in 1949 does not mean that the Chinese have automatically forgotten how Imperial Russia joined the Western powers to exploit the sagging fortunes of the Manchu Government. Russia always made certain that it got a fair share of the Chinese territory being divided by the other imperialist states.

In 1860, after British and French forces occupied Peking, burned the magnificent Summer Palace, and forced the Imperial Court to flee to Jehol, Russia's shrewd Far Eastern diplomat, Nicholas Ignat'ev, offered the "good offices" of Russia in mediating the differences between China and the European powers. The Peking Convention resulted in China's second round of major concessions to the West.[2] Ignat'ev's role as the "honest broker" did a great deal for Britain and France, but the Chinese could see little benefit for themselves. Then, for "services rendered," the Russian Government presented China with its bill—a Russian treaty, by the terms of which China had to give Russia the trans-Ussuri maritime lands and acknowledge Russia's possession of the Amur Valley. The

Treaty of Nerchinsk, in force for nearly 170 years, was negated. Russia's position in eastern Siberia was secure, and the nation's pride in its accomplishment can be judged by the name given to the great port city founded near the Manchurian-Korean border—Vladivostok, "power in the East."

In order to "suppress local revolts and pacify the region," Russian forces in 1878 occupied the Ili Valley deep in the heart of Chinese Turkestan. The Russians reluctantly agreed to withdraw from the region in 1881, but only after the Chinese Government had refused to accept this new loss of territory, threatened war, and agreed to pay Russia a million rubles for the privilege of regaining control of its own land. In spite of the indemnity payment, this was one of the rare occasions in the nineteenth century when China stood up to a European power and refused to concede to its demands.

The Chinese have not forgotten nineteenth-century relations with their aggressive neighbor to the north. Reminding the Kremlin of Russian imperialism in Central Asia, the Chinese have informed the Soviet Government that Russian forces never evacuated all of the Chinese territory they had occupied. Although these recent Chinese claims to ownership of most of Soviet Central Asia seem somewhat ludicrous, the situation becomes ominous when Soviet and Chinese troop movements and border clashes take place along the boundary between Sinkiang and the Kazakh s.s.r.[3]

China also remembers how Russia, guided by the expansionist policies of Czar Nicholas II, extended its political and financial influence into Manchuria and North China during the 1890's and early 1900's. Capitalizing on the Boxer Rebellion, Russia gained extensive railroad rights in Manchuria and annexed Port Arthur.

There is every indication that the humiliations inflicted by Russia on the proud but feeble Chinese Empire have not been forgotten. To the Chinese, imperialistic exploitation appears much the same whether it comes in the form of British traders, French missionaries, American gunboats, Czarist Russian diplomats, or Soviet Russian comrades; whether it masquerades under such terms as free trade, the Open Door policy, spheres of influence, or Communist solidarity.

Although Russian-Chinese relations prior to 1917 contained many points of friction, to find in them the direct causes of the present dispute is a problem of historical speculation. In the relations between the Soviet Union and China after 1917, however, one can certainly begin to trace the historic root causes of the current split. In view of the fragmentation of Chinese politics caused by the

Double Ten Revolution of 1911 and the aftermath of warlordism, the Soviet Government faced the problem of trying to find a Chinese political faction that would complement Soviet national interests in the Far East at the same time that it furthered the cause of Asian Communism.

For the first objective, the Kuomintang Party of Dr. Sun Yat-sen held promise. For the second, the Soviets naturally looked to the young Communist Party of China. For this reason, Sino-Soviet relations until the late 1940's were a sort of triangular affair between the U.S.S.R., the Nationalist Government, and the Communist Party of China. The favor of Soviet recognition and aid would go to that Chinese political group which best furthered the current Soviet policy. Throughout the Stalin era, the "national" interests of the U.S.S.R. dominated the interests of the international Communist movement. In China this meant a Soviet reliance on the Nationalist Government in preference to the CCP. Thus, the seeds of the present-day Sino-Soviet dispute are deeply planted in the history of the CCP itself, and in its historical position vis-à-vis the world in general and the CPSU in particular.

The Chinese Communist Party was formally established by a small group in Shanghai on July 1, 1921. Although Marxist study groups had been organized in 1918 and 1919, Marxism as a philosophy had made far less of an impact on Chinese intellectuals than did the exciting example of the Russian Revolution. Sun Yat-sen had even sent Lenin a congratulatory telegram on the occasion of the Bolshevik *coup d'état*. Lenin was quite pleased. Very few world figures were sending congratulations for his success.

Chinese respect for the new Russian Government was heightened in 1919 when the Council of People's Commissars issued the Karakhan Manifesto. This manifesto renounced all rights and interests gained by the Czarist Government at the expense of China's sovereignty and expressed Soviet sympathy for the oppressed Chinese people.[4] For the Chinese, this new Russian attitude was in pleasant contrast to that of other European and Western powers, who, at the Versailles Peace Conference, had sold out China's interests to appease the Japanese. The Karakhan Manifesto created good will in China, while the Versailles settlement sparked a widespread protest demonstration among students and intellectuals on May 4, 1919. The May Fourth Movement is often called the first real stirring of modern Chinese nationalism.

From 1921 to 1923, membership in the CCP grew, but the Party remained a very small organization. Although the Soviet leaders often repeated Lenin's remark that "the road to Paris lay through Peking and Delhi," they saw little chance for the immediate success of Communism in China. The Chinese Party was tiny and loosely organized. China itself was torn between the government of Peking, Sun Yat-sen's Kuomintang organization at Canton, and other provincial warlord governments. In Marxist terms, it would take some time before the Chinese developed a bourgeois state ripe for the proletarian revolution. Comintern and Soviet agents were sent to China to study the Chinese political puzzle and to advise the Soviet Government about which Chinese faction offered the best long-term possibilities for Soviet interests. Their choice went to the Kuomintang Party. The Comintern agents convinced the Chinese Communists at their Third Party Congress, in June, 1923, that the best hope for a Communist China lay in cooperation with the Kuomintang for the time being. The Communists were encouraged to join and work with the Kuomintang Party. Thus, the policy of the Soviet Government was to put its faith and support behind the Kuomintang, not behind the Chinese Communists. This remained the official Party line in Moscow from 1923 to 1927. It was an extremely difficult position for the Chinese Communists. On one hand, they were to retain their Communist faith and allegiance to the Party, while on the other, they had to cooperate with the bourgeois Kuomintang organization and attempt to gain positions of influence in it. Ideologically, they were forced to walk a most disagreeable tightrope.[5] Nevertheless, they had no choice. They were too weak to resist or defy the orders of Moscow. From the beginning, the Chinese Party found itself not the vanguard of Asian Communism but a pawn in Soviet national policy toward China and the Far East.

Overlooking the predominantly agricultural nature of the Chinese economy, the early leaders of the Chinese Communist Party retained an orthodox Marxism as their philosophy. As a party, the Communists concentrated their activities on winning the loyalty and support of the small proletarian class in such centers as Shanghai, Canton, and Wuhan. As individuals, they concentrated on gaining positions of influence in the Kuomintang organization. At first they ignored, and later officially disapproved of, the activities of Mao Tse-tung, who had begun organizing peasants in Hunan Province in 1925. Mao's approach was summed up in his report to the Central Committee in February, 1925: "This leadership by the poor peasants is very essential. Without the poor peasant, there will be no revolution. To reject them is to reject the revolution."[6] Although he was a founding member of the CCP, neither the Party nor Moscow approved of Mao's unorthodox faith in the Chinese peasantry as a force capable of bringing about a Communist revolution. In 1925, Mao could thus be viewed as a heretic with regard to official Communist policy in China.

By following the orthodox Marxist-Leninist line, the Chinese Communist Party ran into a dead end. By 1926, it was obvious that the Chinese proletariat was too small to be a moving force in society, and the Chinese workers were uninterested in Communism. Also by 1926, the Communists' policy of openly trying to gain influence in the Kuomintang had greatly irritated the right-wing elements of that party led by Chiang K'ai-shek, who had succeeded to Party leadership following the death of Sun Yat-sen in 1925. In Chiang, the Communists found a capable and determined opponent. He controlled the loyalty and support, not only of the right-wing elements in the Kuomintang, but also of the Kuomintang military force which he had helped to build with Russian aid and advice. After March, 1926, Chiang officially banned any Communist from holding a top position in the Kuomintang and began weeding Communists out of the Party. The Russians, who had earlier put faith in Chiang's friendship, were upset over these new developments, but could not do much about it. They did not want to compromise their own professed friendship for the Asian masses by too openly exerting an influence in China that might resemble old Czarist methods of power politics.

In July, 1926, Chiang K'ai-shek launched a northern military expedition designed to bring about a unification of China under Nationalist rule. In 1926–27, the CCP, which was already weakening vis-à-vis Chiang, found itself involved in the Stalin-Trotsky struggle for power—a struggle that had repercussions in all areas of Soviet foreign and domestic policies. The Trotskyites considered Stalin's China policy bankrupt. They advocated, in its place, independent action by the CCP, supported by the U.S.S.R., aiming toward a Chinese Communist revolution. This policy was in line with Trotsky's philosophy of "permanent revolution"—the belief that socialism could not survive in Russia alone and that consequently the U.S.S.R. must work incessantly for the success of world Communism.

Stalin's policy was diametrically opposed to Trotsky's, and was far more realistic concerning China. Stalin saw no immediate hope for a Communist victory in China because the CCP was weak and unreliable, and because the country itself was too backward for Communism to succeed. At the time, Stalin wanted a friendly Nationalist government that would act as a buffer in the Far East against the potential menace of Japanese expansionism. The Kuomintang-Communist alliance in China had to be maintained because it was in the best interests of the U.S.S.R. This approach to China fitted logically into Stalin's ideological doctrine of "socialism in one country." The world revolution was still a long way off; thus it was the duty of all Communists to subjugate their local ambitions to the protection of socialism in the U.S.S.R. Hopes of a Communist government in China were unrealistic. A Nationalist China was possible and was more adaptable to the immediate needs of the Soviet Union.

Although the Stalin-Trotsky struggle was important to developments in China, its importance should not be exaggerated. Whether Stalin was right or wrong in China had little influence on the outcome of his feud with Trotsky. For all practical purposes, by late 1926 the Trotskyites were beaten and Stalin's China policy remained the Party line in Moscow. Even if Trotsky's policy had prevailed, it is doubtful if the outcome would have been much different. Given conditions in China, Trotsky's idea of full support for the Chinese Communists probably would not have succeeded. Stalin's China policy was destined to fail in the end, but at least it was based on a more rational understanding of the Chinese political situation.

Meanwhile, the Kuomintang's northern expedition was proceeding triumphantly. The success of his military campaign against the Peking Government, along with his growing dislike of Chinese Communism, prompted Chiang K'ai-shek to bring an end to Communist influence and presence in the Kuomintang. As his armies approached Shanghai, the local bankers and merchants gave Chiang promises of financial support if in turn he would take measures to end the threat of Communist control in that port city. Chiang accepted the offer, and in the spring of 1927 destroyed the Shanghai labor organizations and the left-wing Kuomintang elements. The Chinese Communists in Shanghai were crushed and driven underground. Relations between them and Chiang were no longer in doubt: There was open civil war.

Chiang's actions in Shanghai split the Kuomintang. Supported by the Communists and by the Kuomintang's Soviet political adviser, Mikhail Borodin, the left wing, led by Chiang K'ai-shek's old rival Wang Ching-wei, broke with Chiang and established a rival Kuomintang organization in the Wuhan area. This was a drastic move, and one lacking in any real support. Backed by his loyal troops, the commercial interests in Shanghai, and the right wing of the Party, Chiang moved up the Yangtze Valley and destroyed the Wuhan Government's inept military force. Then, in April, 1927, Chiang officially established the Nationalist Government of China, with its capital at Nanking. A propaganda war ensued, with Chiang calling the Wuhan Government dupes of Communism and Russia's servants; while Wang Ching-wei retaliated by characterizing the Nanking Government as a warlord dictatorship.

Reaction against the Communists also took place in the Peking area during the spring of 1927. In China's ancient capital, Li Ta-chao, a founding father of Chinese Communism, was killed, other Party leaders were arrested, and the Soviet Embassy was raided by government troops. The raid on the embassy yielded documents indicating that Borodin was taking his orders directly from Moscow and that his role in China as friend and adviser was not for the ultimate benefit of the Kuomintang but only for the benefit of Soviet policy in Asia. These revelations brought disgrace to Borodin personally and to the government at Wuhan. Borodin and other Russians were sent home, and the Wuhan leaders began routing Chinese Communists out of their organization. Cooperation between Wang Ching-wei and Chiang K'ai-shek was again possible. By early 1928, Kuomintang forces were reunited and the campaign to unify China was resumed.

Stalin's policy of Communist cooperation and alliance with the Kuomintang had failed. Of course Stalin could not and would not admit that his policy in China had been wrong. To do so would have strengthened his opponents in the U.S.S.R., and could conceivably have seriously damaged his position in the CPSU. Thus he used an old and familiar tactic. He announced that the unfortunate situation in China was due not to bad policy but to inept execution by Chinese Communist leaders. The founder and leader of the Chinese Communist Party, Ch'en Tu-hsui was accused of Trotskyism, dismissed, and condemned in August, 1927. He was replaced by Ch'u Ch'iu-pai, who had been trained in Moscow and was subservient to Stalin's wishes. With Ch'u, Stalin at last had a firm control over the policies and activities of the CCP. Yet, in 1927, the CCP was weak, persecuted, and torn by internal disputes. From Moscow, the chances of further Communist success in China must have appeared very slim. Soviet advisers suggested that the Chinese Communists go underground and continue resistance against Chiang's "capitalist" government.

By the fall of 1927, there were two Communist factions in China. The regular Party under Ch'u Ch'iu-pai followed an orthodox Marxist line, took its orders from Moscow, and lived a dangerous underground existence in the urban centers. It was still trying to win the support of a disinterested proletariat. The other Communist faction was located in remote areas (known as "Soviet areas" or "Red regions"), such as the mountainous borderland area of Kiangsi-Hunan provinces. The first of the "Red regions" was established in October, 1927, by Mao Tse-tung. The preceding month, in Hunan, Mao had organized a peasant uprising, which became known in Chinese Communist history as the Autumn Harvest Rebellion. It was quickly crushed by Nationalist troops, and Mao himself later admitted that the uprising was badly timed. Chinese Party leaders and Moscow were disgusted with Mao's impetuous activities and his dubious ideology. The CCP Central Committee condemned Mao, but by then he had already lost faith in a Party leadership that had nothing to show for itself except a long history of frustration and failure. Mao ignored the Party rebuke and continued organizing peasants and strengthening the Soviet areas under his command.

In December, 1927, the CCP itself sponsored an uprising in the city of Canton. For a brief time, it succeeded in establishing the so-called Canton Commune Government. Like its famous 1870 predecessor in Paris, the Canton Commune was quickly and bloodily destroyed. This failure brought further disgrace to the bankrupt policies of the Chinese Communists. One might well ask why, weak as they were, the Communists attempted such a pointless action. The answer lay with the Soviet Union. Stalin had wanted to "save face" regardless of the cost to the Chinese Communists. In order to vindicate his policy in China, he had desperately needed some kind of Communist success, and the Canton Commune uprising was thus ordered from Moscow. In the end, the Canton episode further weakened the Chinese Party and Stalin's face was not saved.

To Mao, the Canton affair was an object lesson in the results of blind subservience to the orders of Moscow. Without doubt, Mao was already convinced that if Communism was to succeed in China, it could do so only through Chinese methods. Thus the split in the Party continued. The Communists called it a dispute between left-wing and right-wing elements, but it was really a division between the orthodox Stalinist line and the heretical Maoist line. As such, it was the first fundamental Sino-Soviet split based on different ideological approaches to Communism.

The orthodox Party groups remained underground in urban centers, tied to Stalin's coattails of policy and still working vainly for the dream of proletarian revolution. The history of this faction is a kaleidoscope of ideological and personal struggles for power among the Party leaders. As defeats and frustrations continued, a series of Moscow-trained leaders succeeded one another. Typical was Li Li-san, whose policy was to concentrate Communist attacks on major cities in order to set up urban Communist governments. Li severely criticized Mao's rural soviets and guerrilla war tactics. Li's policy, which was supported by Stalin, ended in 1930 with an abortive attack on the city of Changsha. Li was disgraced and sent back to Moscow for "re-education." Yet even this failure did not deter Stalin from continuing a stubborn and doomed policy approach toward China.

The heretical Party faction continued to concentrate on building and strengthening the various sovietized areas that Mao and others had founded. In 1928, Mao's forces were joined by a group of Nationalist deserters under General Chu Teh. The Chinese Red Army was then officially established under Chu's leadership. Later Chu Teh was to become the military commander of the sovietized areas while Mao supervised the political administration. Unlike Li Li-san's policy, that of Mao and Chu was not adventurous. It was designed to consolidate the Kiangsi-Hunan Soviet, to develop strong guerrilla bands, and to win the allegiance of the poorer peasantry through an extensive program of land reform based on the redistribution of property belonging to landlords and rich peasants. The success of Mao's policy could not be denied. From 1927 to 1934, while the strength and prestige of the orthodox Party leaders rapidly declined, Mao Tse-tung's power was on the rise. Stalin still refused to understand Mao's peasant-oriented Marxism. Even worse from Stalin's point of view, he had no personal control over Mao or his activities. To Stalin, the ultimate anathema was a Communist group attempting to follow a line independent of Moscow's dictates.

In November, 1931, the Communist region in Kiangsi was reorganized and the Chinese Soviet Republic formally established. Mao became Chairman of the Chinese Soviet Government without the approval or blessing of the Chinese Communist Party or of Stalin. In February, 1932, Mao's government declared war on Japan because of the Japanese aggression in Manchuria in 1931. Although his forces were not in a position to offer real resistance to Japan, the declaration of war was a shrewd propaganda move. It condemned Chiang and the Nationalist Government for their failure to defend China. It won support from intellectuals and students who were motivated by nationalistic pride and disgusted with the humiliations inflicted by the Japanese in Manchuria. And it also pleased Moscow. The Soviet Government was becoming increasingly alarmed by the

Japanese menace in Manchuria and North China and by the potential threat that this posed for the Siberian regions of the U.S.S.R.

By 1929, Chiang had defeated his opponents in the north and had unified much of China. This "unification," however, was actually an accommodation between the Nationalist Government and various warlord factions. It looked better on paper than it was in reality. For example, Chiang's success in the north depended greatly on the cooperation and support of the powerful political boss in Manchuria, Chang Hsueh-liang. After 1929, Chiang began to devote himself to the destruction of the various Communist cliques in China, who were the last groups openly hostile to his government.

By 1932, Chiang had succeeded in crushing the orthodox CCP factions in the urban centers. In order to avoid Chiang's persecution, the Party leaders had to escape to the sovietized areas directed by Mao. The Central Committee headquarters was transferred from Shanghai to Juichin in Mao's region. The leaders' political position in the sovietized areas vis-à-vis Mao was very weak, and Stalin's control of Chinese Communism was weakened even more. However, the growing Japanese menace in Asia and the increasing threat of Nazism in Europe precluded any Soviet attempt to salvage the China problem. Stalin was losing his grip on the shattered destiny of Chinese Communism, and Mao Tse-tung was gathering up the pieces.

In 1932, Chiang faced an agonizing decision: Should he, or should he not, give up his anti-Communist civil war in order to concentrate the energy of the Nationalist Government on resisting the increased Japanese aggression against China? There were strong opinions in the Kuomintang supporting both alternatives. He finally decided to continue the anti-Communist campaign while seeking to appease and pacify the Japanese. Chiang has been severely criticized for this fateful choice. His reasoning was that China could never successfully resist Japan until the country was solidly united behind the Nationalist Government. This national unity was impossible as long as the Communists were active. Before Japan could be faced, the Chinese Communists had to be destroyed.

During 1932–34, Chiang launched his first four "extermination campaigns" against the sovietized areas. Although weakened, the "Red regions" survived. The Nationalists' huge expenditure of men and money proved not only insufficient but detrimental to China's long-term interest vis-à-vis Japan. Chiang's extermination campaigns also gave the Communists a magnificent propaganda weapon. Over and over again they pointed out that while the Chinese Soviet

Government was at war to defend China, the Nationalist Government appeased Japan and continued its senseless struggle against other Chinese. The Communists claimed to be the true patriots and implied that the Nationalists' policies smacked of treason. The effect of this propaganda on the Chinese peasant population is difficult to measure. Unquestionably, it hit home to students and intellectuals.

In 1934, aided and advised by military officers from Hitler's Germany, Chiang launched his fifth and largest extermination campaign against the "Soviet areas." Communist resistance was stubborn but began to falter. Mao soon realized that it would be impossible to hold out in Kiangsi. Escaping from Nationalist encirclement in October, 1934, the Communists began one of the most incredible and heroic undertakings in all history—the 6,000-mile "Long March" from Kiangsi Province, through the treacherous hinterlands of China, to a new base in the loess caves at Yenan in northern Shensi Province. Of the 100,000 Communists who left Kiangsi, only 20,000 survived to reach the northwest in 1935. This was the Chinese Communists' supreme test of endurance and faith.[7] Mao himself has described their "finest hour":

> The Long March is also a seeding-machine. It has sown many seeds in eleven provinces, which will sprout, grow leaves, blossom into flowers, bear fruit and yield a harvest in the future. To sum up, the Long March ended with our victory and the enemy's defeat. Who led the Long March to victory? The Communist Party. Without the Communist Party, such a long march would have been inconceivable. The Chinese Communist Party—its leading bodies, its cadres and its members—is not afraid of difficulties or hardships. Whoever is sceptical of our ability to lead the revolutionary war will fall into the muddy pit of opportunism.[8]

The Long March was a turning point in the history of Chinese Communism. It was during the march that Mao Tse-tung was finally elected Chairman of the Central Committee of the CCP. The Moscow-oriented Party leaders had no choice. They had failed; Mao had succeeded. He had the organization and the Red Army; they had nothing. Supported by men like Chu Teh, P'eng Teh-huai, and Liu Shao-chi, Mao assumed Party leadership and effectively destroyed any elements still stubborn enough to resist him. The leadership of the Communist Party of China was welded together during the trials and hardships of the Long March. This experience bound them to one another in sort of an elite club devoted to Mao and to his policies. There are disagreements in this club, but only occasionally have they necessitated a purge. Since 1935, the leadership of the CCP has remained remarkably stable, in startling contrast to the Communist Party of the Soviet Union with its internal feuds, Party terror, and purges.

The Long March further divided the CCP from Stalin and the Russians. Throughout the march, and at the new base in Yenan, the Party was almost completely isolated from Moscow. Stalin's control of events in China virtually ceased. By 1936, the CCP was Mao's party, owed allegiance only to its own cause, and freely established its own policies. Stalin's reaction was to refuse to recognize either Mao's leadership or the validity of his ideas for adapting Marxism-Leninism to the Chinese scene.[9]

In 1936, still determined to rid China of Communism, Chiang put into operation plans for a powerful extermination campaign against the Yenan regime. Suddenly, in December, he was kidnaped and held prisoner in Sian, the capital of Shensi, by Chang Hsueh-liang, the "young marshal" of Manchuria. Tired of the civil war, the Manchurians wanted a united Chinese resistance against the Japanese, who had overrun their homeland. The Communists decided to plead for Chiang K'ai-shek's life in return for his effective promise to stop the civil war and take a firm stand against the Japanese. Chou En-lai went to Sian in order to assure Chiang that if he led a united resistance movement, the Communists would put the Red Army under his command and make the sovietized areas part of the Nationalist Republic. Communist intervention at Sian was a major factor in bringing about the Generalissimo's release from captivity.

Why did the Communists' attitude toward their old enemy change so suddenly? The answer is many-sided. First, the Japanese danger could be effectively resisted only by a united China. The Communists sincerely wanted to help defend the country against foreign aggression. Secondly, they saw a possible end to the Nationalists' extermination campaigns. There was no guarantee that the Communists could have survived a full-scale attack by Chiang's forces against Yenan. Thirdly, Moscow was pleading for an end to the Chinese civil war and for a united front against Japan. Only a month before, in November, 1936, Japan had joined Nazi Germany in the Anti-Comintern Pact. Stalin was desperately worried about a united fascist assault on the U.S.S.R. A strong Chinese war effort against Japan might prevent it.

Regardless of what he felt about Stalin personally, Mao was not pleased with the situation as it existed in 1936. The CCP still firmly believed in the Marxist-Leninist doctrine of the international Communist movement. Stalin and the u.s.s.r. were the leaders of world Communism, and Mao welcomed the opportunity to gain Moscow's recognition and good will. The Sian incident gave Mao that opportunity, while permitting him to retain freedom of action in China. Thus a combination of events revived that illogical alliance of Chinese Communists and Nationalists which had been destroyed only ten years before.

The new alliance was brief and unstable. Not even the binding united-front pressures of war could hold it together. By 1939, the Sino-Japanese War had settled into a bitter ordeal of attrition in which neither side could hope for all-out victory. The Kuomintang-Communist alliance began to fall apart. In 1939, the masks of cooperation, friendship, and united front were thrown off. Nationalist forces were again besieging Communist-controlled regions and fighting Red Army units. The Soviet Union's attitude toward conditions in China did not change after 1939. Engaged in its own life-and-death struggle in the West, the u.s.s.r. hoped to see Japan tied down in China and the Pacific so that Siberia could not be threatened. For this purpose, a united Chinese war effort was needed, and in Moscow's eyes Chiang provided the best leadership for such an effort. Stalin considered Mao and the Chinese Communist Party unreliable, both as Communists and as allies. Thus, during the Sino-Japanese War, Soviet political and material aid went not to the Communist forces but to the Nationalists. Russian guns were being used in China to kill Communists. Mao would not forget this new betrayal.

World War II was another significant turning point in the fortunes of Chinese Communism. Chinese patriotism and national feeling grew and solidified under the pressures of Japanese aggression. The Communists capitalized on the patriotic sentiments that were at last permeating Chinese society to the village level. The ccp played down its Communist ideology and emphasized nationalistic slogans. It presented itself as the persecuted underdog, the only party sincerely devoted to the war against Japan, and the only faction willing to forget past political differences for the sake of China. This posture, as well as more extensive land reforms, won over an ever increasing number of peasants and intellectuals. The Communist Party gained strength and vigorously pursued the war against Japan independent of Soviet aid and advice. The ccp emerged from the war with no obligations to Stalin for its position of prestige.[10]

The spirit and efficiency of the Soviet regions was in vivid contrast to the stagnation, sagging morale, and political corruption that came to infect the Kuomintang Party. The tragedy of China was the deterioration of the Nationalist Government under the impact of World War II, just as the tragedy of Russia in 1917 had been the decay of the Provisional Government under the pressures of World War I. By the war's end in 1945, the Communists offered the Chinese people a brighter prospect for the future than did any alternative political group. The Soviet Union was as blind to the truth of this situation as was any Western government.

Ideological tension between the u.s.s.r. and the Chinese Communists was heightened during the war when Mao published his thesis "On the New Democracy." Mao wrote that China needed the help of a friendly Soviet Union in order to win its freedom from imperialism. Before achieving socialism, however, China would have to go through a democratic stage, based on an alliance of the revolutionary classes. This theory differed widely from the Marxist-Leninist concept of proletarian dictatorship. New Democracy would not only tolerate other political parties, but would also advocate cooperation and alliance with them. In Russia after 1918, political organizations other than the Communists had been ruthlessly abolished. In 1940, Mao rewrote some of Lenin's basic principles in order to fit them to the Chinese scene and the strength of the Chinese Communist Party. The Soviets regarded this as the rankest "right-wing deviationism" and "revisionism."[11] On the ideological plane, the history of Sino-Soviet relations has been the history of uncompromising attitudes. While recently the Chinese accused Khrushchev of cowardly deviation from Leninist orthodoxy, in 1940 the Russians implied that the Chinese comrades were guilty of revising Lenin's words.

Following its six-day war with Japan in August, 1945, the Soviet Army occupied Manchuria. To help replace their own industrial losses in the West, the Russians dismantled Japanese-built Manchurian factories and shipped them to the u.s.s.r. How this has affected subsequent Chinese industrial building efforts is difficult to measure. Surely it was not compensated for by the captured Japanese weapons that the Red Army turned over to the Chinese Communists. Although this Soviet aid was helpful to the Chinese Communists, it is unlikely that this assistance was *the* determining factor in the outcome of the Chinese civil war. Chiang's army retook some of the major Manchurian cities and railroads, but Soviet activities in Manchuria prevented the Nationalists from being able to reoccupy the entire area. Mao's forces were quick to fill the power vacuum in Manchuria. In addition to the captured Japanese arms, this was the U.S.S.R.'s real contribution to Mao's fortunes.

In 1945, Stalin was not thinking in terms of a Communist China. He sought a strong China that could block United States influence in Asia—an influence which in his eyes had replaced Japan as the real menace. For this reason, he still placed his hopes in the Nationalist Government. Again Soviet recognition and aid went to Chiang. Mao was ignored and told to seek reconciliation with Chiang for the sake of a united China. Quite obviously, the strength of the Chinese Communists after World War II was no better understood in Moscow than in Washington. The Russians, too, seemed to believe the myth that Chinese Communists were nothing but a group of "agrarian reformers."

The failure of Western attempts to end the Chinese civil war and to form a coalition government in the country is well known. The civil war continued at a furious pace. Only when the possibility of a complete Communist victory became apparent did the Soviet line change to one of support for Mao Tse-tung. (It is beyond the scope of this chapter to analyze the reasons for the Communist victory.) In October, 1949, the Chinese People's Republic was established as the government of China. Chiang K'ai-shek was forced to abandon the mainland and retire to Taiwan.

News of the Communist triumph in China was received with joy in Moscow, and the U.S.S.R. quickly recognized Mao's government. A Communist China—anti-Western and committed to the aims of world Communism—was more than Stalin had ever dreamed possible. After earlier setbacks in Greece, Berlin, and Yugoslavia, the Communist cause was no longer ebbing but surging forward in a new wave. Yet one wonders if the news from China was really looked upon in Moscow with all the enthusiasm that the Soviets displayed. Far more likely is the probability that Stalin watched the emergence of Red China with mixed emotions. This was no small East European satellite, dependent on the U.S.S.R. for its victory and existence. Here was a huge nation that had achieved a Communist victory with very little help from Russia. Here was a nation that had a population at least three times that of the Soviet Union and was capable of great dynamism when given proper leadership. An agonizing question was haunting statesmen on both sides of the Iron Curtain. Was China to be another satellite nation looking to Moscow for guidance and strength, or was it to be a full partner of the U.S.S.R.

in the Communist world? Was the Communist world a gigantic, monolithic bloc ruled by Stalin's will, or was it a bloc of nations with two capitals—Moscow and Peking? In the late fall of 1949, the answer to that question was in doubt.

Satellite or partner? A partial hint at the answer to the question could be seen in Mao's nine-week visit to Moscow which began in December, 1949. This was his first trip outside China, and it appeared that he was coming to pay homage to Stalin at the throne of world Communism.[12] Mao, however, came to Moscow in 1949 to request Soviet aid and assistance for his new government. In the best Marxist-Leninist tradition, he also came to demonstrate the monolithic unity of world Communism. Thus the answer to the satellite-or-partner question was beclouded at the Moscow meetings by a great display of friendship and solidarity.

On the surface, one would never have guessed that Mao and Stalin had ever been anything but the closest of friends working for years in complete harmony for the birth of Red China. Yet, his meetings with Stalin must have been difficult for Mao. Stalin was not the type of man who could forgive and forget the past. Behind the façade of solidarity, the atmosphere was one of hard bargaining. The Chinese received only a small part of the aid they had requested. For this, they had to pay with foodstuffs, raw materials, consumer goods, and concessions in Manchuria and at Port Arthur. Stalin demanded special rights in China which made a mockery of the Karakhan manifesto of 1919.[13] Mao had to accept Stalin's terms. There was no alternative source of aid to which he could turn.

The most beneficial aid given by the U.S.S.R. was the loan of Soviet technicians, who contributed greatly to China's industrial expansion after 1950. Without their help, Chinese industrialization would have progressed much more slowly.

The Korean War placed serious strains on the newly formed Sino-Soviet alliance, but it also brought certain benefits to both partners. There seems to be little doubt that the North Korean invasion was approved, if not ordered, by Moscow, and that Stalin also "suggested" China's entrance into the war. With the promise of full Soviet aid and support, Mao agreed.

Besides solidifying Communist rule, the Korean War provided China with a great moral victory of national pride. Backward China with its great resource of manpower held the advanced imperialist nations to a stalemate at the 38th Parallel.

The old, cynical story that the Korean War was indecisive because the Chinese had as many men as the United Nations had bullets may have caused wry smiles in the West, but it was no joke in China. As the war stagnated in central Korea, it became an impossible drain on the resources of the People's Republic. Mao believed that the Soviet Union was not doing its share. The promised aid was not forthcoming in sufficient quantities, and China had to pay the ever-mounting cost in manpower and matériel. This was a cost it could ill afford at that point in its history.

By the winter of 1952–53, the Russians were the only people who saw the Korean struggle as anything less than a colossal nightmare. For Stalin, it was the ideal type of war. While the U.S.S.R. remained at peace, building its own power and testing its military equipment, the imperialist West was being drained in Korea. On the other side of the hills, China also was being drained of blood and resources. The People's Republic was dependent on the Soviet Union for help and protection. Certainly the threat of Soviet intervention was a major factor in preventing the United Nations from carrying the war to mainland China. Step by step, the Korean War was forcing Mao into a satellite position instead of partnership vis-à-vis the U.S.S.R. To continue the war could exhaust China to the breaking point. To pull out against Soviet wishes would threaten to shatter the Sino-Soviet alliance and the monolithic Communist world.

Joseph Stalin died in March, 1953. Conceivably, the Chinese took advantage of the resulting power vacuum in Moscow to request, if not demand, an end to war in Korea. The death of Stalin left Mao as the principal elder statesman of the Communist world. In the U.S.S.R., only "little men" like Malenkov, Molotov, and Bulganin were left to fill the shoes of the giant Stalin. No one yet paid serious attention to the former coal miner in the background, Nikita Khrushchev. Mao alone looked like the titan to carry forward the banner of Marxism-Leninism-Stalinism. Thus a new word was added to that trinity of Communist dogma—Maoism.

Mao began building a political-economic system patterned on his own ideas of adapting socialism to the Chinese scene. As early as 1942, he had summarized his basic outlook: "Theory and practice can be combined only if the men of the Chinese Communist Party take the standpoints, concepts, and methods of Marxism-Leninism, apply them to China, and build a theory . . . based on the realities of the *Chinese* Revolution and *Chinese* history [italics added]."[14]

Mao further consolidated the rule of the Communist Party by

various "campaigns": the "Three-Anti" campaign of Party reform and reorganization; the "Five-Anti" campaign against the Chinese and foreign business class; and even an "anti-fly" campaign against the insects of China! Chinese nationalism was further agitated by "Resist America" and "Liberate Formosa" campaigns. Communist totalitarian control stretched from Peking to every village, street, and household of the nation. Central government authority became infinitely greater than the rule of powerful emperors in the past. In classic mandarin tradition, Mao himself began to recede from public view and to assume in the eyes of the people the aura of mystery and divinity that formerly surrounded the Son of Heaven. Thought control, propaganda, and brain washing in China became important tools for the consolidation of Communist power and control.

The Communists launched China on a rapid march toward a socialist system in agriculture and industry. One stage of development was abandoned for another almost before people realized what had taken place—from mutual-aid teams to farmer cooperatives to collectivization of agriculture. Mao was trying to do in five years what the Soviets had taken nearly forty years to accomplish. Both the mistakes and successes found in the development of socialism in the U.S.S.R. were ignored in China as Mao steered his own course.

By 1956, the power struggle in the Russian Communist Party had been pretty well resolved. Nikita Khrushchev emerged to fill the political vacuum left by Stalin. A new era was beginning in the U.S.S.R. Khrushchev realized that Stalinism could not continue unchanged as Khrushchevism. He began his change in the historic anti-Stalin speech at the Twentieth Congress of the CPSU, where he exposed the horrors of his predecessor's regime and ridiculed the pettiness of the cult of personality. The speech also exhibited Khrushchev's own authority and fortitude. It took a new giant to destroy the myth of power that still surrounded Stalin's memory in the Russia of 1956.

The Sino-Soviet split of today can be considered to have had its immediate origins in Khrushchev's 1956 oration. The speech raised Khrushchev to a seat of prestige equal to, if not above, that of Mao. If the cult of personality and totalitarian dictatorship were evil in the Soviet Union under Stalin, was it not obvious that they were equally evil in all Communist states? The immediate results of Khrushchev's policy in Eastern Europe—the revolts in Poland and Hungary—also greatly distressed the Chinese. To them it seemed as if the new Soviet policies were leading to a breakup of the Communist bloc. Chinese representatives flocked to Eastern Europe in an effort to repair the damage and maintain unity. (It has been pointed out that this was East Asia's first direct intrusion into European politics since the conquests of Batu Khan.) Preservation of the Communist bloc was essential to China's interests in 1956. China needed the aid and moral support that the unity of the Communist world supplied. Therefore, the Chinese tried to repair and gloss over Khrushchev's blunders.

After 1956, the animosity between Mao and Khrushchev continued to smolder. At the same time, dynamic events were taking place in China: the blooming and withering of the "Hundred Flowers," the disastrous "Great Leap Forward," and the establishment of the commune system. These developments greatly irked Khrushchev and the Soviets, because with them the Chinese were openly suggesting that the stage of pure Communism could be reached in China more quickly than in other countries.

By the late 1950's, Chinese leaders were questioning the wisdom and necessity of Communist solidarity. How could unity be maintained while Khrushchev was following a revisionist line that they believed was betraying the true principles of Marxism-Leninism? Although the façade of unity was to remain in place for a few more years, the People's Republic was beginning to offer the Communist world an alternative to Moscow's direction. Peking was becoming a new center of absolute Communist truth. The real struggle for leadership between the U.S.S.R. and the Chinese People's Republic began in earnest despite the fact that this diarchy in world Communism was in itself a betrayal of Marxism-Leninism. Now there were two leaders, two roads to Communism for people to follow, and two interpretations of Marx and Lenin, both claiming to be correct. Polycentrism, no longer a theory, had become a reality.

In the late 1950's and early 1960's, new areas of conflict and dispute have added bitterness to the earlier troubles—personal rivalries between Mao and Khrushchev, "paper tigers" and nuclear weapons, the inevitability of war, the Formosa problem, Cuba, and Soviet foreign aid. Why, ask the Chinese, does the U.S.S.R. grant us, a Communist country, so little in relation to our needs, while giving substantial and unrestricted aid to non-Communist states like Iraq, the U.A.R., and India? Of late, the conflict has been intensified by such issues as China's militant border controversies with India, boundary disputes with the Soviet Union itself, and even the race question— with the Chinese viewing Russia as another white nation devoted to the exploitation of the nonwhite races.

Given these past and present differences, the Sino-Soviet dispute does not appear as startling as it appears inevitable. It is the historical combination of these differences that we witness today in the transition of the Communist world from monolithic unity to polycentric disunity. As the *New York Times* recently editorialized: "The Sino-Soviet dispute over 'coexistence' and 'militancy' is in fact a mere disguise for the historic power struggle between Russia and China, now contesting for top influence in the Communist world."[15]

For nearly 4,000 years, China considered itself as *Chung Kuo*—the Middle Kingdom, the center of the universe, the unique possessor of civilization, surrounded by barbarian tribes. Whether Imperial, Nationalist, or Communist, the governments of China in the modern age have been unable to escape this heritage of world outlook. To the Chinese, their nation cannot for long remain a subordinate satellite or even an equal partner. It must be *Chung Kuo*.

From 1917 to 1949, the Soviet Union itself had been a *Chung Kuo*—the center and sole leader of world Communism. Today, the Soviet leaders are understandably reluctant to surrender this position of pre-eminence to the potential giant that is China. Both China and the Soviet Union are learning a lesson that can be found in any grade-school history text. International unions, blocs, and alliances are generally flimsy in the long run, whether based on friendship, expediency, economics, or common ideology. Such alliances have been unable to withstand permanently the pressure of national interest. Today, the heritage and national interests of China and Russia are overtaking and subduing in conflict the bond of union given them by the philosophy of Karl Marx and Lenin.

2. The Sino-Soviet Split: A Reconstructed History, 1956-64

WILLIAM E. GRIFFITH

WHETHER POLITICS is a science seems to be somewhat in question, but that Kremlinology or Pekinology is a science is doubtful. Rather, like the writing of history, it is an art. In particular, it is an art in the same sense as is the writing of the history of ancient Greece or Rome, where the overwhelming majority of the plays of Aeschylus and the books of Livy have been lost. This handicap applies especially to the history of Sino-Soviet relations: Although presumably the archives in Moscow and Peking would reveal much, it is highly doubtful whether we shall have access to them in our lifetime, and we certainly do not have it now. So an awful leap—a "great leap forward" (to speak Chinese)—is the first requirement in the study of contemporary Sino-Soviet relations.[1]

We do have certain tested methodological precedents, however: Before Sino-Sovietology there was Kremlinology. We have learned something about interpreting the absence or presence of persons and the subtle changes of views on this or that subject contained in obscure Communist ideological declarations. Although there is little to learn from personnel changes in the Sino-Soviet dispute, we can learn much from the deciphering of ideological incantations—and I call them incantations because, in a certain sense, the phrase "ersatz religion" best describes the Communist "ideological" disputes.

It would be dangerous to think that the Russians—and, even more, the Chinese—do not believe what they say. Both the Russians and the Chinese subscribe to Lenin's dictum about the unity of theory and practice: Communist ideological declarations not only accompany but reflect and are a total part of a syndrome of ideological, political, economic, and military action. Indeed, detailed research into some episodes of the Sino-Soviet dispute, and particularly the day-to-day course of Soviet-Albanian relations in 1960–61, indicates that on the same day that a foamingly violent anti-Soviet Albanian editorial appeared, the Soviet Union had initiated some new measure of political, economic, or military pressure against Albania.[2]

Yet, in the study of the Sino-Soviet dispute one must always keep in mind the fact that the documentary material is incomplete and inadequate, and much of it is deliberately distorted by the Russians and the Chinese. In the earlier stages of the dispute, there was too little of it, and too much was purposely kept from us. By now, because of the intensity of Sino-Soviet polemics, there is really too much—that is, the more there is the more it is distorted. As Lenin said about statistics, history is a weapon of the class struggle; and Communist documentation is in part a weapon in the Sino-Soviet dispute. But history is always a jealous mistress, the source materials we have are always incomplete, and, for the time being, one can have at best only a preliminary view of the whole situation.

Before we present a chronological account of the Sino-Soviet dispute, let us examine its framework, and in particular the issues involved, as we see them in the fall of 1964.[3] Until relatively recently —indeed, until after the signature of the test-ban treaty in July, 1963—many observers regarded the dispute as "ideological"; and much of the press still uses this term in its references to it. Ideology, history, and political practice, however, are rarely if ever separate in Communist affairs. Specifically, from the very beginning of the Sino-Soviet rift, differences have existed concerning national interests, strategy, foreign and domestic policies, and the organization and control of the international Communist movement. From the very beginning, all these factors were integral parts of the dispute. As the dispute developed, its various components became more difficult to compromise because, given the ideological element in Marxism-Leninism, any dispute over strategy or tactics must be, and is, immediately transferred to the ideological level.

During the last world-wide Communist meeting, at Moscow in November, 1960, Khrushchev is reliably reported to have said that the most crucial issue facing the gathering was that of the "fundamental nature of the present epoch." To us this assertion may seem so unrelated to reality as to be almost an "un-statement," but it does not appear as such to a Marxist-Leninist. What is more, Sino-Soviet differences on this very issue include and imply almost all the other differences as well. The Russians maintain that the world socialist system "is becoming," but the Chinese maintain that it "has become," the fundamental factor of the present epoch. In terms of Communist strategy, this means that Khrushchev felt he could afford to take fewer risks against the West than Mao thought the Russians should take—for Chinese goals. Moscow maintains that the present epoch is primarily one of a largely nonviolent forthcoming world-wide victory of socialism; Peking insists that ours is primarily an epoch of wars and revolution.

To take another example of an ostensibly ideological issue: The Russians maintain that the fundamental present danger to the international Communist movement is dogmatism and revisionism (i.e., the Chinese); the Chinese insist that it is revisionism (i.e., the Russians). It is true that Khrushchev in particular and the Russians in general have revised Marxist-Leninist doctrine. They have proclaimed the existence of what Marxists call a qualitative change in the nature of the world's weapons systems and particularly in the destructiveness of thermonuclear war. They declare that there now exists a division in the camp of the imperialists between the "sober circles" (of whom they considered President Kennedy to be the leader) and the "madmen" (the leadership of which, according to Moscow, is enjoyed by Senator Goldwater). The Soviets conclude from this that war is no longer inevitable, and therefore that it must be avoided. This, in turn, leads to the further Soviet conclusion that "peaceful coexistence is the general line of the international Communist movement until the final victory of Socialism."

The Chinese also maintain that peaceful coexistence is desirable. Peking is not brandishing atom bombs, for many reasons, despite the recent Chinese nuclear test. The Chinese maintain, however, that peaceful coexistence is a tactic, not a strategy, and that it must not be allowed to interfere with wars of national liberation.[4]

The Chinese accuse the Soviets of trying to bring about a Soviet-American *détente* and therefore of not running sufficient risks on behalf of the Chinese, particularly on the issues of the offshore islands and Taiwan. Furthermore—and from the beginning this has played a major role in the conflict—the Chinese accuse the Soviets of promising to give them atomic weapons and then of reneging on the promise. The Chinese charge the Russians with taking an anti-Chinese attitude on various Sino-Soviet border questions—in particular, Sinkiang and the Amur River area. The Chinese also accuse the Russians of supporting anti-Chinese governments, such as that of India, formerly headed, according to Peking, by the American "imperialist agent" Nehru. The Russians deny all these charges and in turn accuse the Chinese of national and racial chauvinism.

The Chinese generally emphasize the importance of supporting Communist parties and extreme radicals in the underdeveloped areas, while the Russians tend to stress the importance of supporting all the "national democratic elements" (e.g., India).[5] But, as is evident from Chou En-lai's embrace of King Hassan II of Morocco and Prince Norodom Sihanouk of Cambodia, Chinese tactics can be —and, especially now, usually are—far more flexible than the Russians' in this respect. Further, Moscow tends to emphasize the peaceful and parliamentary transition to socialism; for example, it supports the potentially successful course of action by the Italian Communist Party. In part, the Russians support peaceful economic competition as the main means for the victory of socialism, because they have too much to lose by risking more violent tactics.

By mid-1963, the Chinese began publicly to challenge the totality of Khrushchev's less extremist domestic policies as expressed in ideological terms by the "all-people's state," while on the other hand the Soviets denounced the "leftist opportunist adventurism" of the Chinese "Great Leap Forward."

Finally—and this is perhaps the most complete of the Chinese challenges and the one to which the Russians can least afford to accede—the Chinese have challenged Soviet leadership and control of the international Communist movement with the intent of ultimately replacing it by their own.[6] The Russians still retain a large majority in this movement: out of eighty-one Communist parties, they have recently asserted that sixty-five are on their side.[7] The Chinese, however, deny that a majority decision can be binding on them; rather, they insist on unanimity—that is, a Chinese right of veto over any international Communist decision. This means that the Chinese insist on their right to agitate against and subvert the present Soviet predominance until Peking has gained majority control of the movement, at which point they would presumably insist on majority rule.

Let us now review the history of the Sino-Soviet dispute in an attempt to reconstruct—partially, incompletely, and probably still in part misleadingly—how it really happened. The sharp intensification of Sino-Soviet polemics after the signing of the test-ban treaty, in July, 1963, produced major revelations from both Moscow and Peking about the previous history of the dispute. According to the Chinese account, which is particularly revealing, Sino-Soviet differences first became serious in the spring of 1956, immediately after the Twentieth Congress of the CPSU. At that time, Peking objected to Khrushchev's denunciation of Stalin, to what it considered his overemphasis on peaceful transition to socialism and on peaceful coexistence (that is, to his policy of *détente* with the United States), to his unwillingness to give more military (atomic) and economic aid to China, to his expansion of Soviet political influence in underdeveloped areas (particularly India), and to his insistence on carrying out such drastic moves as de-Stalinization without consulting Mao.

In the autumn of 1956, the Chinese made various attempts to use the Soviet difficulties with Poland and Hungary in order to expand their influence in Eastern Europe and in the international Communist movement; but their influence was hardly anywhere decisive. After the Hungarian Revolution, their high estimate of the significance of the 1957 Soviet sputnik launching caused the Chinese to increase greatly their attempt to make Soviet foreign policy more extreme—the more so because by that time Peking's short-lived rightist policy phase (the "Hundred Flowers" episode) had been succeeded by the anti-rightist campaign and by a policy of leftist extremism. This new Chinese major shift to the left, which began in late summer and early autumn of 1957, has continued to the present time.

There followed the Moscow international Communist conference in November, 1957. Until fairly recently, this conference was generally regarded as an agreement between Moscow and Peking against revisionism and specifically against Yugoslavia. After all, at this meeting Mao said that the camp of socialism must have a leader, which must be the Soviet Union. This is one of the more striking examples of how the interpretation of Communist terminology can change, for looking at it from an historical perspective this formulation must now be considered to have been an anti-Khrushchev one —a formulation deliberately used by Mao to block Khrushchev's *rapprochement* with Yugoslavia, thereby to weaken the general Soviet foreign policy of an international *détente,* and thus to increase Chinese influence. The Chinese have now revealed that shortly before this meeting, on October 15, 1957, Moscow had promised Peking some form of atomic aid. Without such a move, it is doubtful whether the November, 1957, meeting would have resulted in any Sino-Soviet agreement.[8] It is now quite clear that the November, 1957, meeting in no way reflected a genuine meeting of minds between Moscow and Peking; rather, it was a serious and essentially indecisive Sino-Soviet confrontation.

What happened thereafter confirms this view. In May, 1958, the Chinese took the lead, both in time and in intensity, in the renewed attack on Yugoslavia. At the same time, they initiated the people's communes and the "Great Leap Forward," moves which must now be considered to have been caused, at least in large part, by their realization that they could not possibly hope to obtain the massive Soviet economic aid and that without it rapid Chinese economic development required extremist measures. During 1958, it now also appears, the Russians attempted in some way to obtain more military influence in China, probably to get a commitment for Soviet control over atomic warheads if and when they gave any to the Chinese.

It is 1959, at the latest, that must be considered to have been the "year of no return" in Sino-Soviet relations. In view of the most recent revelations, after the summer of 1959 neither Moscow nor Peking anticipated a reconciliation; on the contrary, both anticipated a probable total rupture. Their actions since then have been primarily determined by the desire of each to fix the blame for the final rupture upon the other and, in the process, to gain as much influence as possible in the struggle for leadership in the international Communist movement. In the summer of 1959, as thereafter, the accelerating deterioration of Sino-Soviet relations was characterized primarily by a constantly intensifying Chinese offensive against Soviet influence in Communist parties and international Communist front organizations. This, in turn, resulted in continually intensifying Soviet countermoves in order to block, reverse, and eventually render ineffective this Chinese offensive.

In June, 1959, as we now know, Khrushchev formally withdrew the Soviet offer of atomic aid to Peking.[9] That summer, he apparently unsuccessfully attempted to intrigue with dissidents in the Chinese leadership, headed by the Minister of Defense Marshal P'eng Teh-huai, who tried either to force Mao to change his anti-Soviet and domestically extremist line or, failing that, perhaps even to replace him. P'eng's attempt was crushed by Mao at the Lushan Plenum in July and August, 1959.[10] At the same time, the Soviet attempt to prevent the Chinese from demonstrating their predominance over the Indians, and specifically from maintaining the foothold they had won in Ladakh, finally failed.[11] In September, 1959, the Chinese initiated the first major border incident against the Indians, whereupon the Russians, disregarding Chinese attempts to dissuade them, publicly declared themselves neutral on this issue.

All these 1959 events represented one of many cycles in the Sino-Soviet dispute, which at least since 1959 has been characterized by a process of cyclical escalations: first, deterioration; then partial improvement; and finally, a renewed and sharper deterioration. As has been shown by subsequent revelations, these cycles were much less significant in reality than they appeared to be at the time. Essentially tactical in nature, they largely revolved around the problem of the level of public Sino-Soviet polemics rather than around any major change in relations. As, over the years, Sino-Soviet relations worsened, Moscow and Peking's rivalry for influence within the international Communist movement increased. The Chinese tactic has never been the initiation of a total rupture; on the contrary, Peking wishes to remain nominally within the international Communist movement, to use its veto against any hostile Russian actions, to increase factional activities with the ultimate aim of obtaining a majority, to split individual Communist parties, and to establish new Communist parties as well as new front organizations under Chinese control. To foil these moves, the Russians have been continually driven toward initiating a formal split.

The course of the dispute from 1960 onward is much more familiar, and the new revelations concerning it are much less significant than those concerning the previous period. It might, therefore, be summarized briefly. In April, 1960, Peking published a series of articles, *Long Live Leninism!*, which made public the ideological controversy. In June, 1960, Chinese factional activity in the international Communist front organizations became first apparent in Peking at a congress of the World Federation of Trade Unions. Later that same month, at a Romanian Party Congress at Bucharest, Khrushchev launched his first overt (but unpublished) attack against the Chinese, which resulted in violent verbal polemics between him and the Chinese delegate P'eng Ch'en. The Soviets also began extensive economic pressure against China; they cut off economic aid and withdrew all their specialists.

The Russians also probably tried (unsuccessfully) to carry out a coup in Tirana to overthrow the Albanian leadership.[12] By 1960, only the Albanian leadership had clearly joined the Chinese. They did so essentially because Hoxha, with reason, so feared a Soviet-Yugoslav *rapprochement* that he found China the ideal (being both powerful and distant) protector for Albania against a Soviet Union which appeared again to be moving toward an alliance with his deadly enemy Yugoslavia.

The eighty-one–party Moscow meeting of November, 1960, appeared initially to have been a relatively successful attempt at compromising Sino-Soviet differences; its final communiqué seemed clearly pro-Soviet. But, as we have since learned, its real course was quite different. The violent Sino-Soviet polemics in Bucharest in June were followed by even more violent ones in Moscow in November. There the Chinese flatly refused to accept a Soviet-sponsored ban on factional activity within the international Communist movement. The Soviets rejected a Chinese proposal for a joint Sino-Soviet directorate of the movement which would have institutionalized the Chinese veto. All in all, the November, 1960, Moscow meeting made Sino-Soviet relations much worse.

Following this meeting, the steady but not yet public deterioration of Sino-Soviet relations was clear only from the worsening of Soviet-Albanian relations. From November, 1960, to October, 1961, there were relatively few Sino-Soviet polemics; in terms of the cyclical model, therefore, this period should presumably be considered one of lull. Sino-Soviet polemics simply became more esoteric; the *rapprochement* between the Soviet Union and Yugoslavia intensified; and during the spring and summer of 1961 (as we now know in detail), the Soviets continued their unsuccessful political and economic pressure against, and the Chinese their support of, the embattled Albanians. Thus although relatively little seemed to happen, in fact much did occur. This became clear when, at the Twenty-second Congress of the CPSU, in October, 1961, Khrushchev publicly denounced the Albanians (a step to which Chou En-lai took public exception), and when, in December, Moscow broke off diplomatic relations with Tirana.[13]

Chou En-lai did more at the Twenty-second Congress. After his pro-Albanian speech,[14] he placed on the grave of Stalin a wreath with the inscription "To the great Marxist-Leninist J. V. Stalin," and immediately departed for Peking. Shortly thereafter, Khrushchev had Stalin's body removed from its tomb. An outbreak of violent polemics against the Albanians—not only from the Soviets but also from many other Communist parties—reached its high point in December, 1961–January, 1962. Thereafter, again apparently in a cyclical fashion, they declined.

We now know what we did not know at the time: Because both the Chinese and the Russians desired to appear opposed to the break, which they disliked but anticipated, and also because of the conciliatory initiatives of certain other Communist parties, there developed in the spring of 1962 a Sino-Soviet exchange ostensibly concerning the summoning of another international Communist meeting. This discussion not only came to nothing but further exacerbated Sino-Soviet relations.

It did, however, reveal something more about the tactical positions of both sides. The Chinese terms for agreeing at that time to such a meeting remained the same. They placed clear and narrow limits on mediation, and, considering the inevitable Soviet reaction to them, they further worsened the controversy in the direction of a total public rupture. In the first place, Peking demanded the suspension of public polemics. (This represented no major obstacle; one must always, and in principle, favor the suspension of polemics.) Secondly, the Chinese demanded bilateral and multilateral talks; that is, not only the Chinese and the Russians should meet, but other parties should participate as well. The final Chinese demand was the most difficult for the Russians to accept: Soviet-Albanian relations must be "normalized," and the Russians should take the initiative in this respect; that is, Khrushchev should go to an "Albanian Canossa." One may also assume that the Chinese insisted upon upholding the November, 1960, Declaration's excommunication of the Yugoslavs; that is, they insisted that Khrushchev must abandon his *rapprochement* with Tito. The Soviet terms were: firstly, the end of public polemics; secondly, bilateral (or, if necessary, multilateral) meetings, although at this stage the Russians preferred an immediate international meeting; and lastly, implicitly, the revision of the November, 1960, Declaration to declare that dogmatism rather than revisionism (i.e., Mao rather than Tito) represented the main danger to the international Communist movement.

During the summer of 1962, Sino-Soviet relations continued to worsen. Moscow's moves were primarily, and not surprisingly, organizational. (Any strong, reformist movement prefers this tactic.) They included intensification of the *rapprochement* with Yugoslavia and greater multilateral integration with CEMA. Weaker but more orthodox, the Chinese concentrated primarily on ideological moves, in particular on a series of anti-Soviet esoteric ideological articles. The Soviet-Yugoslav *rapprochement* proceeded apace throughout the spring and summer of 1962, and by September Moscow and Belgrade had reached almost complete public agreement on foreign policy and party organization, although not yet on ideological issues. Furthermore (as we learned a year later), in April and May, 1962, serious unrest developed in Sinkiang, which resulted in the flight of probably up to 50,000 Kazakhs and Uighurs over the border to the Soviet Union, where their friendly reception further angered the Chinese. The Russians also admitted Outer Mongolia to CEMA and adopted a more favorable attitude toward the Common Market.

Meanwhile, the Chinese were building up to a border war with India, where, since 1959, and especially in Ladakh, the Indians had been trying to regain the territory that the Chinese had occupied during the 1955–59 period. Throughout 1962, the Chinese publicly warned the Indians that they would resist Indian attempts to dislodge them. On October 12, Nehru declared that India was going to throw out the Chinese by force of arms, but he actually did nothing about it before the Chinese attacked in force in Ladakh and the North-East Frontier Agency on October 20. The results of the Chinese attack in India have been almost entirely favorable to the Chinese. The Indian Communist Party split as a result of the attack, and its pro-Chinese faction has been steadily gaining in influence. After initial wavering because of the Cuban crisis, the Soviet Union adopted an ostensibly neutral but actually (as the Chinese correctly stated) pro-Indian policy. Finally, the Chinese attack on India resulted in a major intensification of the Sino-Soviet dispute, all the more so because it occurred at the same time as the Cuban crisis.

Fundamentally, it seems that the October, 1962, Cuban missile crisis represented a hasty, risky Soviet attempt to slow down (if not to overcome) rapidly increasing American strategic lead in invulnerable second-strike nuclear deterrents. It intensified the Sino-Soviet dispute, because the Chinese felt that it confirmed what they had maintained about Khrushchev's wanting a *rapprochement* with the United States at the expense of China and Cuba. It also revealed serious Soviet-Cuban differences which since that time have been temporarily papered over by relatively short-lived agreements between Khrushchev and Castro. After the crisis, the Cubans temporarily adopted a neutral position in the Sino-Soviet dispute.[15]

The accentuated intensification of the Sino-Soviet dispute resulting from the Sino-Indian and Cuban crises led in early 1963 to a rapid deterioration of relations between Moscow and Peking. Sino-Soviet ideological exchanges increased in intensity, explicitness, comprehensiveness, and vitriolic character. A series of five Communist congresses in Europe, staged by Moscow as a form of pressure against the Chinese, ended with a scene in the East German Congress in January, 1963, at which the Chinese delegate's speech was drowned out by other delegates stamping their feet in protest.[16] Tito's visit to Moscow at the beginning of 1963 further solidified the Soviet-Yugoslav *rapprochement* and further enraged the Chinese.

During the spring of 1963, however, the cyclical nature of the dispute again appeared. Sino-Soviet exchanges between February and July led to the Moscow meeting of July, 1963, but they further intensified polemics and thus condemned the meeting to failure in advance. The Russians charged the Chinese with wanting to get rid of Khrushchev. The Chinese declared that the world Communist movement was on the verge of a split. They brought the Sino-Soviet boundary issue into the open; they declared that the Russians insisted on dominating all the Communist parties ("by waving their baton"); and, in accord with their own racist view, they insisted that the centers of the world revolution were really in Asia, Africa, and Latin America—areas in which, they added, the Soviet Union was selling out the national liberation struggle to the American imperialists.[17] In any new international Communist meeting, the Chinese insisted on continuing factional activity and retaining a Chinese veto. They also continued to demand that the Russians apologize to the Albanians and that the Yugoslavs be excommunicated as American agents. Mao refused to go to Moscow but said that Khrushchev, if he wished, might come to Peking. On the other hand, the Russians publicly made known their intention to revise the November, 1960, Declaration so as to brand Mao rather than Tito the main danger to international Communism. Thus, several months before it occurred, the July, 1963, Sino-Soviet meeting in Moscow was already doomed to failure. During this period the Chinese also intensified their efforts to disrupt the international Communist front organizations, to set up new Afro-Asian organizations under their control, and to establish or support anti-Soviet Communist parties and groups. The "neutralist" Communist countries, those trying to balance between the Russians and the Chinese, gradually were forced to take sides. In May, 1963, for example, North Viet-Nam opted (albeit not totally) for the Chinese. Tito increased his anti-Chinese activity. Castro again appeared pro-Soviet. Surprisingly, Romania successfully defied the Soviet Union on the issue of multilateral economic integration in CEMA and appeared, while remaining pro-Soviet, to be flirting with the Chinese.

Then, on June 14, two weeks before the July Sino-Soviet meeting, the Chinese published a twenty-five–point letter to the Russians.[18] This was an ideological platform for a split, a total and explicit attack on the domestic as well as international policies of Khrushchev since the death of Stalin, and therefore a bid to replace the Russians in the leadership of the international Communist movement. At the same time, a series of Sino-Soviet diplomatic incidents developed.

While the July, 1963, meeting was still under way in Moscow, the East-West test-ban-treaty negotiations began. During the meeting, Sino-Soviet ideological polemics intensified. On July 14, the Russians came out with an "open letter" amounting to a major rebuttal of the Chinese ideological platform, which made it quite clear that the meeting to iron out the differences had failed.

The collapse of the meeting and the signing of the test-ban treaty touched off a new series of overt, violent Sino-Soviet polemics. These completely abandoned esoteric terminology for all-out, explicit denunciation, perhaps best typified by the Chinese statement that Moscow's signing of the test-ban treaty was treason to the international Communist movement. The Chinese revealed the significance and details of the border and atomic issues. Chinese factionalism within the international movement greatly increased, and it became clear that the Chinese intended to set up a whole series of new Communist parties where they could not take over old ones. They also began the publication of a long series of detailed and violent articles—what might be called an ideological *roman fleuve*—against the Soviet Union.

The next major episode was the frustrated Soviet attempt in September-October, 1963, to call an international Communist meeting to excommunicate the Chinese. The Russians had become convinced that only excommunication could stem the danger of continued and increasingly extensive subversion by the Chinese. Although in September and October, the Russians did not engage their full prestige toward this end, they did reprint in *Pravda* resolutions by small Communist parties (such as those of Portugal and Paraguay) calling for the expulsion of the Chinese. But the attempt did not work, and the Russians called the meeting off for the time being. On October 25, Khrushchev declared that polemics should be suspended and that the issue of an international meeting was not vital. He did so, it seems, largely because three Communist parties—the Poles, Romanians, and Italians—publicly objected to excommunicating the Chinese. It may be assumed that they did so because such a Soviet-sponsored excommunication might sometime be turned against them. This incident—one of great significance in international Communism—was the first time that a clear (albeit still implicit) Soviet move was abandoned (if only temporarily) because of pressure by other pro-Soviet Communist parties. For some months thereafter, the Russians presumably suggested resumption of Sino-Soviet negotiations to the Chinese. Peking, however, intensified its world-wide factional activity and, at the end of March, 1964, explicitly called for Khrushchev's removal and for an international conference of Communist parties to revise the November, 1960, Declaration.[19] Furthermore, in July, 1964, Mao went so far as to accuse the Russians of illegally occupying both East European and Japanese territory[20]—a move clearly designed to embarrass the Russians by raising territorial issues among socialist countries. The Russians countered by issuing renewed, extensive polemics against the Chinese, by extending a new call for an international conference,[21] and by revealing that the Chinese leaders had offered to barter with the Russians over the fate of Mongolia as early as 1954.[22] In turn, Romanian, Italian, Polish, and Cuban dislike of the proposed conference again became evident; and Khrushchev's fall in October, 1964—in part precipitated over the issues of what tactics to use against Mao—made it even less likely that the conference, already imperiled, would be successful.

The Russian Communists are thus faced with a very serious problem—one that, in terms of an ideal resolution, is quite insoluble. The Russians' permanent dilemma may be stated as follows: A recalcitrant and powerful ally of a superpower, particularly within a world-wide ideological context, must either be brought to heel or excommunicated. How can the Russians accomplish this when China remains defiant and has so loosened Soviet control over their minor allies that they will not cooperate? But, on the other hand, how can the Russians refrain from doing it when, if they do not, the already loosened control of these allies loosens still further?

3. Poland

M. K. DZIEWANOWSKI

As BOTH A RECENT British visitor to Eastern Europe and a Canadian professor have observed, Poland is a Communist country with a difference.[1] In most fields, this is a difference to her advantage. Despite the marked domestic recompression of the scope of freedom that had existed in Poland in 1956–57, cultural ties with the West are strong, and cultural exchange not only goes on but has even been extended to university students. Western radio broadcasts are no longer jammed.

Although Poland is different from the other Soviet-controlled countries of Eastern Europe, the distance separating her from them has been steadily diminishing, because of the slow and subtle changes going on both in Poland and in the other satellite countries. During the early 1960's, the Gomulka regime continued its retreat from the achievements of the unfinished revolution of October, 1956 —the revolution that established Gomulka as First Secretary of the Central Committee of the ruling Polish United Workers' Party. Yet, despite the progressive tightening of the police regime, Poland has remained more free than other Soviet-controlled countries, although Hungary and Romania have been rapidly catching up. The all-pervading fear, which had been characteristic of the Stalin era, has

56

not returned, despite the gradual re-emergence of the secret police and the increasingly brutal reprisals against intellectuals.

Despite the spread of the government-supported "agricultural circles"—which were intended to serve as steppingstones to some sort of "socialist organization of agriculture"—Poland has been pursuing a rather Bukharinist agrarian policy: Land has not been collectivized and, defying the innumerable regulations and limitations, farmers have enjoyed a relative measure of prosperity. Thus, agriculture in Poland is more like that in Yugoslavia. Well over 90 per cent of the land is in the hands of individual farmers, who produce more per acre than do the collectivized agricultural enterprises of most other satellites.[2]

On Sunday mornings, almost all peasants go to church to hear Mass.

> It is not easy to call to mind a country in the West where religion appears to be so strong a force. In the towns there are fewer practicing Christians than in the villages, but even in urban areas an appreciable proportion—perhaps 30 to 40 percent—of the population attend Mass regularly. Religion is strong among university students, too. While estimates vary on this point, it would seem that at least 50 percent of students are churchgoers, and some place the figure as high as 80 percent.[3]

Yet, friction with the Roman Catholic Church has been mounting—particularly since the intensification of the atheistic campaign sponsored by the Party, and the passage of the School Reform Law of July, 1961, which finally eliminated religious instruction from schools and placed severe limitations on it outside the school premises, and even in church buildings. Yet, in spite of the growing tension in church-state relations, the Catholics of Poland—with their own University of Lublin, Theological Institute, 37 periodicals, 14 publishing houses, 40 seminaries, and a group of deputies in the Diet—have enjoyed a broader sphere of relative religious freedom than have the other captive peoples.

While in the sphere of culture Poland has been relatively better off than other countries of Soviet Eastern Europe, the same cannot be said about her economics; here the situation in the early 1960's has been steadily deteriorating. Already in 1962, Gomulka had announced a new austerity program, drastically reducing the planned industrial growth rate for the last stretch of the Five-Year Plan ending in 1965. Likewise, in view of the serious foreign trade deficit, production targets for industries using imported raw materials have been especially severely cut back.

What are the reasons for the worsening of Poland's economic situation? They are numerous. While the chief export, coal, has dropped in price, Warsaw has had to pay more for the machinery and raw materials it needs for its further industrial expansion. The tightening of the Common Market has adversely affected Polish export trade. But it seems that a faulty system of planning and management has been the chief long-term source of Poland's economic difficulties. There is no doubt that Polish planners erred on the optimistic side. The success in surpassing relatively moderate targets in 1960 resulted in upward revision of plans in 1961, and thus created unexpected difficulties. The unusually vigorous winter of 1961–62, as well as a mediocre harvest in 1963, aggravated these difficulties and caused alarming shortages of food and fuel, the prices of which were sharply increased as a result. The Poles reacted with a flood of malicious stories lampooning the inefficient regime. ("Has Poland already reached the socialist stage of development, or will the situation deteriorate still further?")

Between 1960 and 1963, productivity increased about 15 per cent (according to the official announcement), rather than 20 per cent, as had been expected. Wages rose faster than productivity. More workers were hired than had been planned, in order to reach the desired targets. The quality of consumer goods did not improve much, and unsold goods began to accumulate. Moreover, the balance of foreign payments deteriorated, because imports increased more rapidly than had been anticipated. Consequently, on November 30, 1963, anticipating the policy of the Soviet Union, Gomulka announced at the Central Committee's Plenum that the current Five-Year Plan would have to be reviewed in order to allow for larger investment in agriculture, and especially for building more fertilizer plants "in the next few years." If fertilizer production had not lagged in the 1950's, he said, Poland might not have had to import grain in recent years.[4]

The formation of the Common Market frightened Warsaw because it threatened to reduce those Western markets which the Poles consider as vital. But, unlike the Soviet Union (which, at least initially, tried to ignore and boycott the Market), the Poles adopted a more positive attitude and accepted it for what it was—an important phase in the consolidation of the Western world, and a symptom of vitality of the allegedly decaying capitalistic system unable to oppose the dynamic socialist world. Even before the establishment of the Common Market, Warsaw had been in the vanguard of the East European countries trying to maintain close economic ties with the

West. After all, nearly 40 per cent of Polish exports go to non-Communist countries.

Now, with the Common Market presumably here to stay, Poland, together with Yugoslavia, has been trying to persuade the Council for Economic Mutual Assistance (CEMA) to liberalize its attitude toward the Market and to seek negotiations that would "keep open channels of trade with the West."[5] This is in tune with the general attitude of the Poles: Making virtue out of necessity, they are loyal to the *Macht im Hintergrund,* while trying to maintain their traditional ties with the West. Keeping trade channels open is partly an economic necessity and partly a concession which an essentially unpopular regime has to make to the people as a price for reluctant and half-hearted collaboration.

Their lingering ties with the West and the ambiguous autonomy of the Gomulka regime, as well as a greater sophistication of some of the Polish Communists and their non-Communist "stooges," allow Moscow to use its Polish comrades in a variety of ways. The first use is diplomatic. A typical example is the Rapacki Plan, proposed by Warsaw in 1957, providing for a denuclearized zone in Central Europe that would encompass both Germanies, Czechoslovakia, and Poland. The idea was rejected outright by the NATO powers, but it never completely vanished from the diplomatic scene. In the spring of 1963, the plan was dusted off and, in a somewhat altered form, put forward again by the then acting Foreign Minister, Marian Naszkowski, as a partial remedy for the tensions in Europe. Another attempt was made toward the end of 1963. Speaking at a ceremony opening the "Friendship Pipeline" in Plock on December 28, Gomulka, while outlining a broad plan for easing tensions between East and West, suggested a freeze on nuclear arms in Central Europe as a step in the direction of creating a supervised zone of security in Central Europe—obviously an allusion to the old Rapacki Plan.[6]

Warsaw has also been playing a role in the Moscow-directed maneuvers toward a *modus vivendi* with the Vatican. The private audience with the Pope which the Catholic deputy and member of the Council of State, Jerzy Zawieyski, had in the spring of 1963 probably had something to do with these efforts.[7]

These steps had been preceded by a series of gestures on the part of Warsaw. In an address to the Peace Congress held in Warsaw on June 12, 1962, Gomulka quoted and praised Pope John XXIII. After stressing the Soviet bloc's desire for peace he said:

It is from this point of view that we approach the statement made by Pope John XXIII when he appealed twice in his message of September and December of last year to men at the helms of government and responsible for the fate of nations. The anti-war attitude of the head of the Roman Catholic Church converges with peaceful policy of the socialist states, regardless of all the differences separating Marxism-Lenism from the philosophy guiding the activities of the Church.[8]

However, the death of Pope John XXIII, as well as the policy of increasingly painful administrative pinpricks systematically administered by the Polish Communist regime to the Catholic Church, soon rendered these gestures futile.

The role of Poland as a bridge was thus frustrated in the field of religion—but not so in the field of political propaganda. Some Warsaw diplomats and non-Communist intellectuals, including several "progressive Catholics," traveling in the West, have utilized their contacts with influential people in the West to peddle Soviet concepts of coexistence and sell certain ideas about possible implications and consequences of the Sino-Soviet conflict for Eastern Europe.[9]

This brings us to Poland's attitude toward the great political conflict of our times.

The Sino-Soviet conflict broke into the open in April, 1960, on the ninetieth anniversary of Lenin's birth. The anniversary, celebrated throughout the Communist world, gave Peking the opportunity to call once more for eradication of imperialism in all its forms, by force if necessary. Acrimonious polemics followed. The Peking Congress of the World Federation of Trade Unions in June, 1960, and the Romania Party Congress in Bucharest later that month further sharpened the tone of the controversy, with the Russians defending stubbornly the idea of peaceful coexistence while the Chinese scornfully rejected it as cowardice and even treason. Soon it was revealed that what lay between Moscow and Peking was an axe, not an axis.

The Polish reaction to the Sino-Soviet controversy cannot be fully understood without looking at least as far back as the upheaval of 1956. Then the Polish people, including most of the Party, had received with great satisfaction the statement by the Chinese Government, which approved the never fulfilled Soviet declaration of October 30, 1956, "on the principles of development and further strengthening of friendship and cooperation between the Soviet Union and other socialist states." "Because of the unanimity of ideology and aim of struggle," we read in the Chinese declaration:

It often happens that certain personnel of socialist countries neglect the principle of equality among nations in their mutual relations. Such a mistake, by nature, is the error of bourgeois chauvinism. Such a mistake, particularly the mistake of chauvinism by a big country, inevitably results in serious damage to the solidarity and common cause of the socialist countries. . . . As a result of these misunderstandings and estrangements, a tense situation has sometimes occurred which otherwise would not have occurred. The handling of the 1948–49 Yugoslav situation and the recent happenings in Poland and Hungary are enough to illustrate this.[10]

The gratitude which the Polish Communists felt toward Peking was expressed a few months later by Prime Minister Cyrankiewicz. In January, 1957, while greeting his Chinese counterpart Chou En-lai, in Cracow, Cyrankiewicz thanked him for this assistance. In 1956, the Chinese friends, said Cyrankiewicz, fully understood that ". . . the coexistence of nations should not be like the coexistence of various fish . . . living in one lake, the bigger devouring the smaller ones. We are fighting against *all forms of national oppression* [italics added]."[11]

The attitude taken by Poland toward the "Great Leap Forward" was cautious but considerably less negative than that of the Soviet Union. At the Twelfth Plenum of the Party's Central Committee in October, 1958, Gomulka declared politely but firmly:

There is no doubt that what is now happening in the People's Republic of China is a special phenomenon resulting from the historical development of China. In our situation the problems are somewhat more difficult, and it is completely impossible to copy automatically the Chinese experiment in our country.[12]

At the Peking meeting of the World Federation of Trade Unions at the beginning of June, 1960, a Polish Politburo member and a close personal friend of Gomulka, Ignacy Loga-Sowinski, while avoiding polemics with the Chinese, firmly supported the Soviet position on coexistence. Trying to flatter his hosts, Loga-Sowinski attempted to use the well-known slogan of Mao Tse-tung, but married it with the Soviet one, thus producing a strange Sino-Soviet propagandistic hybrid: The east wind will prevail over the west wind as a result of a peaceful coexistence.[13] An equally conciliatory line was followed by Ochab, the Polish delegate to the Romanian Party Congress in Bucharest in July, 1960, which Gomulka proudly stressed in his programmatic speech in Katowice.[14]

During the second half of 1960, the Polish press tended to avoid the Sino-Soviet dispute. "We are not doing any more gymnastics," said a higher Polish functionary to the German journalist Hansjakob Stehle, then a press correspondent in Warsaw. The bureaucrat indicated that in Poland—except for Boleslaw Piasecki, chief of the leftist Catholic PAX, who praised the Chinese at a private meeting in 1960—no one was enthusiastic about Peking's thesis. On the other hand, he continued, it was not necessary for the Poles to attack the Chinese head on, since in 1956 the latter had already shown understanding for Poland's "own road."[15]

Thus, from the very beginning of the controversy, Gomulka, a pragmatic, down-to-earth man, showed his characteristic distaste for tricky and (for him) rather illusive, ideological finesse and doctrinal hairsplitting. He emphasized, rather, the practical sides of the issue. As in his mediation attempts in the Soviet-Yugoslav dispute, he now preached the necessity of maintaining the unity of the Communist camp in order to promote "victory of socialism in peaceful coexistence" and to avoid a potentially disastrous split that might damage all Communist regimes. This was the gist of the speech with which Vice-Premier Zenon Nowak was sent to the Albanian Party Congress in February, 1961.[16]

Arbitration could not alter the basic fact that, from the very beginning, the official Polish point of view had been rather close to the Soviet one, and that, on most essential points, it opposed the Chinese approach on all three main issues of the controversy: (1) the possibility of peaceful coexistence with capitalism; (2) the effects of the thermonuclear war on the two great antagonistic systems; and (3) the expediency of temporary, tactical compromise with the common enemy. Consequently, most Chinese or Albanian attacks on Moscow—or, for that matter, on Yugoslavia—were considered, automatically, assaults on Warsaw. To these ideological sympathies one should add the geopolitical position of Poland, her economic dependence on the Soviet Union (for iron ore, oil, and spare parts for the Soviet-built factories) and the hard fact that China has little to offer in the field. All this would have predetermined Poland's attitude even if the Polish party differed from the Russians ideologically.

Gomulka voiced this basic ideological solidarity with Moscow often, persistently, but with caution. In his report to the Central Committee of the Polish United Workers' Party on November 22, 1961, he said:

Nothing speaks more convincingly for the peaceful policy of the socialist countries than the fact—already proved to the whole world —that they can develop their economy more rapidly than capitalist

countries in times of peace. War is a terrible obstacle to their economic development. . . . Today, in the era of genocidal thermonuclear weapons and ballistic rockets, war has become unacceptable
to a sane mind.[17]

Characteristically, throughout the report Gomulka attacked not
China but Albania, and he mentioned China only once as supporting
the erroneous views on coexistence voiced by Tirana:

The concepts of dogmatism and sectarianism do not properly reflect
the nature of the position of the leaders of the Albanian Party of
Labor and their policy, which is not a policy but senseless adventurism. Thus, for instance, in a speech delivered recently in
Tirana, Enver Hoxha accused the leaders of the Soviet Union of being afraid of imperialism and therefore of postponing from year to
year the settlement of the German problem and of the West Berlin
question. This is a mixture of conceit and adventurism . . .[18]

Thus, while supporting Moscow, the Polish Party faithfully
imitated the Soviet example, and for a long time avoided direct attacks on Peking. All the anger was emptied on the Albanian
whipping boy:

To justify the willful acts committed by them in the past and still
committed at present in their country, the leaders of the Albanian
Party of Labor, by defending Stalin's methods of activity condemned
by the 20th Congress and by the whole international workers movements, break away from this unity. They also break this policy of
the USSR and of other socialist countries. International Communist
opinion, including that of our party, regards their position with indignation and condemnation.[19]

This tactical line was continued throughout 1962 and most of
1963. At the same time, Gomulka was maneuvering behind the
scene in order to patch up the rapidly deepening rift, as he had done
in the case of the Soviet-Yugoslav quarrel. His spokesman, Mieczyslaw Rakowski, Editor-in-Chief of *Polityka,* became, however, more
and more outspoken:

Hoxha and Shehu have been stating more or less clearly for quite
some time that they oppose the policy of peaceful coexistence as the
general line of our movement. In February, 1961, at the Fourth Congress of the Albanian Party of Labor, Enver Hoxha, in his general
report, confined himself only to a repetition of that part of the Moscow Statement [of November, 1960] which dealt with the aggressive-
ness of imperialism and its desire for war. However, he did not
mention at all the possibility of avoiding wars under the present

circumstances. . . . Enver Hoxha and Mehmet Shehu pursue a policy which clearly attacks the unity of the international Communist movement.[20]

Thus, in 1961, the Twenty-second Congress of the CPSU, which publicly castigated and outlawed China's chief ally, Albania, had confronted Gomulka with a difficult situation. He obviously was surprised by the move, of which he had no previous knowledge. Moreover, the methods used now against Tirana were strongly reminiscent of those that Stalin had applied with Belgrade in 1948 —methods which Gomulka repeatedly and emphatically rejected on various occasions. His reluctance to adopt the neo-Stalinist means of muzzling his *Communist* opponents was expressed soon after the Congress by his spokesman Rakowski:

> The unity of the Communist movement is not a taboo which forbids discussion and debate. Our rejection of the cult of personality takes place at a time of conflict which is by no means at an end. The emergence of different attitudes and methods of approach is perfectly natural in view of the present complicated conditions. The present epoch demands, in fact, re-evaluation of many conceptions and opinions which have been established over the decades. . . . The possibility may not as a matter of course be excluded that mutually conflicting and mutually contradictory problems may arise within the Communist camp. The most important thing is that the unity arising from the conflict should not be artificial or illusory.[21]

Thus, for nearly three years, Gomulka, while loyally supporting the Soviet viewpoint, never openly attacked the Chinese. On September 8, 1963, however, he took a firmer position. Soon after his return from the Soviet Union, in his first frank public comment on the Sino-Soviet controversy, Gomulka gave full expression to his accumulated resentment against Peking as aggressor in the dispute:

> We are surprised and filled with bitterness by the attitude of the Chinese People's Republic Government which adopted a negative attitude toward the Moscow agreement on banning nuclear tests, and in this connection attacks the Soviet Union and blackens it, trying to represent its policy in a false light. Leaders of People's China, as we can see, do not link the problem of their country's security with the unity and fraternal alliance of the States of the socialist camp, but, blinded by the desire to possess their own nuclear weapons, are splitting the unity of the commonwealth of socialist states and the international socialist movement, thus doing a service for the enemies of socialism and warmongers.[22]

On September 6—that is, two days before Gomulka's speech—the Chinese *People's Daily* editorially criticized the Soviet Union for its attitude toward independence of other Communist states. The paper claimed that it was the Chinese restraining hand "firmly opposing the erroneous methods of great-power chauvinism" which in October, 1956, "prevented the Soviet Union from subduing the Polish comrades by armed force."[23]

Nevertheless, while pledging ideological loyalty to Moscow, for a long time Warsaw was trying to cultivate good cultural and economic relations with both Peking and Tirana. The congratulatory telegram sent to Mao Tse-tung on his seventieth birthday (December 26, 1963) by the Polish Communist Party is a good indication that Poland is continuing its efforts to prevent deterioration of Sino-Polish relations. The telegram referred to Mao as "Dear Comrade" and paid compliments to his "Communist record" and his achievements in "building Socialism" in China. The telegram wished him "a long life and fruitful activity . . . for strengthening of the unity of all socialist forces for our common Communist cause."[24]

In February, 1964, however—probably on Moscow's insistence —the first symptoms of retreat appeared. Ominously, the monthly review *Chiny* (*China*), organ of the Sino-Polish Society of Friendship, stopped publication.

So much for the official Polish reaction to the Sino-Soviet controversy. As far as unofficial reaction is concerned, one must distinguish between *"le pays légal"* and *"le pays réel,"* the rulers and the ruled. The apolitical masses were delighted. There are many reasons why the anti-Communist Poles—that is, an overwhelming majority of the people—should be happy about the split. First of all, their drab, dreary, monotonous existence has been brightened by the sight of the two Eastern giants falling apart, hurling recriminations and even threats at each other. What a wonderful spectacle! How exciting! The Polish *Schadenfreude*—which soon found its expression in dozens of malicious stories about the great controversy—was reflected in a popular saying: "One gangster, Khrushchev, quarrels with another gangster, Mao, about the third gangster, Stalin."

After the first spontaneous emotional reaction, some sobering thoughts followed. Mao's apocalyptic vision of an atomic Armageddon obviously has left the Poles shuddering and dampened any possible enthusiasm for Peking. The Poles tend to agree with Khrushchev that the bomb does not respect class principle and that the thermonuclear peace is indispensable to both the proletariat and the bourgeoisie—hence their enthusiastic approval of the test-ban treaty and the *détente* in East-West relations.

The Poles do not harbor a deep-seated, atavistic apprehension of the yellow, slant-eyed Mongol invaders—an apprehension still rather strong in Russia as a heritage of the "Tatar yoke" under which the Muscovites lived for over two centuries during the Middle Ages. Nevertheless, the Poles did experience the Mongol invasions, and a vague fear of the "Asian hordes" and the enormous Asian land mass still lingers in the Polish subconscious. At the beginning of the century, the National Democrats believed that, despite the past, despite the numerous points of friction, Polish and Russian national interests were fundamentally not incompatible in the long run. Only a generation ago, the leader of the National Democratic Party, Roman Dmowski, while analyzing the plans of a possible German (and, perhaps, European) crusade against the Soviet Union, bluntly warned his countrymen against getting involved in a conflict with Russia: ". . . the time may come when those who are now dreaming about partitioning Russia will anxiously ask whether she is strong enough to withstand the pressure of China . . . this moment may not be very far away."[25]

The residue of National Democratic thinking is still rather strong in Poland, and this line of reasoning may be found both among representatives of the *"pays réel"* and the *"pays légal."* Both Gomulka and his predecessor, Bierut, often quoted Dmowski whenever the fundamentals of Russo-Polish relations were discussed. A humorous expression of this school of thought is the well-known saying. "How lucky we are to have such a strong buffer state between us and China!"

The inner Party reaction to the Sino-Soviet split has been complex and has undergone many changes. Initially, many Polish Communists felt that the controversy could produce positive results for their Party as well as for the bloc. Equal relationship had been advocated by the Polish comrades for a long time, although during the Stalinist period theirs was "the voice of the turtle." They remembered that in the crucial days of October, 1956, the Chinese intervened in Moscow on Poland's behalf. The "liberal" wing hoped that the widening of the split would keep Gomulka from proceeding too rapidly with the recompression, especially with the tightening of his cultural policies, if only in order to avoid the impression of leaning toward Peking. On the other hand, the Stalinists expected that the conflict would result in an overthrowing of Khrushchev by their ideological cousins in Moscow.

After the summer of 1963, however, the situation became menacing to the Polish ruling Party. Most tactical considerations were thrown overboard, while the long-range implications of a final break soon became obvious to most leaders: It would not only damage, beyond repair, the world movement as a whole, but could also seriously undermine the very existence of the Communist regimes in Eastern Europe. Peking's racial arguments undermined faith (or whatever remained of it) in Communism's claim to universality and brotherhood of all races within the movement. In Poland, where Communism never had deep roots anyway, this has posed new and serious problems.

What are the prospects for the near future? It seems that the leaders of every minor Communist Party have a vested interest in a measure of friction between the two giants. But such a friction should be controllable and short of a final break. A limited antagonism is good for the minor parties, because it allows them room for maneuvering, for playing off one against the other. But a total split threatens all Communists and deals a deadly blow to the myth of the movement as the wave of the future. Consequently, Gomulka's attitude is ambivalent. As a Pole, he should welcome the Moscow-Peking rivalry in order to build out of it a larger measure of autonomy for himself and his Party at home, as well as a stronger position within the Communist camp. As a Communist, however, he has been frightened by the widening of the split. The growing possibility that it may become permanent is a grave menace to world Communism, to the Polish United Workers' Party, and to all the Communist regimes in Eastern Europe. In his speech in Berlin on January 17, 1963, Gomulka admitted frankly that "The Soviet Union is the decisive main strength of the socialist camp, without which no socialist state could hold out against imperialism. No Communist or labor party, especially no party in the socialist countries, should forget that."

Because all Communist parties have nothing to gain and much to lose from the final split, the Polish Party leader (helped here by Janos Kadar) has made numerous and persistent representations to the two great rivals, imploring them, in the name of the superior interests of the movement, to refrain from any rush moves. Reportedly, Gomulka often warned Khrushchev that the split might endanger the stability of the satellite regimes.

Gomulka's uneasy and apprehensive attitude is symptomatic of his sense of insecurity. He realizes that an independent Polish Communist Party would not be able to hold power for long, that it would either be swept away or would have to share power with other groups while probably evolving in the direction of social democracy. That is why he has been sticking to Moscow without reservation and, unfortunately, without any worthwhile political compensation. Thus, he now pays the price for his retreat from the gains of the unfulfilled and betrayed October, 1956, revolution and for his estrangement from the overwhelming majority of his countrymen.

Nevertheless, almost automatically, the split has enhanced Poland's position within the Soviet Empire. First of all, Gomulka's repeated mediation—although perhaps occasionally irritating to Moscow, which is sensitive to any independent initiative of its satellites—rather strengthened his role as the most important among the lesser Communist leaders. As long as China was within the bloc and was on reasonably good terms with the Kremlin, Warsaw's role was insignificant. With China outside the camp, Poland has been promoted to second place in the Soviet alliance system. She is the largest and most populous of the Soviet satellites (31 million inhabitants), and her army is the largest (257,000 men and 3,000 tanks, organized into 14 divisions, 4 of which are armored). In economic potential, Poland ranks third, behind East Germany and Czechoslovakia. She occupies a key strategic position, astride the vital lines of communications between Moscow and East Berlin.[26]

A series of setbacks suffered by Moscow in its contest with the Chinese for the loyalty of the Communist parties of the underdeveloped countries, combined with the French diplomatic recognition of Peking, may profoundly alter the international situation and open new vistas to Poland—but only if the Polish leaders are willing to take advantage of such opportunities (which is by no means certain). As an acute observer of the East European scene put it: "In theory, a Communist party may well have the opportunity when the two giants have a falling-out, to gain its complete independence; in practice, it may not want to be independent."[27] Gomulka's aim seems to be to consolidate the moderate autonomy he enjoys and not to expand it.

General de Gaulle's Chinese gambit has profoundly altered Russia's geopolitical situation. It may foreshadow a sort of simulated encirclement of the Soviet Union by the rising antagonistic powers of Asia plus a group of dynamic European states. The global aspects of Paris' diplomatic recognition of China have been recently discussed by Professor George Liska:

> The encirclement [of Russia in Eurasia] might become really serious at a later date, when West Germany has drawn consequences from

the fact that it shares territorial and other grievances against Soviet Russia with Communist China and that the Atlantic policy is apparently incapable of satisfying, even partially, these grievances. Rather than be wedged in between two irredentist powers or reduced to the position of the inferior party in an entente with the United States, the Soviet Union may eventually be willing to seek an understanding with the Western European states. In the anticipated circumstances, the Soviets would have to pay for such an understanding with concessions to the Germans in East Germany and to the French in the area between Germany and Russia. The latter concessions would tend to moderate the scope of the former and, in addition, the Soviets might receive a symmetrical reduction of American presence and influence in Western Europe. Successful or not, a global strategy of European unity has the advantage of timeliness over the contrary strategy of freezing the nuclear *status quo* and putting the Eastern European issue on ice as part of an effort to promote a continuing thaw in the postwar version of the East-West conflict.[28]

It remains to be seen what consequences for Eastern Europe may evolve from de Gaulle's bold move. One cannot exclude the assumption that, together with the growing attraction of an increasingly prosperous and dynamic Western Europe, the French step, together with recent denunciations of Soviet imperialistic territorial acquisitions both in Asia and in Europe, may eventually reopen the issue of the Soviet-controlled part of the European continent —an issue which for a long time was diplomatically closed.

It seems that the opening of a dangerous new frontier in the Far East is bound to make Moscow rethink her policy in Eastern Europe, in order to stabilize and consolidate the latter area. One may ask, therefore: Will the consolidation of the Soviet camp be achieved by consulting more frequently with the satellite countries and taking into account their peculiar domestic needs, or by tightening the screw? Would Moscow under the new leadership set up in October, 1964, try to return to the Stalinist method of running the satellites by preaching the medieval patristic principle *Timor Domini est initium sapientiae* (The fear of the Lord is the beginning of wisdom)? Or has the Kremlin learned that, in the long run, by ruling less sternly it may well rule more firmly? Does Russia, at this crucial historical moment, need more allies or more satellites?

Does the Sino-Soviet dispute mean a gradual transformation of the Soviet camp in the direction of a relatively pluralistic (although not necessarily polycentric) Communist commonwealth of autonomous (if not completely "free") nations, the evolution of which had been foreshadowed by the Soviet declaration of October 30, 1956?

Or does the rift constitute a hindrance to further domestic liberalization, as well as an obstacle to loosening what is left of the Soviet
camp?

Only time will tell. But Moscow's passive attitude toward the
changes going on in Romania, as well as the magnitude of the problems to be faced by Russia in Asia, seems to forecast a limited appeasement of domestic national aspirations for greater autonomy at home
as well as a greater flexibility within the Communist camp. Moscow's
preoccupation with its great conflict with China is bound to produce
profound global repercussions. The slow but nontheless perceptible
increase in domestic autonomy in most Communist states—which
resulted from the erosion of official ideology that has followed in the
wake of the Sino-Soviet conflict and the consolidation of Western
Europe—is bound to set the stage for a new historical relationship
within the Communist camp.

4. Hungary

FERENC A. VALI

POLITICAL DEVELOPMENTS in post-World War II Hungary appear to occur in cyclical movements. The 1945–46 liberalization was followed by the Stalinist era of terror, which, after the Soviet autocrat's death, was succeeded by the "thaw" and the unsuccessful anti-Communist revolution of 1956. Soviet military intervention suppressed the revolt and brought a new wave of violent oppression. Since the early 1960's, the cycle has moved toward another period of relaxation, placing Hungary next to Poland among the most liberalized East European Communist countries. The sequence of events in Hungary is characterized not only by the extremism of cyclical motions, such as the nadir of Stalinist terrorism and the paroxysmal zenith of the 1956 revolution, but also by their frequency. Neither the Soviet Union nor any of the Soviet dependent states has gone through such political oscillations as Hungary within less than two decades.

The present relaxed period began early in 1961, after the forced collectivization of agriculture was completed. After the Twenty-second Congress of the CPSU, there was a further relaxation, and still another followed the Hungarian Eighth Party Congress, in

71

November, 1962. Since then, during 1963 and later, Hungarian politics has remained in a state of relative equilibrium.

It is highly characteristic that the Hungarian Party directives for the Eighth Congress, published in August, 1962, used such language: "The Party invites those sectors of society which previously did not sympathize with [the Party] and even opposed its objectives, to join in helping to build socialism."

It is now admitted, implicitly if not officially, that class struggle has ended. Educational institutions have been directed not to screen applicants according to their class origin.[1] Admissions are based simply on qualifications of students. At present, the official approach to non-Party people is based on Janos Kadar's dictum, pronounced in December, 1961, before a meeting of the People's Patriotic Front: "Who is not against us is with us." This was an explicit reversal of the principle held by the Stalinist dictator Matyas Rakosi, who had once stated: "Who is not with us is against us."

Kadar's "Communist gamble"[2] is an appeal to the common-sense "live and let live" motto. Instead of claiming (as the election results are supposed to confirm) that the majority of the people are enthusiastically pro-Communist, he is ready to admit that at least for the time being they are not. Indeed, he recognizes that even the people who, according to him, favor the regime, do so for selfish reasons, and not for the love of Marx and Lenin.[3] Such reasoning, though not convincing to everybody, is bound to obtain a more cooperative response than intimidation and terror.

Since 1962, important and widespread shifts in personnel have taken place. Incompetent Communist Party members or "opposition elements"—meaning, this time, Stalinists who opposed the Party line—were demoted or removed and sent back to their original professions. They were replaced either by non-Party experts or by better qualified, younger Party members. Equality of employment opportunities between non-Party people and members of the Party was announced and generally adopted. Party members were even warned that those who could not cooperate with non-Party experts would be removed. Efficiency was to take precedence over Party membership and even Party merits.

These trends caused apprehensive tremors among the *apparatchiki,* and among the middle and lower-rank segments of the Party. The middle cadres, the majority of whom still tend to be Stalinist, were the most affected. The anti-Stalinist purge culminated in August, 1962, when former dictator Matyas Rakosi (who had been living in the Soviet Union since July, 1956), his deputy and successor, Erno Gero, and twenty-three other Party members, were expelled from the Party. Abuses and illegalities under the "cult of personality" system, as well as formation of "factions," were officially adduced as reasons for the expulsions. Simultaneously, the victims of Stalinist purges, including many former Social Democrats, were rehabilitated (a number of them posthumously) and readmitted into the Party. With these measures, it was announced that the Party had finally liquidated the "personality cult." Henceforth in socialist Hungary, all law-abiding citizens might live and work in peace.

To perfect this edifice of tolerance and appeasement, the Presidential Council issued an amnesty decree on March 22, 1963, which, claimed the Hungarian press, led to the release of all political prisoners. However, the decree excluded the men who had been condemned for espionage and treason, even though during the Rakosi era many of them (including Cardinal Mindszenty) had been convicted for such offenses in rigged trials. Also excluded were prisoners condemned for murder and arson—among them many of the Freedom Fighters who had been condemned for just such alleged crimes during the 1956 revolution. Conversely, those who had violated "socialist legality"—that is, those who caused death, torture and illegal imprisonments during the Stalinist era—were amnestied by the decree without any qualifications or time limits.

Control over literature and the press also was relaxed. Reports and articles are now less slanted toward Soviet Communist views. Writers and artists were permitted to reorient themselves according to their predilections—that is, toward the West. Oral criticism of economic and even political conditions was widely tolerated at the meetings of factories and agricultural collectives. Travel restrictions were eased both for those wishing to visit Hungary and for Hungarians who wanted to go abroad. In 1963, some 70,000 Hungarians were able to visit Western Europe. In the same year, 20,000 went to the Soviet Union and nearly 200,000 traveled in neighboring Communist countries. Nevertheless, the easing of travel restrictions remained in sharp contrast with the elaborate "technical obstruction system" along the Hungarian-Austrian border. In the last years, the border has been made impenetrable by huge concrete posts and electric-fed wires, in addition to the mine fields and barbed-wire fences—and a view of the "live" Iron Curtain has become a fashionable sightseeing program for tourists visiting Vienna.

The latest period of Hungarian "democratization" coincided with the de-Stalinization process in the Soviet Union, and with the exacerbation of the Sino-Soviet conflict. Links of causality between these occurrences and the developments in Hungary can easily be ascertained. But these influences are by no means exclusive. To a considerable extent, the lessening of tensions in Hungary was conditioned by determinants peculiar to Hungary alone.

The Hungarian Communist Party issued a lengthy declaration on January 20, 1963, condemning those parties that "proclaim dogmatist and sectarian views, thus endangering the unity of the workers' movement."[4] This declaration resembled that of the Soviet Central Committee published in *Pravda* on January 8, 1963, in which the Albanian Communist Party (and implicitly the Chinese) was accused of "belittling the forces of imperialism" by asserting that the United States was a "paper tiger," and of resorting to other "pseudo-revolutionary slogans."

What distinguishes the Hungarian declaration from its Soviet pattern is a strong protest against the Albanian (but, really, the Chinese) interpretation of the Hungarian Revolution. The Albanians asserted that the real cause of the "counterrevolution" had been the ill-considered condemnation of dogmatism and of the cult of personality. The Hungarian declaration revealed that Budapest had sent a special letter to Tirana rejecting such "erroneous interpretation" of the events of 1956. In addition, the declaration praised the attitude of the Hungarian Communists during the revolt: "When necessary," it declared, "we swam against the current; we did not refrain from using extreme measures against culprits and traitors." In order to demonstrate unanimity and strength, the Hungarian leaders expressed pride in having executed, along with his associates, the revolutionary Prime Minister Imre Nagy.

Apparently after more than eight years, the Hungarian Communist leadership still remains under the spellbinding influence of the 1956 revolution. Come what may, they have to discuss it, and to try to impress an audience of disbelievers (who know better) with their version of the story: that Western imperialists, exploiting the discontent created by Rakosi's "cult of personality," fomented the uprising of the handful of "counterrevolutionaries" which the workers, with Soviet assistance, successfully defeated. Thus, as a result of the Sino-Soviet conflict, the specter of the past revolution once again has to be banned and explained away.

No doubt exists in the minds of the adult Hungarians that the Kadar regime was installed in 1956 by Soviet armed forces. For this reason alone, although for other reasons also, Kadar and his ruling party clique must support the Kremlin's policy, both externally and internally. It is necessity and not gratitude that compels Kadar to join the Russian forces. Gratitude has never been a Marxist-Leninist incentive for action. Moreover, the Hungarians do not believe that Kadar has any strong personal convictions except a marked instinct for survival.

Accordingly, Kadar is a "centrist" and a Khrushchevite by necessity. His past imprisonment under Rakosi, conferring on him in the eyes of many the halo of anti-Stalinism, separates him from the dogmatists and sectarians and, therefore, from the pro-Chinese elements in the Hungarian Communist Party. He was selected by the Soviets as First Secretary of the Party because in contrast to his predecessor, the arch-Stalinist Gero, he had the reputation of being a "liberal," anti-Stalinist Communist. Subsequently, he became the pliable tool of the Soviets in the struggle against the Imre Nagy faction of the Party with its revolutionaries and their revisionist adherents. This circumstance forces Kadar and his associates to be strongly opposed to revisionism, which in Hungary alludes to approval of the revolution and condemnation of Soviet intervention. Revisionism also signifies the vague concepts of a democratic-pluralistic Communism-socialism (as developed by Imre Nagy) as well as nationalist and anti-Soviet attitudes. All of these ideas, as Kadar must realize, are fairly popular among some Party circles and extremely popular (as a disguised expression of their anti-Communism) among the people at large.

In contrast, dogmatism-sectarianism in Hungary is even more strongly identified with Stalinism than anywhere else. The reason for this is that the terroristic system of Rakosi utterly compromised Communism even in the eyes of many of its devoted adherents. Rakosi's system exposed all the weaknesses inherent in the Marxist-Leninist political and economic structure, and eventually lined up the entire nation against the regime. Moreover, for no apparent or rational reason, it killed, tortured, and imprisoned thousands of persons, including hundreds of faithful party members.

Accordingly, the Kadar regime must wage a struggle on two fronts: against both the revisionists and the dogmatists. Its maneuverability is thus severely restricted. The future of Kadar and his tight ruling clique is linked with the Russian antirevisionist and antidogmatist line. Such a policy compels the Hungarian leadership unhesitatingly to adopt a pro-Soviet attitude in the intra-Communist dissonance.

The Hungarian Party leaders must have been painfully affected when reminded by the Peking *Jen Min Jih Pao* (*People's Daily*) that they were bailed out in 1956 by the Soviets only upon insistence of the Chinese Communist Party:

> At the critical moment, when the Hungarian counterrevolutionaries had occupied Budapest, for some time [the Soviet leadership] planned to adopt a policy of capitulation and abandon Socialist Hungary to the counterrevolutionaries . . .

> But . . . the Chinese Party and other fraternal parties, persevering in Marxism-Leninism, firmly demanded the repulsion of the assaults of imperialism and reaction, and the safeguarding of the socialist camp and the international Communist movement. We insisted that all necessary measures be taken to smash the counterrevolutionaries.[5]

The Hungarian Central Committee and the Eighth Party Congress have clearly sided with the official Soviet attitude toward Peking and Tirana. The East European Communist regimes, including Hungary, may have gained a higher level of autonomy as a result of circumstances incidental to the Sino-Soviet rift. But Kadar and his ruling clique have much to lose and little to gain by further intensification of the conflict. A better insight into Kadar's views on this subject may be gained from the interview he granted to the editors of the Hungarian Communist Party daily, *Nepszabadsag*.[6] Questioned on the Sino-Soviet issue, the First Secretary of the Hungarian Socialist Workers' Party and Hungarian Prime Minister emphasized the necessity of conducting, "within limits," the interparty discussions in this matter. He complained, however, that:

> Recently an unhealthy dispute and open polemics with regard to the most important statements of the 1957 and 1960 Moscow meetings have developed within the framework of the international Communist and workers' movement. There is no doubt that this dispute is harmful from the point of view of the unity of the Communist movement.

> It would be desirable to stop this dispute, and to concentrate our efforts in the otherwise favorable international situation on increasing the force of the international Communist movement and its chief strength: unity of action in the socialist system.

Kadar further insisted that "the interests of the international workers' movement demand the termination of this public dispute and the end of debating methods inadmissible in the Communist movement." In his opinion, the Sino-Soviet dispute, if continued, should not be aired in the press, "to be read and seen by all our enemies."

Underlying his party's support for the Soviet position in the Sino-Soviet rift, Kadar vowed to promote "the protection of Marxist-Leninist doctrines against all sorts of distortions—both dogmatist and revisionist." The most noticeable feature of this interview was the constant pleading for a termination of the dispute. "We might repeat," Kadar concluded, "that an end should be put to the open dispute."

In addition to Kadar, only Gomulka, among the other satellite leaders, is known to have emphasized to Khrushchev the need for a peaceful compromise with the Chinese. It should also be noted that on April 3, 1964, Khrushchev, at the last minute, was persuaded in Budapest to substitute parts of his speech which contained violent attacks against the Chinese for a much milder version.[7]

Strangely enough, Kadar seems disinterested in the greater measure of Hungarian independence which might result from a further aggravation of the Sino-Soviet dispute. He evidently feels that following the Soviet line is not only the most expedient way, but in fact the only way, for the Hungarian Communists to tread. As long as he can prove this, he will have little trouble with his left-wing or right-wing critics. For as long as Hungary must subordinate her interests to those of the Soviet Union, it is unnecessary and even impossible for the Hungarians to search for what might be in the best interests of their country. If the Hungarian Politburo, the Central Committee, or the people at large were permitted to discuss Hungary's domestic and foreign interests irrespective of Soviet interests, unforeseeable and dangerous results might follow. Such discussion could lead to the position that Imre Nagy so vigorously defended before and during the revolution of 1956—in his writings and by his deeds. Although much is said today about the "counter-revolution," a nearly complete blackout still surrounds the person and the writings of the former Prime Minister. In the house of the hanged man one should not speak of the rope.

There is no contradiction between Kadar's desire to maintain Soviet responsibility for Hungary and his endeavors to strengthen his regime. The Hungarian Communist Party leadership is fully aware of its country's political and economic weaknesses. It believes that cooperation and unity between socialist countries guarantees greater safety and progress than would a polycentrism in which Hungary and her Communist neighbors would be left largely on their own.

For the Hungarian Communists, if not for all East European

satellites, polycentrism is a somewhat alien concept. At this juncture, only Moscow and Peking appear as rallying centers for ruling and nonruling Communist parties. Individual characteristics undoubtedly are emerging in the other Communist countries. Nevertheless, their particular "roads to socialism," if juxtaposed with the earlier Stalinist monolithic uniformity, may better be termed "polymorphism." They have acquired multiform application and adaptation of Communist political and economic principles, but without entailing an ambition to become a center for the direction of other parties.

The postrevolutionary era of repression in Hungary was out of tune with the general political trend in the Soviet bloc countries. Although events in Poland, and especially in Hungary, slowed down, and at times even halted, the process of decompression initiated by Stalin's successors in the Soviet Union, the negative effects of the year 1956 were eventually overcome. Following the experiences sustained by the Hungarian Communist Party, the example of the evolutionary "thaw" in Russia must have been, in itself, a determining factor in Hungarian policy.[8] To follow Moscow's line of de-Stalinization undoubtedly appeared distasteful and risky to leaders of some parties, notably those of Czechoslovakia and East Germany. In Hungary, however, where the post-1956 neo-Stalinism was a reversal of an all-too-dangerous decompression, the urge to imitate Moscow's successful experiment of relaxation was more insistent than in the Communist countries where Stalinism had never before been significantly weakened or uprooted.

In addition to its having been suggested by Khrushchev,[9] Kadar's decision to embark on a path of "democratization" may have been prompted by other mutually agreeable grounds fostered by circumstances in Hungary. First of all, the beginnings of the liberalization drive coincided with the completion of agricultural collectivization that had violently antagonized the usually passive peasantry. Faced with almost universal unpopularity, the regime felt compelled to embark on a campaign to gain sympathy among the intellectuals and industrial workers. The most important "lesson of the revolution" for Kadar must have been the realization that it would be impossible, in the long run, to rule against, rather than with, the support of the masses. In order to strengthen the regime, it became necessary to secure the effective support of as many as possible, instead of claiming a popular support which in reality was mostly fictitious.

At the time of their ascension to power, Kadar and his circle of adherents had planned "to do it differently"—that is, to abstain from the terror and dictatorial methods practiced by Rakosi. However, the time of their takeover was inappropriate for any such implementation of benevolent intentions. Soviet military intervention had tainted Kadar in the eyes of the very workers whom he was trying to persuade into abandoning their resistance to his puppet government. In December, 1956, the Workers' Councils refused to cooperate unless Soviet forces were withdrawn from Hungary, a condition which Kadar could not have fulfilled even if he had so desired. Then, following Soviet advice, he and his associates resolved to adopt the methods of terror and violence which characterized the present regime during the first three to four years of its existence.[10]

Thus, it may be argued that Kadar, with the help of his "enlightened" advisers, Deputy Prime Minister Gyula Kallai and the leading Party Secretary Bela Biszku, undertook to implement the "liberal" policy which he was prevented from carrying out as First Party Secretary during the revolution (when it was too late), and immediately after the revolution (when it was premature). The Communists, of course, deny that there is a "liberalization" in Hungary. They prefer to call it "our popular system aimed at the development of our social life and social system," or the "deepening of democracy."[11] Whatever description the Party uses, this new chapter of Hungary's history is, in considerable measure, a leaf taken from Imre Nagy's book.

De-Stalinization also enabled Kadar to rid himself of some of his Party opponents, making the higher and middle echelons of the Party more coherent and loyal. The Central Committee decisions of August, 1962, not only ousted a number of Stalinists from the Party, but also rehabilitated 190 unnamed former Party members. The latter were mostly Social Democrats who had become members of the Party after the merger of the two workers' parties in 1948, but who subsequently had suffered eclipse under Rakosi. The old Social Democrats still commanded great prestige and influence among the industrial workers. Their rehabilitation (even if posthumous) not only repaired former injustices, but also gained new proselytes for the regime. As practiced by Kadar, democratization is designed as a guarantee that no return to the Stalinist-type terrorism shall ever be contemplated. But as yet, no promises have been made with regard to the postrevolutionary terrorism. In this respect, the regime has by no means crossed a line of no return.

Communist Hungary lost much of her international status when Kadar and his ruling clique were installed by the Soviet Army. For a number of years, Budapest vainly tried to restore its lost prestige and secure the same standing that the other Soviet-bloc countries enjoy in the West and among the uncommitted nations. When the Kadar regime was condemned by the United Nations General Assembly, many countries downgraded their diplomatic missions stationed in Hungary. A number of years passed before the quisling character of the Hungarian regime was, at least partially, erased from the memories of the non-Communist world. At the time of this writing, the United States has still not re-established normal diplomatic relations with postrevolutionary Hungary.

This lack of international prestige was felt in the regime's external relations. The awareness of its international disrepute also lowered the internal authority of the regime in the eyes of the Hungarian people. Status and prestige could be regained only by "good behavior." While Rakosi's prerevolution Hungary was not overly concerned with her position in the eyes of the world outside the Iron Curtain, the present government found it necessary to strive systematically for an improvement of its international contacts, even to the extent of presenting to the outside world an often unreal or fairytale image of conditions in Hungary. The internal relaxation was also motivated by the regime's desire to offer a more favorable picture of the country which it governed.

Today Hungary's position in the United Nations weighs heavily on the role she seeks to play in the international scene, especially in Africa and Asia, where some of her exports are directed. In 1956 and later, the Soviet Government and the "Hungarian authorities" (*sic*) were condemned in resolutions passed by the General Assembly. These resolutions demanded: (1) the withdrawal of Soviet forces from Hungary; (2) free elections in Hungary under United Nations supervision; and (3) observance by the Hungarian authorities of fundamental human rights and freedoms. Although they were not rejected, the credentials of the representatives sent by the Hungarian regime to the United Nations were not recognized. Neither the Soviet Union nor the Kadar Government complied with any of these resolutions, which they considered an infringement on Hungary's "domestic jurisdiction."

After 1957, support for condemnatory resolutions in the General Assembly gradually declined until it became unlikely that the two-thirds majority required for censure could be obtained if the "Hungarian Question" remained on the agenda of future sessions. The United States, the primary promoter of earlier resolutions, therefore proposed a draft resolution which opened the way for a graceful removal of the Hungarian issue from the agenda of the Assembly.

On December 18, 1962, the General Assembly passed a resolution reaffirming "the objective" of earlier decisions and requesting the Secretary General "to take any initiative that he deems helpful in relation to the Hungarian Question." Secretary General U Thant visited Hungary in June, 1963, but nothing is known of his conversations with the Hungarian Government. He refrained from submitting any report to the 1963 General Assembly, and the "Hungarian Question" was no longer placed on the agenda. At the present time, the credentials of the Hungarian delegation are again fully recognized.

The American attitude of caution in the resumption of normal diplomatic relations with Hungary is influenced by the problem presented by the Roman Catholic Primate of Hungary, Cardinal Mindszenty. Strangely, the tenacity and steadfastness of this man have placed him in a position where he has partial control over conditions that are pondered seriously in Washington, Budapest, and Rome.

Cardinal Mindszenty sought refuge in the United States Legation in Budapest on November 4, 1956, when the Soviet military intervention threatened his safety. Prior to the revolution, he had spent eight years in prison serving a life sentence handed down at one of the rigged theatrical trials arranged by the Stalinist regime. The Kadar Government failed to ask for his surrender in 1956 or 1957 because his practical internment in the American Legation building appeared to serve its interests. Thus, it can be considered to have acquiesced in the right of asylum granted to the Cardinal. By 1963, however, the presence of Mindszenty in the United States Legation became embarrassing to the Hungarian Government as a blatant reminder of the revolution. At present, it appears that one of the prerequisites of the resumption of normal relations between the United States and Hungary is the settlement of the Mindszenty case.

Cardinal Mindszenty would leave the Legation and Hungary only upon an order from the Pope. Early in 1963, the Vatican dispatched to Budapest Cardinal Koenig of Vienna, who, with the consent of the American and Hungarian authorities, held long conversations with Mindszenty. The negotiations concerning the fate of Mindszenty are linked with the position of the Catholic Church in Hungary. The Kadar Government refused to accept the bishops appointed by Rome until an agreement, signed by Hungary and the Vatican on September 14, 1964, settled some outstanding questions. Mindszenty, however, was not mentioned in the agreement, and, at the time of this writing, no arrangement appears to have been made that would, in this respect, terminate the present stalemate in the relations between the Vatican and Hungary and between the United States and Hungary. Despite his long isolation from the people of Hungary, the Cardinal still commands enormous prestige throughout the country.

The seismic tremors of the Sino-Soviet conflict have now reached East Europe and brought about estrangements and *rapprochements* between the Communist powers of that region. As far as Hungary is concerned, the resumption of cordial ties with Yugoslavia for the first time since 1958 is one such noteworthy result.

Khrushchev's altercations with Mao had allowed him to resume cordial relations with Tito, the archrevisionist, who had (for the second time) been denounced and excommunicated in 1958. It was in March, 1958, after Kadar had visited Tito, that the Hungarian leader was believed to have attempted mediation in the dispute over the Yugoslav Draft Party Program, published on March 14, 1958. However, after the new break of Party relations between the members of the Soviet bloc and Yugoslavia, Hungarian-Yugoslav ties were restricted entirely to diplomatic essentials.

Personal relations between Yugoslav and Hungarian leaders were again taken up when Tito traveled to Moscow in December, 1962, and on his way back was met by Kadar in Budapest. In September, 1963, Kadar visited Yugoslavia and had talks with Tito, Rankovic, and others in Karadjordjevo, near Belgrade. It was reported on that occasion that Kadar had invited Tito to visit Hungary. In January, 1964, a large Yugoslav delegation led by Aleksandar Rankovic came to Budapest for interparty talks, followed in September, 1964, by Tito himself.

An intensification of political and economic ties with Hungary, as well as frequent visits between Party leaders, seems to indicate resumption of Yugoslav diplomatic interest to a degree unparalleled since the time of the Hungarian "thaw" in 1956. At that time, Tito cherished the idea of closer cooperation between Yugoslavia and Hungary. He hoped to bring Hungary's internal and external politics into closer agreement with Yugoslavia's own political situation, in contrast with the politics of other Communist states in the area.[12] In other words, the Chinese conflict with the Soviet Union, along with the Soviet-Yugoslav *rapprochement,* permitted Tito to revert to his earlier scheme, which had been cut short by the revolutionary events in Hungary in 1956.

Another effect of the Sino-Soviet schism may be a gradual alienation among the various East European Communist states, which so far have been held together by the overriding authority of the Soviet Union. Among those countries, Romania appears to have made the most extensive use of her enhanced autonomy by opposing other bloc countries in the economic and cultural spheres. Romania has departed from the policy of toleration toward her national minorities, especially the large Hungarian minority in Transylvania. She has been repealing measures that allowed cultural autonomy, maintenance of minority schools, and other manifestations of separate national identity, and has reintroduced former methods of discrimination, oppression, and forcible Romanization of the minority groups.[13]

Although Romania's unfriendly policy has been adversely received in Budapest, the Kadar Government so far has made no overt *démarche* of protest. Nevertheless, a certain chill in the Hungarian-Romanian relations has recently been noticeable. Any further dissipation of Soviet paramountcy in the area will probably continue to elicit dormant animosities between the historically inimical nations of the Danube Valley, unless such animosity is counteracted by acts of foresight and toleration.

Romanian intractability has obviously provoked displeasure in Moscow. As yet, the Kremlin has failed to counter or openly condemn the bolts or extravagances of the Romanian Communist Party. It may, however, find a roundabout way of invoking such a warning by authorizing Hungary to expose the alleged Romanian deviations from the correct path of Leninist nationality policy. Pressures from Hungary against Romania, and vice versa, have been frequently used in the past by other superpowers claiming paramountcy over the area, in order to prevent one or the other party from following diversions which were considered harmful to the overlord's interests.

The impact of Kadar's popularity campaign on the people of Hungary may be surmised but not as yet conclusively judged. The concessions that the regime has made to gain popular sympathy have certainly been received with satisfaction by all those favorably affected. The enjoyment of even a controlled freedom, which previously was denied, has induced a certain benevolent disposition toward the regime among many people. This feeling, however, is based on comparison with the even worse conditions the Hungarians had the misfortune of experiencing previously. Expressions of these comparative appraisals often mislead casual visitors or gullible observers. The present phase of Communist rule is thought by most Hungarians as better than any other Communist regime they have witnessed. But this by no means amounts to an approval or endorsement of Communism. For the time being at least, the Hungarian people simply do not see any possibility of having anything other than a Communist government.

It is a highly significant symptom of popular thinking that the present relaxation is attributed to the effects of the revolution of 1956 rather than to the generosity or wisdom of the regime. It is no longer thought, as it was in 1957, that the revolution was fought in vain. A fascinating analogy exists between popular belief in the 1860's when concessions made by the Austrians to the Hungarian national demands were attributed to the tragic revolution of 1848–49, and not to the change of heart of Vienna.

The Sino-Soviet feud has caused tremors, not only within the Party, but in wide segments of the Hungarian population. Reactions among the people vary from the simple *Schadenfreude* over Soviet troubles, to anxiety that Chinese-prompted Stalinism might find its way back into the Kremlin, and from there into Hungary. Whatever the popular ideas about this interparty conflict are, developments along this line are carefully watched by all politically conscious Party and non-Party Hungarians alike. Fantastic rumors about the Soviet difficulties—such as troop concentrations and defense preparations in Central Asia and the Far East—are rampant and eagerly listened to.

The present period of relative relaxation and liberalization in Hungary may be viewed as a policy alternative chosen by the Kadar Government for reasons of expediency rather than of necessity. This is a significant circumstance which differentiates the present Hungarian "thaw" from the post-Stalinist one. In other respects, too, the present situation is potentially far less explosive than that of the summer of 1956.

The Hungarian Communist Party, although certainly not homogeneous, is no longer paralyzed by a split in its leadership as it was after Rakosi's ouster in July, 1956. The leading clique and its faithful 10,000 men are truly in control over an estimated 40,000 middle ranks and the remaining 450,000 indifferent, conformist, or opportunist Party members. Executed or imprisoned after the revolution, the potential leaders of the rightist Party opposition have been eliminated; the prominent leftists have been removed from key positions, and were expelled from the Party in the big purge of 1961–62. In this way, the formal unity of the Party has been assured.

The present "thaw" did not coincide with, nor was it conditioned by, a change of the leading personnel of the Hungarian Communist Party and government. The *dramatis personae,* Kadar and his circle, who introduced the recent changes, are the very same leaders who earlier had practiced terror and absolute oppression. No alternative leaders have appeared on the political horizon, nor has dual leadership affected continuity, as it did between 1953 and 1956, when Rakosi and Imre Nagy fought for power. No "changing of the guard" may now be expected, for the simple reason that there is nobody who is—or, in actuality, can be considered—by the masses as an alternative to Kadar and his ruling group.

This is not to suggest that there exists no dissatisfaction and that no elements ardently desire a change. But relaxation—more often a stimulus for further demands than a political safety valve—whets the appetite of dissatisfaction only when discontent is manifested in some organized form. This time, the Hungarian regime has seen to it that no Party factions, pressure groups (like the Petofi Circle in 1956), and other mouthpieces of opposition (like student organizations) are able to utilize the decompression to request more than is given. Political and social concessions have been initiated by the Communist leadership and not upon ostentatious demands of the others. "Khvostism"[14] no longer prevails as it did in 1956.

The greatest barrier preventing the Kadar regime's popularity drive from becoming a genuine success is the person of Kadar himself. The continuity in the leadership of Party and government works both ways: it forestalls rivalries, but at the same time perpetuates the stigma attached to the leadership. Contrary to Gomulka, who had been placed at the head of the Polish Communist Party against the will of Moscow, Kadar had been thrust upon Hungary by an invading foreign army. Regardless of how actively Kadar attempts to popularize his person by descending among the people, talking in common-sense terms, and endeavoring to please workers and intellectuals, the mark of Cain will continue to plague him.

As long as the present decompression remains a planned and controlled relaxation, it will not be fraught with the dangers that accompanied the "thaw" of 1956. The Security Police (under whatever name it operates) is now under strict Party control and, although it has not ceased to be efficient, it is more restrained and discreet than earlier. Arrests are less arbitrary, and, while secret trials are still held, prison terms are shorter and death sentences fewer. Whether the Hungarian armed forces are now more reliable than in 1956 is a matter of conjecture. Ultimately, the regime might still depend on the Soviet forces which, while trying to be "invisible," continue to surround Budapest and other important cities.

In spite of internal relaxation, greater independence in her relations with the Kremlin, and the Communist schism, the presence of the Red Army points to the dependence in which Kadar's Hungary continues to live. When Kadar casually remarked in May, 1963, that "Soviet troops will leave Hungary only when the Americans will pull out from somewhere,"[15] he fully revealed the fact that developments in Hungary and in the entire East European scene depend ultimately on events outside that area. The evolution of the German problem, other developments in the Cold War, and the Sino-Soviet conflict are among the issues that will certainly impinge on the future of Hungary.

5. Czechoslovakia

H. GORDON SKILLING

THE SINO-SOVIET dispute placed the leaders of Communist Czechoslovakia on the horns of a dilemma. This stemmed from their decades-old tradition of unquestioning obedience to Moscow and the Communist Party of the Soviet Union, and the long-standing tradition of Stalinism in their domestic practice of government. The Chinese Communist challenge to Soviet leadership of the bloc, and its condemnation of Soviet policy and ideology, touched on one of the most sensitive aspects of the relationship of all Communist states with the U.S.S.R., by raising the question of the rightness of Soviet direction and forcing these states to choose between the leadership of Moscow and Peking. At the same time, Khrushchev's increasingly dramatic assault on the Stalinist pattern forced Communist states such as Czechoslovakia, which had not seriously modified this pattern, to decide either to embark on the dangerous course of de-Stalinization or to find themselves increasingly out of step with their Soviet model. Were they to choose Moscow or Peking, and, if Moscow, would this mean the gradual breakup of the Stalinist system and the dissolution of their own power?

Khrushchev's anti-Stalinist course was profoundly unsettling for Czech and Slovak Communist leaders, and some of them sympathized with Peking's defense of the Stalinist tradition. They could not easily adjust to Khrushchev's adaptation of Leninism to the new conditions of the latter half of the century, and repudiate the more familiar orthodoxy of the Chinese. Nonetheless, their utter devotion to the Soviet Union made it virtually certain that they would opt for Moscow rather than Peking, and without hesitation or doubt. Even had Moscow insisted on immediate and drastic dismantling of Stalinism in Prague, it is doubtful if the regime would have dared, or wanted, to follow Tirana's example in defying the Soviet Union and relying on China. In any case, the Soviet Party gave no sign of urging immediate changes in Czechoslovakia's course at home, and, on the contrary, seemed satisfied with Prague's acceptance of the Soviet position on foreign policy and ideology in the dispute with China. For the time being, therefore, Prague's embarrassment was reduced, and the choice of Moscow was rendered more palatable. Nonetheless, the perplexity involved in this choice was likely to reappear, because of either Soviet pressure to conform or domestic pressures resulting from expectations of change awakened by the leaders' verbal onslaughts on Stalinism.

Prague's loyalty to Moscow—or, perhaps, its subservience—had deep roots in the history of the Communist Party of Czechoslovakia.[1] Klement Gottwald, leader of Czechoslovak Communism from 1929 to 1953, had been placed in his position largely by the action of Stalin and the Comintern and had had a reputation as a devoted follower of the Moscow line. During the entire wartime period, Gottwald lived and worked in Moscow, where he had also spent several earlier years, and was a faithful exponent both of the sectarian tactic of the period of the Russo-German pact and of the "people's front" policy after 1941. Rejecting the left-wing criticism of some other Czech and Slovak Communists, who favored an immediate advance to proletarian revolution and dictatorship, Gottwald espoused the Soviet doctrine of a more gradual approach to socialism, by a "national path." This involved accepting a substantial degree of democratic freedom, and necessitated the compromises of cooperation with President Benes and the other coalition parties. The Prague regime was thus less fully Communist than its counterparts in Sofia, Bucharest, and Belgrade, and, after 1947, even those in Warsaw and Budapest. Although Gottwald adopted this policy at Moscow's behest, this only partially communized country represented in some measure an Achilles' heel of the Communist bloc, especially as the conflict with Yugoslavia began to develop. The early willingness of Gottwald's government to associate itself with the Marshall Plan suggested the dangers that threatened in Prague, as long as full Communist control had not been established.

All this was drastically changed by the Communist seizure of power in 1948. In one leap, Czechoslovakia was transformed from a somewhat backward satellite into one of the most advanced, with complete Communist rule achieved and, at the same time, with more massive support for the regime than in most other Communist countries. Viewed from Moscow, Czechoslovakia, during the next five years, must have appeared as the model ally, acting in utter solidarity with the Soviet Union in world affairs, and moving rapidly toward the complete transformation of Czechoslovak society on the Soviet model. In the Communist bloc, no member proclaimed the primacy of the CPSU more vociferously, or denounced the Yugoslav heresy more venomously, than Prague.

Until the death of Stalin in 1953, there was no conflict between the faithfulness of Prague to the course of Soviet policy and its fervent imitation of the Stalinist pattern of rule. Indeed, one presupposed, and was identified with, the other. The Communist leadership was thoroughly Stalinist, both in origin, as the creation of Stalin, and in methods of rule. The Stalinization of public life proceeded pell mell, with the copying of all major Soviet practices and institutions, frenetic mobilization of the economy, strict Party control of cultural life, and the exaltation of Gottwald as the supreme personal ruler. Most notable of all was the succession of political trials, involving the execution of leading figures, such as Rudolf Slansky and Vladimir Clementis, and the imprisonment of hundreds of others. Slansky and his colleagues were accused of conspiring with Tito and committing the heresy of "national Communism," but, for the most part, suffered more for their association with the police apparatus, or their Jewish, German, or Slovak origins, than for their belief in a distinctive Czechoslovak path to socialism. Slansky was no Gomulka or Tito, but a devoted Muscovite, no less subservient to Stalin than Gottwald. Only Clementis, the former Foreign Minister, stood for a more liberal and nationalist brand of Communism, and as a Slovak, for resistance to the centralism of Czech Prague.

Even the death of Stalin brought little significant change. There was no real "thaw" in Czechoslovakia, and the "new course" of the early years was extremely modest. The revolt in Pilsen was motivated mainly by economic complaints, and was easily subjected to control. Apart from the coincidental death of Gottwald—appropriately within a few days of Stalin's—there was almost no shift in the corps of leaders who had been in power at Gottwald's side for five years and were thoroughly Stalinist in outlook. His successor as President was the veteran Antonin Zapotocky, and as party chairman, Antonin Novotny, a Party *apparatchik* of the new generation but a product of the Gottwald period. Persons active in Stalinizing various spheres of life—such as the Slovak boss, Viliam Siroky, the former security chief, Karol Bacilek, and the information head, Vaclav Kopecky—remained in high office. Lip service was paid to the need for de-Stalinization, but only token changes were made in basic practices and institutions. Indeed, in some respects, Czechoslovakia intensified Stalinist repression, in particular in a series of show trials in 1954. Apart from smaller fry caught up in the Slansky case, the new purge was expecially aimed at Slovak Communists of a more nationalist outlook, such as Gustav Husak, the head of the Slovak Board of Commissioners, and the distinguished writer, Ladislav Novomesky.

The basis was thus laid for Czechoslovakia's remarkable political stability during the momentous events of 1956 in Hungary and Poland. As Hungarians and Poles were moving forward during 1955 and early 1956 to broadened freedoms, and experiencing severe internal tensions, comparable manifestations among Czechoslovaks, especially among students and writers and even within the Party, met with little general popular support, and were early counteracted by firm action of the authorities.[2] The leadership was united, and no revisionist or nationalist spokesman, comparable to Nagy or Gomulka, was available. During the October days, the Prague regime showed no overt sympathy with its neighbors to the north and south, and, after the crushing of the Hungarian revolt, it was among the first to approve publicly the intervention of Soviet armed forces. Had Prague chosen to associate itself with Budapest and Warsaw, a general crumbling of Soviet and perhaps Communist power might have ensued in the entire region. Prague, however, stood firm, as a reliable point of strength in the Soviet power structure in Eastern Europe. Soviet military intervention in turn saved the Prague leaders from the disaster that might have followed successful Hungarian resistance.

The Hungarian revolt, and its bloody consequences, tended to discredit liberalizing efforts in Eastern Europe, and to weaken the position of Khrushchev in Soviet politics and in the bloc. Chinese influence, exerted briefly on the side of relaxation of Soviet control in Eastern Europe, now came increasingly to favor a harder line. The slow and cautious attitude of the Czechs toward de-Stalinization seemed to have been vindicated, and must have awakened some admiration among the Chinese as well as among Soviet critics of Khrushchev, such as Molotov. Nevertheless, Khrushchev himself had no reason to complain, for the Czechs showed no signs of lining up against him in the critical months at the end of 1956 and in early 1957. In the summer of 1957, during the crisis in the Soviet Party, the "anti-Party group" of Molotov, Malenkov, and Kaganovich found no open sympathy among Czechs and Slovaks, and Khrushchev's victory was warmly greeted in Prague. By the end of the year, the Czech leaders were throwing their full support behind the new intransigence, endorsing the Moscow manifesto, and fully joining the anti-Yugoslav and antirevisionist campaign.[3] After the Congress of the League of Communists of Yugoslavia, in May, 1958, the campaign against Yugoslav revisionism reached a high pitch of intensity.[4] During a visit to Moscow in early July, 1958, Novotny took the occasion to declare: "We shall always remain loyally by your side. We shall devote all our power toward strengthening our socialist camp and the international revolutionary movement." The contradiction that may have once threatened Czechoslovakia between its devotion to Moscow and its unwillingness to de-Stalinize was removed at a time when de-Stalinization itself seemed to be out of line with the unity and stability of the Communist bloc as a whole.[5] Nonetheless, the constant attention of Czech and Slovak leaders to the dangers of revisionism and bourgeois nationalism, especially in Slovakia, suggested that beneath the surface of unanimity and orthodoxy, dissatisfaction and unrest were stirring.[6]

As we now know, a new menace to bloc unity and Soviet preeminence was beginning to appear in the shape of "dogmatism," a term used at this time to refer esoterically to the Chinese views on the strategy and tactics of world Communism. It became increasingly clear, especially by the time of the Bucharest and Moscow conferences of Communist parties in 1960, that beneath the façade of unity a serious divergence of view was manifesting itself, and that Communist China, supported in particular by Albania, was challenging a whole series of Soviet policies and theories, including Khrushchev's denigration of Stalin and Stalinism. It was at these conferences that Czechoslovakia might have opted to follow the Albanian lead, and to associate itself with the critics of the revisionism of Khrushchev and the CPSU. There was no sign, however, that any of the Czech or Slovak Communist leaders, or the members of the Party as a whole, entertained any sympathy for the Sino-Albanian viewpoint or even considered the possibility of independent action. On the contrary, everything pointed to the willingness of the Czech and Slovak delegates at these conferences to continue their traditional unconditional support of Moscow and Khrushchev and to refuse to encourage or support the critics on the "left" or "dogmatic" side of the controversy.[7] No doubt, the pragmatic Leninism of Khrushchev had a greater appeal to the practical Czechs than the more revolutionary and orthodox version of the Chinese and Albanians. Even on the issue of Stalinism, which began to obtrude more and more openly into the Sino-Soviet dispute, the Czechs and Slovaks were ready to associate themselves with the Soviet verbal onslaught on Stalin, hoping, no doubt, that they might avoid the necessity of taking genuine steps to modify their own Stalinism. They were ready, without any reluctance, to express their full agreement with the main lines of Soviet foreign and domestic policy.[8]

A new climax in the Sino-Soviet dispute was reached at the Twenty-second Congress of the CPSU in November, 1961, with Khrushchev's open denunciation of Albanian Communism and the publicly expressed disagreement of the Chinese with this action. It is impossible to know whether the threatening open split between Moscow and Peking produced serious differences of opinion among Czech and Slovak Communist leaders. As far as the published evidence goes, by choosing Moscow they resolved any dilemma that might have existed in their minds and any differences in their ranks. Support for the Chinese line seemed to be nonexistent among the leaders. Novotny showed no desire to emulate Hoxha. There was not even a sign of an attempt to steer a middle course or to use the situation to play China against the Soviet Union in Communist bloc politics. Novotny, in his report to the Central Committee on the Moscow Congress,[9] proclaimed his full support for the Soviet standpoint and criticized the Chinese Party for the attitude it expressed on the Albanian question. The Czechoslovak Party, he said, had done everything possible to guide the Albanian leaders to a right stand, sending letters and issuing declarations, but now regarded them as breaking the ranks and following an entirely wrong course. His vigorous assault on the Albanian Party, and on the "anti-Party group," as well as his open censure of the Chinese, suggested how closely he was ready to involve himself personally on Khrushchev's side in the controversy.

As in 1956, so in 1961, Prague took a firm stand, without hesitation, at the side of Moscow, and showed its complete reliability in a moment of crisis. In particular, the Czechs endorsed the Soviet policy of peaceful coexistence, leaving no doubt of their belief that nuclear weapons had rendered this policy the only sane course to follow.[10] The Soviet policy of *détente* with the West harmonized with the burning desire of Czechs and Slovaks to avoid a world war, and involved no real sacrifice of essential Czechoslovak national interests. The idea of peaceful competition in the economic sphere fitted in well with the important role of the advanced Czechoslovak economy in the bloc and in its program of technical assistance to the underdeveloped world. This policy had a much greater appeal to the businesslike and practical Czechs than the pursuit of the will-o'-the-wisp of revolution in Asia and Africa. The Soviet effort to put aside the Berlin question, as well as to moderate somewhat the hostility toward West Germany as part of the price of coexistence, did not unduly endanger Czechoslovakia, and removed a danger spot which might otherwise quite easily have produced a nuclear showdown. The policy of coexistence did not necessarily involve too close an association with Western powers, such as the United States, Great Britain, and France. Some modest and cautious expansion of commercial, and even cultural, relations with these countries was permissible and even desirable, provided that they did not threaten in any way the closest solidarity with the Soviet Union and did not permit too great an extension of Western influence among a people once accustomed to look westward for their ideas and their trade.

Czechoslovakia did not use the opportunity of the Sino-Soviet dispute to demand a widened autonomy for itself within the bloc nor did its leaders sympathize with the efforts of some Communist states to achieve such autonomy. The idea of polycentrism was absolutely and unconditionally rejected. "Does not polycentrism," Koucky asked the Central Committee, "under the present conditions necessarily weaken internationalism?"[11] The "only center" of the Communist movement, wrote Party ideologist Fojtik, was the Communist Party of the Soviet Union.[12] Although the idea of polycentrism was still identified in Czech discussions with the revisionism of Yugoslavia, in fact, of course, it was the Chinese and the Albanians who, while paying lip service to monocentrism, had done much more to advance the idea of competing centers of power and decision-making in the Communist world. The Czechs were adamant in rejecting any tendency toward a splitting up of the Communist bloc, whether from the revisionist or the dogmatist side. Indeed, both heresies were more and more treated as equal dangers, originating in nationalism. "The common denominator of both revisionism and dogmatism is nationalism, a position of national exclusiveness, the betrayal of proletarian internationalism, the severance of fraternal bonds with the CPSU and the other Marxist parties . . ."[13] For the Czechs, proletarian internationalism still required the loyal acceptance of Moscow as the only legitimate center for formulating the ideology and making the policy of the Communist world. Czechoslovakia herself had few real friends within the bloc, having little but contempt for Romania and Bulgaria, herself enjoying little but scorn from Yugoslavia, Hungary, and Poland, and separated from the East Germans by traditional fear of all Germans. Her own best recourse was the closest solidarity with Moscow, where, through direct relations and her own reputation as a loyal and dependable ally, she could achieve more than by a dramatic assertion of autonomy.

Nevertheless, the Twenty-second Congress must have brought disturbing thoughts to Czech leaders because of the resumption of the campaign against Stalin, expressed symbolically in the removal of his body from the mausoleum and the public denunciation of his crimes. Moreover, Khrushchev's assault on Albania was explained in terms of that country's continuing Stalinism. No doubt, the real points of controversy were the Albanian defiance of Soviet foreign policy and Khrushchev's ideological revisions, but Albania had certainly done less than other states to reform its Stalinist system, and had hardly even indulged in verbal de-Stalinization. Czechoslovakia, which had also changed little of the old order, was thus placed in an embarrassing position. Could she continue to restrict her support of Khrushchev to matters of foreign policy, ideology, and bloc relations, and avoid a modification of her own domestic pattern? Could she continue to limit herself to de-Stalinization in words, without actually rectifying political and economic practices inherited from the Stalin days? There was an increasing anomaly in the continuance of Czechoslovak Stalinism, and a deepening dilemma for Czech and Slovak Communists about their future course.

The Czech leaders sought to resolve their dilemma by making gestures in the direction of de-Stalinization, but without serious efforts to democratize or even to rationalize the existing totalitarian system. At the Central Committee meeting following the Twenty-second Congress, Novotny admitted that the cult of personality had had undesirable results in Czechoslovakia, too, but sought to give the impression that the worst consequences had been largely eliminated by actions already taken. The main blame for Stalinism was placed on Slansky. The only definite steps proposed were the removal from Prague of the massive Stalin monument, which represented "a commemoration of the cult of personality," and the re-interring of Gottwald's body, the display of which in the mausoleum was said to be out of harmony with the principle of collective leadership. During the ensuing year, the cult of personality was repeatedly denounced, and its evil effects in all fields of life were lamented. The need for freedom in cultural and economic life, and for popular participation in political life, was constantly advocated. The agencies of the Party were to be made organs of collective leadership, and freedom of criticism within the Party was asserted. These statements, however, were paralleled by equally insistent declarations of the need for discipline, for centralized decision-making, for criticism only from a Party standpoint, and for Party control of culture and the economy.[14] It is clear that the timid measures to encourage a greater degree of freedom and rationality in the conduct of affairs, even if sincerely meant, were to be narrowly circumscribed, and were hardly likely to bring about a substantial and meaningful modification of society, even to the extent accomplished in the Soviet Union, and still less to that in Poland.

An important reason for the Czechoslovak failure to adjust to the new spirit of Moscow was the lack of alternative leaders representing a more liberal or national viewpoint and capable of giving a "new look" to Communism in Czechoslovakia. Most of the leaders were veterans from Gottwald's days or were his comrades from the 1920's—such as Bacilek, Dolansky, and Siroky, who were not able to adapt to the post-Stalin climate. A new generation, represented by Novotny himself, and by Hendrych, Kolder, and Lenart, were *apparatchiki* trained in the Gottwald period, and carrying on, in a bureaucratic and Partyminded manner, the old ways and the old ideas. Leadership for a liberal Communism could hardly be offered by a former Social Democrat, such as Fierlinger, as wedded to the old order as the veterans, or by the one spokesman of the managerial or technician classes, Oto Simunek. There was no former leader of stature, like Gomulka, who had survived the purges and might emerge from prison, to assume the mantle of leadership. The top circles had no representative of the home resistance movement, and most "Westerners" had been eliminated during the Slansky purges. Among the intellectuals, no significant revisionist had emerged during the thaw of the 1950's. The one person, Rudolf Barak, who, in spite of many years as Minister of the Interior, seemed to possess the ability and popular appeal required for leading a more liberal course, was imprisoned in the spring of 1962 on charges of embezzlement. On the other hand, there was no extreme Stalinist, such as a Chervenkov or Rakosi, waiting in the wings, and no need for a drastic purge of Stalinists comparable to that in Bulgaria or Hungary. The leadership seemed to possess the unity as well as the orthodoxy necessary to continue the old line.

The leaders were fearful of taking steps that might have threatened their own position or the Communist system as a whole. Although ready to attack Stalin in words, they could not even bring themselves to demolish the visible symbols of Stalinism. It took a full year after the Twenty-second Congress for the Stalin statue to be removed, or for the body of Gottwald to be reinterred. The leaders were no doubt fully aware of the ridicule into which the continuance of these symbols of Stalinism brought them and of the shock that would be caused by their removal. Even more delicate and dangerous was the rehabilitation of the many persons who had suffered injustice during the Stalin period. Some of them had been released and allowed to resume normal lives, but there had been no revision of the verdicts and no public rehabilitation of outstanding persons such as Clementis and Novomesky. A commission to investigate the trials continued its work, without, however, completing or publishing its findings. The threads of these investigations no doubt led often directly to persons such as Bacilek, Siroky, and Novotny, who had had a large share in the purges of the 1950's and were themselves deeply involved in the crimes of Stalinism. An ominous event in early 1962 was the arrest of Rudolf Barak, who had been in charge of the re-examination of the trials, and had perhaps found out too much.

When the Twelfth Congress of the CPC met in Prague, after postponement, in December, 1962, it was widely expected that there would be indications of a shift of course, perhaps with the removal of some of the most extreme Stalinist leaders and a more definite reckoning with Stalinist ways. Nothing of the kind occurred. No significant changes were made in the top command; there was no more than a stepped-up verbal denunciation of the cult of personality, including a more extended criticism of Gottwald's alleged errors. Although the trials of the 1950's were criticized, the idea of a possible rehabilitation for Slansky was expressly rejected. Indeed the Congress was largely absorbed by the consequences of the grave economic crisis that had plagued the country throughout the year, and confirmed the decision to revert to a more centralized direction of the economy to meet these problems.

A much more significant feature of the Congress was the intensified public criticism of the Chinese, who until then had been largely spared open attack and had been criticized vicariously in the person of the Albanians. The Prague Congress was part of the tide of denunciation of Peking which had begun to rise at earlier party congresses in Sofia and Budapest. Vladimir Koucky in particular made a full-dress assault on the Chinese defense of the Albanians. Novotny himself, in his final address to the Congress, bitterly condemned the Chinese attitude, and called for "unity" in the Communist movement and cooperation with the CPSU, on the basis of close alliance and friendship with the U.S.S.R.[15] There were friendly words for Yugoslavia, and the sharpest of criticism was reserved now for "dogmatism," especially as expressed by the rejection of the Soviet policy of coexistence.[16] When the Chinese later launched a savage attack on the Czechoslovak Congress, and spoke of "certain people who today betray Fucik's heritage and instead of death, prefer a life on their knees, a life in a kennel," the Czechs replied with an equally savage attack, denying the charge of "right opportunism," restating the case against "dogmatism and sectarianism," and proclaiming their continued belief in the CPSU as "the vanguard" of the international Communist movement.[17]

Novotny also used the occasion of the Congress to express his complete approval of the closer integration of the economies of the U.S.S.R. and the East European states, a policy to which Khrushchev was increasingly assigning an important role in the strengthening and unification of the bloc. Czechoslovakia was ready to associate itself closely with an international division of labor within the Communist camp, at least in Eastern Europe, and with the unified planning organs proposed in this connection. This would help, said Novotny, to create a "unified economy" within the Communist world, and to overcome dependence on the capitalist states. Although this policy, if fully applied, was bound to involve difficult adjustments of Czechoslovak production to the needs and capacities of the bloc as a whole, the Prague regime was ready to accept these implications of the division of labor, and no doubt felt that, with an advanced industrial economy, its gains would be greater than its sacrifices. When later economic integration met with some resistance from Romania, Czechoslovakia was not sympathetic with the Romanian viewpoint, and tended to side with the Soviet Union and other more developed states on the need for greater integration.

In the early 1960's, it was difficult to know whether or not Moscow was pressing Czechoslovakia to make changes in its leadership and policy. Was Khrushchev insisting that eventually Czecho-

slovakia must bring its obsolete domestic ways into greater harmony
with the Soviet Union? Other states, notably Bulgaria and Hungary,
had taken the imperative of de-Stalinization more seriously. On the
other hand, Poland had made a considerable retreat from the position of 1956. Even in the Soviet Union, many backward steps were
taken, and it was impossible to discern a straight and undeviating
forward line in the reform of the old. It was still conceivable that
Khrushchev was not really interested in de-Stalinization at all, except as an instrument in his struggle for power. He may have been
satisfied with East European support in his conflict with China, and
may not have insisted on internal reforms. It seems more likely that
Khrushchev sought a more rationalized totalitarian society at home
and abroad—one that remained basically totalitarian and continued
to exhibit "partisan" or "ideological" as well as "rational" elements.
In the case of Poland, he was perhaps pressing for a retreat, and in
the other East European states, for a somewhat more rapid advance,
without, however, making this a condition of his aid and approval.
Moreover, all of the states now had more freedom in domestic affairs, and could not be forced into actions distasteful to them.
Albania was a warning of what might happen elsewhere if too much
pressure was applied, and reinforced the lesson of Yugoslavia in
1948. It was not desirable to push these states too far in a liberal
direction, for the experience of Hungary and Poland in 1956 had
demonstrated the dangers of this course. Certainly for Czechoslovakia one of the advantages of the situation was that she could use
her new-found autonomy in order to avoid making serious changes
in her system, while continuing to throw her support to Moscow in
foreign and bloc affairs.

There was another element to be reckoned with, namely, the
aspirations and expectations of the rank and file of the Communist
parties, and of the people in general. The hopes of a moderation
of Czechoslovak Communism had been awakened before, in 1953
and 1956, only to be frustrated by the continuance of a hard course.
Expectations had been awakened anew after the Twenty-second
Congress, only to be again disappointed.

During the spring of 1963, the long-delayed impact of the campaign against Stalinism finally made itself felt, to the surprise of the
world. There had, however, been hints of a changing mood and a
new temper. Dissatisfaction and anger were steadily accumulating—
particularly dissatisfaction with the slow pace of de-Stalinization and
with the fact that the victims of the terror of the 1950's had not

been rehabilitated, and anger at the continuance in office of leaders tarred with the brush of Stalinism.[18] The Party leaders became increasingly afraid that their critics were taking advantage of the spirit of de-Stalinization to undermine their position. Novotny and others lashed out at the alleged influence of bourgeois ideas among Czech Communists. He warned against any criticism that ignored the progress allegedly made in de-Stalinization and that touched the Party and its leadership.[19] These statements did not, however, prevent the explosion of feeling that finally occurred in April and May, 1963, at successive congresses of writers and journalists in Bratislava and Prague.[20]

The outburst of the writers against the evils of Stalinism and against the delay in de-Stalinization was not entirely spontaneous, for the Party itself had to some extent prepared the ground for it by re-examining the political trials of the 1950's. Although the full report was not made available until the late summer of 1963, the general trend of the investigation was known earlier and no doubt encouraged the critics to voice their pent-up wrath and discontent. The ferment was largely confined to writers—and indeed to Communist writers at that, but there can be little doubt that they were giving expression to the long-suppressed feelings of wider circles of the public, non-Communist as well as Communist. There can be equally little doubt that the wave of criticism escaped from the control of the Party apparatus, and went far beyond anything officially desired. This was particularly true of the speech by M. Hysko at the Congress of Slovak Journalists,[21] when he openly condemned leading Party figures, such as Prime Minister Siroky and the dead Kopecky, and repudiated the official Party reports of the 1950's which had been the basis of the trials and purges. Hysko devoted much of his attention to what he thought was the unjustified attack on Slovak nationalism at that time, and to the necessity of rectifying the entire treatment of the Slovak question since then. Like many other writers, he singled out for blame the failure to correct the consequences of the cult of personality in the seven years since the Twentieth Congress in 1956. Indeed, the tide of criticism had advanced so far as to require the sternest warning by Novotny himself, in a speech in Košice,[22] directed not only at Hysko personally, but at others, including the editorial boards of newspapers that had published these comments and had themselves wandered onto a "dangerous path." In a spate of other articles and speeches, Novotny and others tried to curb the dangerous current of criticism, and to justify all that the Party had already done in de-Stalinizing.

The wave of criticism, stirred up in part by the action of the Party itself, in turn pushed the Party still further along the unwelcome path of de-Stalinization. The earlier removal of Karol Bacilek and Bruno Kohler, in April (and revealed only six weeks later), had been the first straw in the wind. The final report on the trials,[23] exonerating all the culprits of the legal charges against them, went far beyond anything that had been hinted at, and indeed contradicted the leaders' earlier efforts to narrow the scope of the re-examination. Even now, certain leaders were not fully rehabilitated in a political sense, although their legal convictions were pronounced entirely without foundation. Slansky, in particular, was not given a full political rehabilitation, nor were leading Slovaks, such as Novomesky and Husak. Nonetheless, the report, condemning the trials as total fabrications and rehabilitating many who had been executed or imprisoned in 1953 and 1954, cast a dark shadow on the past of the Party, including the post-Stalin years, when a rectification of the trials had been so long resisted. The report further discredited the regime in the eyes of the public and the Communist rank and file, and weakened those leaders who had been responsible for these events, both of commission and omission, and who still remained in office. This was demonstrated in September, with the removal of Siroky from the prime ministership, and the displacement of a number of Gottwald's other prominent associates from the government.

Novotny himself weathered the storm, and by these moves—to a large extent taken unwillingly, and forced upon him by public pressure—had strengthened his own position, at least for the time being. With a new and relatively unknown and untried team, he could now proceed on his largely unchanged course, hoping that the stains of Stalinism had been removed from his regime. A visit to Moscow at the end of the year gave testimony that he continued to enjoy the confidence of Khrushchev. In the increasingly open conflict between China and Russia, the Czechoslovak Party sided fully and unconditionally with the Russians, stepping up its ideological onslaught on the Chinese position in theoretical articles and in speeches.[24] At the same time, the regime continued its campaign against dissidents at home, justifying it with Khrushchev's dictum rejecting the concept of coexistence in culture and ideas.[25] Yet the ferment continued, with leading literary organs and figures continuing to express their thoughts in a manner that brought down upon their heads the condemnation of the Party.

The latest example of continuing tension was an address by Vladimir Koucky, chairman of the Party's newly formed ideological commission, and the main speaker at a special session of the Central Committee devoted to ideological work.[26] Assailing those people who still alleged that the Party had not yet faced squarely the problem of the personality cult, and who regarded any emphasis on the necessity of unity and discipline as "a sign of dogmatism and even of a 'turn back,'" Koucky declared: "Only the Central Committee represents and expresses, after the Congress, the will of the whole Party." He went on:

> I must emphasize these elementary principles because there are comrades who quite clearly keep overlooking them. They seem to think that Party discipline is a kind of fetter good enough for the rank-and-file Communists, while they, the "intellectually mature," may do whatever they wish. They present problems of a clearly inner-Party character even to the non-Party public, and they pretend not to see that the Party is in the course of solving them, or that it has actually already solved them; they attempt to force upon the Party discussion of questions about which they prove to be incredibly ignorant; they claim for themselves the right of a monopoly to interpret Leninism and lose no opportunity to lecture the Party organs. It is impossible to remain silent in these circumstances. Especially when in the same breath these attempts are dishonestly presented as a defense of the line of the Twelfth Congress, which they one-sidedly distort and revise.

> Unfortunately, a certain part of our press offers its pages to these people, and now and then they even get a word in on some programs on radio and television. *Literarni noviny* and especially Bratislava's *Kulturny zivot* have played in this connection an unpraiseworthy role. Particularly on the pages of the latter appear regularly articles that are politically not serious and theoretically devious, wrongly orienting the reader. . .

Later, Koucky censured

> . . . cultural periodicals, especially *Kulturny zivot,* which as a rule, do not react at all even to the criticism of Party organs or even to *Rude pravo,* when in this paper the anti-Leninist character of their arguments is clearly and unequivocally proved. Replies based on Party positions, sent to their editors, are often not published at all, or done so in distorted form. This is inadmissible, an opportunist liquidation of the partisan exchange of views.

On the same day that this was being published in *Rude pravo,* the editor of one of the papers under attack, Pavol Stevcek, was summing up the past year in his own journal, the organ of the Slovak writers.[27] Speaking of the year 1963 as one of "rebirth," of "anti-dogmatism," and of "truth," he said it was also a year of "social-ism," but a new kind of socialism:

> . . . socialism . . . has acquired characteristics and attributes known before only in medicinal doses. It has become human, it has humanized itself. The specter of dread, for instance, of the conse-quences of criticism, of error, of frankness, of the one true face of a man in opposition—this fear has gone. People once again give the right meaning to the words formerly included in the "idealistic vocabulary," such as conscience, honor, truthfulness, etc. The feeling of security and safety, the awareness of freedom, the duty to be courageous and to think, the task of forming one's own mind, one's own personality—all this was not always allowed. Now a man with-out such features will not feel himself at home.

He concluded: "The year 1963, the good old friend, is departing. It should stay, however, in history, in our consciousness, in our tasks of tomorrow. And in our newspapers."

In the same issue, the writer Ladislav Mnacko tried to draw up a balance sheet for the "remarkable year of 1963," and called it "a year of discussions, ideas and acts, frequently still timid and con-cealed, but all the more important . . . For the first time at the Congress (Twelfth Party Congress), one frankly and responsibly discussed questions that had been hushed up, concealed and sup-pressed for a long time. It gave the go-ahead signal to discussions and through this to the discovery and examination of the truth and to its evaluation."

Wrong views had been expressed, he admitted, but not surpris-ingly, "after so many years of shutting oneself in and only searching for a way in private." But even wrong views "expressed by anybody, above or below" can be useful, "if one replies to it truthfully and correctly." "Not by forcible means, but by the power of convincing arguments." He concluded: "The discussion continues, it probes even more deeply, and it ought never to stop. On the contrary, in a so-cialist democracy, it is discussion that is the most effective corrector of mistakes and a guarantee against the possibility of new deforma-tions in all branches of our life."

What of the future? Czechoslovakia has for so long been regarded as the docile satellite, as the "Good Comrade Schweik" of Com-munism, that the events of 1963 came largely as a surprise to the outside world, and no doubt to the Czechs and Slovaks themselves. The ferment of 1963, and in particular the courageous stand taken by the Slovak Communist intelligentsia, supported by their Czech associates, suggest that we have underestimated the potentialities of these two nations. We have been inclined to regard the Czechs and Slovaks as passive, and even cowardly, equating their attitude under Stalin and Khrushchev to their entire history, and forgetting that there have been occasions in their past (in 1848, 1914–18, 1938, 1943, and 1945, for instance) when some Czechs and some Slovaks have shown their unwillingness to accept an unwanted rule and their readiness to accept the risks of opposition, exile, and even revolt. We have tended to assume that the tradition of Masaryk and Benes, short-lived as it was in terms of national independence, but going back to deeper roots before 1914, had been snuffed out by expatriation and persecution, forgetting that devotion to these great figures was still widespread among the older generation, and was not likely to be entirely expunged from the consciousness even of a new generation reared under Communism. We have tended also to forget that a strong radical intellectual tradition, going back to the nineteenth century, although serving as a favorable condition for the triumph of Communism in 1945–48, has also left a legacy of Marxist and socialist thought which could not but be repelled by the excesses of Stalinist distortion of socialist and Communist ideals. We have also assumed that Czech and Slovak national consciousness had been more or less wiped away by the years of sovietization and apparent acceptance of Soviet domination, and could not stimulate resistance to Soviet rule and its excesses. We have failed to see that the subjection of Slovaks to centralized Czech Communist rule has not dimmed the feeling of Slovak nationalism, even among Communists, and could produce a brave response. We have also tended to assume that the failure of Czechoslovakia to de-Stalinize had been accepted by Czech and Slovak Communists and that rehabilitation and reform were not burning desires of a movement disillusioned by the terror of the 1950's and the deceit of the early 1960's.

These factors must be taken into account in our evaluation of the future of Czechoslovakia in the Communist bloc. The split of Russians and Chinese, and the de-Stalinizing course of Khrushchev at home, have unleashed forces in the Communist world, including Czechoslovakia, that will be difficult to curb. No doubt, the issues are not finally settled. Leadership changes in the Soviet Union, or even policy changes by the Kremlin, might pave the way for a harder course at home and abroad—and even a settlement of the Sino-Soviet split—accompanied perhaps by a reduction of the leeway now enjoyed by the smaller countries of Eastern Europe. It is more likely, however, that there will be a continuance, and a widening, of the split, and even a total break, and the steady increase of the area of maneuver of the East European states. Soviet influence, and some measure of Stalinism, will remain, of course, but in constant tension with strivings for national autonomy and a reform of Communism. Efforts to restore full-blown Stalinism and complete Soviet domination, if they take place, might produce explosions comparable to the similar efforts by Rakosi in Hungary in 1956.

Prediction is difficult in politics, and has not been notably successful, especially about the Communist world. Czechoslovakia's future will be affected by the development of world Communism as a whole as well as by conditions at home. It is not likely that Prague, at least under its present leaders, will embark on a course of complete independence from the Soviet Union. Loyalty to Moscow will no doubt be maintained, but not in the subservient manner of the past. Assuming, as we must, that Czechoslovakia, like Albania, has the *ability* to act somewhat independently, the decisive question will be whether she *desires* so to act. Up to the present, Czechoslovakia has believed that the main policies of the u.s.s.r. since Stalin do not conflict sharply with its basic national interests. Peaceful co-existence, relaxation in Berlin and regarding the German question, peaceful competition, economic integration within the bloc, technical aid to the underdeveloped world, a modest cultural and economic interchange with the West—all are acceptable and even welcome. The thorny issue of de-Stalinization has for the moment been surmounted without a shock to the regime and to Novotny's personal position. A reversal of the Soviet line, manifesting itself particularly in a tougher policy or in other features not now foreseeable, might, however, face the Czechoslovaks with decisions such as those faced by Albanians or Romanians, and force them to choose a more independent stance. The forms of "national Communism," as diverse in the future as they have been in the past, are not likely to be the same in Czechoslovakia as in other countries.

Much will depend on the evolution of Czech and Slovak leadership, and the outcome of the play of forces within Czechoslovakia. Novotny, lacking any real hold on the people's loyalty, or even the loyalty of the Communist rank and file, is hardly strong enough to turn the clock back. His greatest strength, perhaps, is the absence of an alternative, or rival, among the men whom he has placed in authority. His eventual replacement by someone with more popular appeal and a less tarnished past, perhaps even by Barak, is possible. Apart from Novotny, the top leaders are new men, products of the Party apparatus—yet free of direct association with Gottwald—and, like Khrushchev, more concerned with the practical tasks of running the system efficiently than with traditions or doctrines of revolution. They are not liberals, and have no understanding of democratic processes in politics or freedom in culture. Any trend toward "liberalization" will be a cautious and controlled one, as in Poland and Hungary at present. Ferment is still at work, however, in intellectual circles. There is less risk in open criticism, and the absence of terror ties the hands of the regime. Persuasion of the Party apparatus is less effective. Tension continues to exist, not only between writers and the Party career men, but also within the Party itself, between the "Party-minded" and the "liberal-minded." It is not accidental that Novomesky, for instance, is a member of the Party's central ideological commission. In the continuing struggle ahead, the forces that manifested themselves in 1963—more liberal conceptions of Communism, Slovak national feeling, and even traditional Czech national consciousness and democratic thought—will stand as obstacles to a retrogressive course, and as possible stimuli of a more progressive development in the future.

6. Romania and Bulgaria

J. F. BROWN

THE HISTORICAL contrasts between Romania and Bulgaria are obvious to anyone who is even slightly acquainted with the Balkans. They are contrasts of which both of these neighboring nations have been, and are still, only too aware—and too proud. And yet, during the relatively brief periods of their independent existence, these two countries have been linked together by many observers as having the same political and economic characteristics which can be described as Balkan—in the pejorative rather than the geographical sense of that term.

There is a good deal of justification for this. Economically, both countries have been overwhelmingly agrarian and industrially backward. Their internal politics have been associated with instability, violence, and the inevitable drift toward dictatorship. Expansionism and irridentism have, at varying times, been the main planks of their foreign policy. After 1945, the dull, gray blanket of Stalinist Communism descended on both countries. Both initiated domestic policies of ruthless socialization and industrialization. For many years, both were considered to be model satellites of the Soviet Union, as backwaters of servitude from which nothing original was heard and little was expected. Now, however, they present a study in contrasts. One of these countries, Romania, has broken its mold and is showing a new and challenging face; the other, Bulgaria, as if trying to contribute its fair share to the growing contrasts, seems intent on remaining truer to its stereotype than ever before. The contrast is by no means all-embracing. But it covers the most interesting and vital subject in the Communist world today—relations with the Soviet Union, and hence the whole subject of Communist unity or disunity.

ROMANIA

The hope that proletarian internationalism could supplant nationalism in Eastern Europe has been disappointed several times since 1945. Nationalism constantly re-emerges as the dominant force in the area. This was so in Yugoslavia, Poland, Hungary, and Albania, and it is the case now in Romania. In Romania, however, nationalism has expressed itself differently and perhaps more interestingly than in the other countries, and its manifestation has been caused by different factors.

Romanian Communism never had a strong tradition. Much of it came to the country in the mind and the suitcase of Nathan Katz, a Jewish emigré from Russia, who changed his name to Constantine Dobrogeanu-Gherea and became perhaps the only serious theorist the Romanian Communists have ever had. It was an internationalist creed in a fiercely nationalistic land; it drew its inspiration from Russia, a country that most Romanians feared and despised; many of its proponents were Jews among a nation strongly anti-Semitic. Between the two world wars, the Romanian Communist Party probably never had more than 2,000 members. It was considered not only un-Romanian but also anti-Romanian.[1]

In 1945, Communism was imposed on Romania by Russian troops. The Romanian Communist Party sanctioned the ceding to Russia of Bessarabia and Northern Bukovina. It condoned the most blatant type of Russian economic exploitation, first through open looting and then through the notorious Sovroms.* With Russian troops in support, it quickly tightened its grip on a demoralized and sullen nation. To inflate its own puny size, it opened its ranks to the scum of society—former fascists, Iron Guardists, careerists, opportunists, criminals—and disgusted the mass of the people even more. Even the most tyrannical dictatorship, if it is to function at all, needs the support of some sections of the population. In this respect,

* Soviet-Romanian joint companies, which served as effective instruments of economic exploitation of Romania by the U.S.S.R. They were disbanded after de-Stalinization.

the Romanian Communist dictatorship could hardly have made a worse start. All it had was quiescence, with practically no basis for operation.

Its first step on the long road toward identity with the Romanian people came about 1950 with the imposition of a series of purges. Many of the unsavory elements which had joined the Communist Party immediately after the war were weeded out. The Party was drastically trimmed, and a new cadre policy was aimed at the rising generation. The purges culminated in 1952 with the downfall of two Soviet-trained Jews, Ana Pauker and Vasile Luca, and the victory of Gheorghe Gheorghiu-Dej and his "home" group of Communists. This group was composed of ethnic Romanians who, violently distrusted though they were and in many respects still are, were homegrown products who understood, and were understood by, the people they governed.[2]

Obviously, back in 1952, Gheorghiu-Dej was not conscious of what he was doing in this respect. He did not purge Pauker and others so as to lead the Party toward some kind of mutual identity with the Romanian people. For some three to four years, he had been engaged in a life-and-death power struggle with the Pauker group. At a time when "home" Communists like Rajk, Kostov, and Gomulka were falling in other countries around him, he must have been fairly close to political or even physical extinction. He may have owed his salvation and final victory only to the vicious bout of anti-Semitism, shortly before Stalin died, which saw the end of Slansky in Czechoslovakia and Pauker in Romania. Now, of course, Gheorghiu-Dej speciously maintains that, by getting rid of Pauker and Luca, he was the first in the bloc to de-Stalinize, that this was part of a grand design by the true Romanian Communists to lead the country to better things. His claims have anti-Semitic and even anti-Russian overtones. Spurious though they are, they show a certain skill in the manipulation of public opinion and popular prejudices.

Gheorghiu-Dej was interested in power. He had finally won it in 1952, and was intent on keeping it. The events of the next five or six years showed that he could be as ruthless as any dictator in achieving this end. These were the years of the "new course" after Stalin's death when Gheorghiu-Dej, to stay afloat, combined concession with terror. At the Twentieth Congress of the CPSU, Khrushchev upset the calm. Gheorghiu-Dej's recipe was the same as after Stalin's death —purges in the Party accompanied by an almost Ottoman-type intimidation of the population at large. By 1958, he had the situation again in hand. Soviet troops left the country in the summer of that year and, at the head of a now thoroughly united leadership, he could plan for the future.

It was probably at about this time that Gheorghiu-Dej convinced himself (or was convinced by others) that a more positive policy was both opportune and necessary. Ever since he had assumed the Party leadership in 1945, he and his group had had to spend most of their time fighting for power, protecting it, and consolidating it. Now came the time for them to deepen it and broaden its base. They also had to run the country. Their previous efforts had failed in most respects—nowhere more so than in the economy, where their planning had been as ambitious and as ruinous as in the other satellites. For this, of course, they had themselves largely to blame. In mitigation of their guilt, however, it could be argued that Romania had to pay tremendous war reparations to the Soviets, and had the additional burden of the Sovroms, which were not disbanded until 1954–56 (an act for which Gheorghiu-Dej is now quietly claiming credit). A further burden was the political instability which characterized the whole of Eastern Europe for the half-decade after Stalin's death. By 1958, however, these handicaps no longer applied; nor did another—the absence of technical intelligentsia—which had played a large part in undermining the Communist economic effort.

Immediately after the war, the Communist Party had rejected the old bourgeois-trained technical intelligentsia, on the ground that they were "rotten and unreliable." Much of the economy, therefore, had to be managed either by uneducated Party hacks or by fledglings with little training and no experience. But very early, the regime had provided for the education of many technical cadres. It was, in effect, forming a new class, ambitious for both place and privilege, and, one may assume, not entirely devoid of patriotism. This class presented both a challenge and an opportunity to the regime. Its ever-growing numbers had to be satisfied by posts in an expanding economy; if its demands were met, it might become a large and powerful base on which the regime could rest and rely. What Romanian Communism had always lacked—a strong base of support—was, by about 1958, in an advanced stage of formation. The regime was also fortunate in having, in its leading ranks, men who were both convinced Communists and able economists, like Alexandru Barladeanu, now Romania's CEMA delegate; Gheorghe Gaston-Marin, the planning chief; and Gogu Radulescu, the chief trade expert.[3] These leaders were able to win the confidence of the upcoming elite. Finally, Gheorghiu-Dej himself is believed to have developed an interest in technical and industrial matters sufficiently genuine to make him realize that too much Party interference would be unwise.

The regime could harness the ability, the ambition, and the patriotism of this class if it adopted a comprehensive industrialization policy. One must assume that the Party leadership was not prompted simply by power cynicism but also by a genuine national pride in what it was doing and by a Marxist-Leninist desire for heavy industry as an economic base.

Gheorghiu-Dej had no reason to believe that the Soviet Union or its CEMA partners would object to Romania's program of economic expansion. As late as 1960–61, the Soviet Union still seemed to be advocating that each CEMA member should build its own integral economy. Specialization and the "international socialist division of labor" were talked about of course, but they seemed no threat to Romania since they meant specialization by *branches* of industry rather than by whole industries. The Romanian Party, therefore, at its Congress[4] in June, 1960, approved a six-year plan and a fifteen-year economic program designed to make Romania another Belgium by 1975. (The most important single project in this program was a gigantic metallurgical combine to be constructed at Galati—a combine, which, by 1970, was slated to produce 4 million tons of steel out of a national total of 7.5 million.) After this, however, the Soviet Union, probably spurred on by economically advanced satellites like Czechoslovakia and East Germany, began to change its attitude toward CEMA cooperation, to think in terms of specialization by whole industries, and evidently to advocate that a country like Romania should concentrate on agriculture and industries such as the petrochemical industry, for which it already had a good basis. The Romanians may have gotten wind of these intentions as early as the Twenty-second Congress of the CPSU in October, 1961. Throughout 1962 and early 1963, Soviet intentions were becoming clear, just when the Romanians were enjoying success in their efforts and when their "economic miracle" was becoming a common topic of conversation in both East and West.[5]

The dilemma of Gheorghiu-Dej is not difficult to imagine. As a leader, he had made prudence the hallmark of his political activity; he was so successful a trimmer in his relations with the Kremlin that he had remained in power for well over fifteen years. Yet a basic policy on which he had embarked, in the confident belief that there would be no opposition, had been challenged by the very country that was not only the acknowledged master but the one to which

Romania looked mainly for trade and aid in carrying out her program.[6] On the other hand, Gheorghiu-Dej knew that if he bowed to Soviet wishes he would lose prestige in the Party, and his Party would lose prestige among the people, and especially among the class on which it was mainly depending for support. Then came the momentous event that rescued him—the eruption of the Sino-Soviet dispute.

With shrewdness, Gheorghiu-Dej soon recognized the implications of the Sino-Soviet dispute for the East European satellites. He saw that they now had more scope for maneuver vis-à-vis the Kremlin than ever before. On the overt basic issues in the Sino-Soviet dispute, he is wholly pro-Soviet; there is virtually no danger of his ever becoming a Maoist. To him, Mao became a means of winning concessions from the Russians. He knew that Khrushchev was pre-occupied with China, that he could not afford another Albania in Eastern Europe. He realized the possibilities of the situation, and he had a problem that forced him to exploit these possibilities. Thus, there followed in 1963 what can perhaps be described as "flirtations" with China. Throughout the year, in contrast to the press of the other satellites, there was no real attack on the Chinese and only one mild criticism of them in the Romanian press. While the rest of the East European bloc was reducing its trade with China, Romania increased hers by 10 per cent. In the same year, Romania quietly returned her ambassador to Tirana and increased her trade with Albania.

In the summer of 1963, two even more serious events occurred. Moscow took the most violent exception to Peking's letter of June 14, containing the twenty-five conditions on which discussions should be based in the bilateral talks between the two parties. Every regime in Eastern Europe, therefore—except the Romanian—simply printed the Tass statement saying that the letter contained slanders and distortions and would not be published. Romania published a long account of the letter and itemized all twenty-five points.[7] This was open defiance of Khrushchev. The question of the Chinese letter probably was closely linked with the most striking example of Romanian divergence that had yet occurred—the absence of Gheorghiu-Dej from the East Berlin "little summit" at the end of June—a conference which all other East bloc leaders attended. Evidently fearing that he would be a minority of one at such a meeting, he stayed away, thus revealing the worst rift in Eastern Europe since the Albanian affair.

All this occurred also during a year of provocative interviews with Western journalists on the Romanian view of CEMA and of flamboyant Romanian commercial sorties to the West which had begun earlier and which were now paying off with startling success. These sorties cannot be considered solely as part of the now general East European attempts to trade with the West. Many of them were designed to get equipment either that Romania's CEMA partners would not provide or that was superior to what they could provide.[8]

Romanian defiance of the Soviet Union brought Gheorghiu-Dej a popular support much broader than that which he could get from his new technical intelligentsia. He had done little to stimulate, and nothing to deserve, the support of the toiling masses from which he himself had sprung. Though the standard of living had risen, it remained pitifully low; the "economic miracle" was based on this hard fact. The great masses of the population had little indeed for which to thank the Gheorghiu-Dej regime. But in one respect, he satisfied their emotions, if not their needs. He knew that one of their strongest sentiments—or prejudices—is anti-Russian feeling. He must have been aware, therefore, that his defiance of the Soviet Union on the CEMA issue would win the emotional support of the masses. The sight of their regime, unpopular though it might be, standing up to the Russians (and here the term "Russian" is much more appropriate than "Soviet") not only had a positive appeal but also diverted attention from the fact that the issue at the center of the dispute—Romanian insistence on comprehensive industrialization—would limit greatly the possibilities of an early improvement in the general standard of living. This may have been the main reason why Gheorghiu-Dej, once he had resolved on his policy, began to make sure that the masses knew what he was doing. He did not, of course, publish his case in *Scanteia,* but he made sure that every Party member was informed, and the Party members were by no means sworn to secrecy on the matter. These actions of "quiet publicity" seem to have taken place shortly after the February, 1963, meeting of the CEMA's Executive Committee in Moscow where Romanian economic policy was evidently subjected to severe criticism.[9]

Gheorghiu-Dej appealed further to the anti-Russian emotions of his people by acts designed to play down the Soviet presence and influence in Romania. In late 1962, Romanian scholars attacked the Soviet historian, Ushakov, for a book in which he gave the Romanian Communists insufficient credit for the role they now claim they played in the liberation of their country in 1944. (Ushakov had simply accepted the old Stalinist version, which gave the whole credit to the Red Army.) The Romanian Communists now insisted that they had played the major role, and even gave some credit to King Michael and certain bourgeois groups for having seen the writing on the wall and for having cooperated with the Communists. The truth of this version is fortunately not the subject of this essay, but two points should be noted. The first is the Party's attempt to represent itself as the inheritor and torchbearer of all that is finest in the Romanian progressive tradition and to embody itself in the nation; the second is that, though the Romanian people are not likely to be taken in by the claim for Communist predominance in the 1944 events, they are not likely to be averse to this disparagement of the Soviet achievement. Their emotions have been fed by other gestures of anti-Russian nationalism—the renaming of streets, squares, cinemas, etc. More important were the closing of the Maxim Gorky Institute in Bucharest, which had always been the bastion of Soviet cultural influence in the country, the demolition of the Russian bookstore in Bucharest, and the suspension of the Romanian edition of the Soviet *New Times*. All these acts were noticed and talked about. They won credit for the regime among circles in which normally there would have been opposition or dislike.

It can be argued, of course, that what the Gheorghiu-Dej regime did was nothing more—and perhaps in some respects less—than what was done in Hungary and Poland shortly after the 1956 events, and that, therefore, this is nothing exceptional. But the point is that similar actions in Hungary and Poland were concessions to angered populations, which had shaken the foundations of the East European system. They were concessions to which Khrushchev had to agree in order to save something bigger. In the Romanian case, they took place against a far different background. Though Gheorghiu-Dej could point to the previous Hungarian and Polish examples, he knew very well, as did Khrushchev, that his action was another facet of a policy that had made Romania the "odd man out" in Eastern Europe.

There is yet another aspect of policy by which Romania would qualify for this rather enviable title. It is not completely clear why Khrushchev decided at the Twenty-second Congress of the CPSU to begin his second bout of de-Stalinization. But he was obviously staking some of his reputation both at home and abroad on the success of his policy of political and economic relaxation. This policy had also become an issue in the dispute with China. He was, therefore, anxious that the spirit of his own domestic policy be reflected in Eastern Europe. This has generally taken place. Poland, despite its retrogression, still leads the field. In Hungary, Kadar saw the Twenty-second Congress as the "green light" for his own policy. In Czechoslovakia, Novotny is in danger of being overrun by the forces he relutcantly set in motion. In Bulgaria, at least a spectacular beginning was made. Even in East Germany, there is some attempt at economic rationalization, if only in lieu of de-Stalinization. But in Romania, either out of some morbid, Byzantine fear of the people he governs or from a realization that a trickle soon becomes a flood, Gheorghiu-Dej has maintained his rigidity. Although the atmosphere is more relaxed than it was in Stalin's time, Romania remains a repressive police state. By August 23, 1964, all political prisoners had probably been released, but de-Stalinization still had a very long way to go. Gheorghiu-Dej's reaction to the Twenty-second Congress of the CPSU had been a masterly exercise in diversion. Every blame for the excesses—and not even he could deny them—was heaped on the Pauker clique, which was purged in 1952 and (according to him) finally disappeared from the scene with the fall of Chisinevschi and Constantinescu in 1957. Proceeding from the fact that, in the early years, the Muscovite Pauker was the driving force in the country, Gheorghiu-Dej disclaimed all responsibility for the Stalinist crimes and then capped his argument by implying that, since Pauker fell in 1952, the Romanian Party had actually de-Stalinized a year before Stalin's death. Therefore, at the end of 1961 there was no point in talking about something that had been completed in the middle of 1952![10] Having argued thus, he proceeded, in the next four months, to herd the country's remaining free peasants into kolkhozes.

Gheorghiu-Dej could not have genuinely responded to the Twenty-second Congress without endangering himself. Having been in power for so long, he could not have repudiated the past without undermining the present. But while appreciating his dilemma, Khrushchev must have been irked by such obvious disregard for his own policy. Had the Romanian regime been loyal and malleable in other respects, Khrushchev might have condoned this course of action. But, as matters stood, this was one more lapse from the standard of acceptable behavior.

Where has this policy led Romania in her relations with the Soviet Union? Where will it lead her? These are the most important questions now being asked about the Gheorghiu-Dej regime.

It is still difficult to see Romania as another Albania in the making. A glance at the map showing Romania's juxtaposition to Russia would itself justify skepticism. But Gheorghiu-Dej has defied the Soviet Union on a number of important points. In domestic policy, he claims de-Stalinization is irrelevant, and he has quietly but obviously initiated a widespread de-Russification process. Within the framework of CEMA, his obstinacy was mainly responsible for upsetting the Kremlin's schemes for area-wide economic integration. In intrabloc policy, he has used China to put pressure on—or to blackmail—the Soviet Union. Even in foreign (i.e., extrabloc) policy he has shown signs of independence.[11] He has made little secret of the fact that he often prefers good new Western equipment to anything the East can offer.

It is probably correct to assume (as has been done earlier in this chapter) that this defiance of the Soviet Union was prompted mainly by the regime's desire to win its point on its comprehensive industrialization program. But it seems that the animosity engendered by this defiance persisted after the issue that caused it was settled. Most observers agree that the strong objections of the Soviet Union and her more advanced CEMA partners (such as East Germany and Czechoslovakia) were finally dropped at the CEMA "summit" meeting of First Party Secretaries in Moscow in July, 1963. One can assume, therefore, that Romania's obstinacy won the day and that her flirtation with China and her ambivalence on the whole Sino-Soviet dispute had contributed to this victory. But after the victory, this ambivalence became not less but more marked. There was no settling back into the comfort of true satellite status. De-Russification continued; de-Stalinization was still soft-pedaled; top-level commercial delegations were still sent to the West. Most important of all, the Romanian attitude toward China took a sharp turn even further from Russia than ever before.

What the CEMA dispute, and the tactics used in it, had shown was that things would never be the same again between Khrushchev and Gheorghiu-Dej. The causes and the consequences of the dispute had evidently created a momentum which could not be slowed down. There was no reconciliation. Instead, there was dislike on the one side and fear on the other. Once his victory had been won, therefore, Gheorghiu-Dej had not less need of Mao but rather more need of him. The Chinese leader, with whom he has basically nothing in sympathy, had become the guarantee of his security. This being so, the Romanian leadership had two things to fear. One—a real reconciliation between Khrushchev and Mao—seemed almost impossible; the other—the formal expulsion of China from the world movement—seemed, in the autumn of 1963, a very distinct possibility. With China publicly expelled from the movement, Khrushchev would have a much freer hand in bringing his satellites to heel. With China still in the movement, there would still be that element of uncertainty and fluctuation that would give small powers room for maneuver. Romania, therefore, put herself in the van of the growing number of countries or parties urging restraint, an end to the polemics, and a renewal of some form of Moscow-Peking contact. The first public example of this was Premier Ion Gheorghe Maurer's article in the November, 1963, issue of *Problems of Peace and Socialism,* in which he indirectly chastised both disputants, called for a renewal of bilateral contacts, and supported the summoning of a world conference of Communist parties only after the necessary preparations had been made. Maurer's article, together with other appeals that had been made earlier, may have done much to deter Khrushchev, who was believed to be anxious at that time to force the issue with the Chinese. The most dramatic example came in March, 1964, with the departure of the Maurer delegation to Peking—a move that can, again, best be interpreted as an eleventh-hour attempt to prevent the final irrevocable split that would leave Gheorghiu-Dej alone with Khrushchev.

In mid-April, 1964, the Romanian Communist Party's Central Committee held a plenary session to hear a report on the talks that the Romanian delegation had held with the Chinese leaders in Peking and with Khrushchev at Gagra on its journey home. The declaration issued at the end of this plenum (and published on April 26, 1964) supported the U.S.S.R. on virtually every major issue in the Sino-Soviet dispute, but it rebuked both disputants for engaging in polemics. Categorically declaring Romania's complete independence within the bloc, it advocated in effect a relationship similar to that prevailing in the British Commonwealth. It repudiated entirely the proposals for a joint planning body within CEMA, on the ground that it would infringe on national sovereignty; this was the *leitmotif* of the whole declaration.

This essentially anti-Soviet document was published shortly after a gathering in Moscow in celebration of Khrushchev's seventieth birthday—a gathering at which Gheorghiu-Dej was the only satellite leader not present. His absence, and the subsequent publication of the Romanian Central Committee's declaration, showed that, while definitely remaining in the socialist camp, Romania was serving notice that, for her, the concept of satellite status was no longer valid.

In May, 1964, a Romanian economic delegation led by Planning Chief Gheorghe Gaston-Marin obtained highly beneficial economic arrangements with the United States. Politically, this U.S.–Romanian conference was a logical culmination of what Bucharest had done and said over the previous two years.

Tremendous ties bind Romania to her Russian neighbor. Over 40 per cent of Romania's foreign trade is with the Soviet Union; about 70 per cent of it is still with the Eastern bloc. Her economic, cultural, and diplomatic links with the West are growing but are still tenuous. The West, and still less China, could not fill the void left by an economic boycott from the East. If the Soviet Union embarked on any economic sanctions against Romania, she could cripple Gheorghiu-Dej's industrialization drive, which was the primary issue of the quarrel and the issue on which the present leadership has staked its reputation. For the moment, Gheorghiu-Dej's leadership is strong and his Party is solidly behind him. It is true, also, that the worse his relations with Russia became, the stronger would become his popular support. The Romanian people would strongly support a major gravitation to the West and would be willing to endure even further sacrifices.

In their stand regarding national sovereignty and in their opposition to CEMA integration, the Romanians cleverly shield themselves with quotations, not only from Marx and Lenin, but also from the 1957 and 1960 declarations, and they even paraphrase certain remarks of Russia's leaders. The Kremlin therefore finds it difficult to denounce them openly or to take overt action against them—especially in view of the delicate situation in the world Communist movement. The Romanians know this, and they depend on the fact that the Russian leaders also know it.

BULGARIA

The Bulgarian Communist Party began its period of power after World War II with most of the advantages that its Romanian counterpart seemed to lack. It was the oldest Communist Party in the Balkans—a fact in which it took considerable pride. Immediately after World War I, it was one of the most powerful political parties in the country, and even during its period of outlawry, after 1925, it continued to make a strong showing under the cover of various front organizations. It could boast champions of brilliance and influence. Its founder, Dimitar Blagoev, had established Marxist circles in St. Petersburg as early as the 1880's. He was followed by men like Rakovski, Kolarov, and Georgi Dimitrov, all men of power in the international Communist movement, and behind them was a galaxy of lesser men who contributed much to the Bulgarian Communist legend. Finally, Bulgaria itself was traditionally pro-Russian.

Today, less than twenty years after its assumption of power, the Bulgarian Party is bereft of inspiration, brilliance, and pride— bereft, in fact, of everything except its servitude to the Soviet Union. While its neighbor Romania has been in the act of shaking off Soviet dominance, and while other East European countries have at least been at pains to make their loyalty to Moscow less ostentatious, Bulgaria has made itself almost a caricature of the model satellite. While others seek their salvation in loosening their ties, Bulgaria seems intent on replacing hers with hoops of steel.

Lack of confidence born of failure has produced this situation. The failure began early, when confidence was still running high and the strains of jubilation had hardly died down. Violence has always been traditional in Bulgarian politics, and the Communists in 1923 and 1925 had made their own contributions to it. But in 1945, there was no pressing reason for the continuation of this tradition. The mass of the Bulgarian people were not anti-Russian; the Bulgarian Communists were strong and secure. The country's class structure was egalitarian when compared, for example, with that of Romania, Hungary, or Poland. Many non-Communists of skill and experience might have placed their services at the country's disposal if a mild, conciliatory policy had been adopted. But the triumphant Communists pursued a policy of purge and repression which, with the exception of that later carried on in Hungary, was the most ruthless in Eastern Europe. Potential support was brusquely spurned; collaboration was confined to the puppet Agrarians and certain "non-Party" politicians who became perhaps more despised than the Communists themselves. Nowhere in Eastern Europe was this brutal policy less necessary and more senseless.

Having shocked the people, the Bulgarian Party proceeded to shock itself. The struggle between "home" Communists and "Muscovites" was a familiar one in all the new ruling parties. In Bulgaria, it led to a particularly acute struggle, since it coincided with the deaths of the two "grand old men" of the Party, Georgi Dimitrov and Vassil Kolarov. Had either one lived, he could probably have bridged the gulf and avoided the dissension which so gravely weakened the Party. But Dimitrov died in 1949, and Kolarov a year later. The shock of their deaths would have been serious psychologically even had the succession problems been only personal and not factional. Dimitrov's logical successor as Party leader was Traicho Kostov, a "home" Communist, who showed signs both of energy and of a certain independence from Moscow. In his group were able and confident men. Against them was Vulko Chervenkov, who had gone to the Soviet Union in 1923 and been a prominent teacher in the Comintern school in Moscow. The execution of Kostov at the end of 1949 and the death or imprisonment of other members of his group had repercussions that are still being felt. The situation in Romania was very much the opposite. In Bucharest, the "home" Communists under Gheorghiu-Dej defeated the "Muscovites." Romania did have its Patrascanu; but Patrascanu was something of a lone intellectual without a real following, and his execution in 1954 did not have the same effects as the execution of Kostov five years earlier.[12]

The Chervenkov period in Bulgaria was typical of Eastern Europe in the period from 1950 to 1956. It was closely analagous to the Bierut period in Poland and the Rakosi period in Hungary. All three followed the victory of "Muscovite" factions of the Party against "home" factions; all three were stigmatized by repression and terror; all three were characterized by ruthless industrialization and collectivization. "Stalinist" repression at home was accompanied by complete subservience to Moscow abroad. But in Poland and Hungary, this period was followed in 1956 by a violent reaction, which led (sooner in the case of Poland than Hungary) to a break with the past and a new start. This gave a new vitality and a completely new look to the Polish and Hungarian parties. It brought to the fore men who could respond to the situation and who tried to identify themselves with the aspirations of their nations. In Bulgaria, the Chervenkov period produced no violent reaction. There was nothing like the same anti-Russian nationalism in Bulgaria as in Poland or Hungary, nor, despite the alienation of a large section of the population, were there similar conditions and opportunities for revolt.

The pressure in Bulgaria produced a change of men but not of character. The Party remained as dispirited and uninspired as before. In March, 1954, as part of the game of musical chairs that took place in Eastern Europe after Stalin's death, Chervenkov was succeeded—at least nominally—as Party leader by his protégé Todor Zhivkov. Zhivkov has continued as First Party Secretary ever since, but for several years after his appointment he was overshadowed by older, more powerful figures. For two years, in his capacity as Premier, Chervenkov remained as powerful as before, but after the Twentieth Congress of the CPSU and Moscow's *rapprochement* with Belgrade it was obvious that he had to go. The premiership was taken over in April, 1956, by Anton Yugov, a "home" Communist, a former associate of Kostov, and a person of some stature. A personal enemy of Chervenkov, Yugov had been in eclipse for several years after the death of Kostov. But he was seriously compromised in the eyes of the people because of his brutality as Minister of the Interior in the first years of Communist power, from 1945 to 1948. Even had the circumstances allowed it, he was certainly not the man to revitalize the regime.

In some respects, the situation in the Party became even worse after 1956. There had been no strong pressure or violent events to give it the shock it needed. Chervenkov had been demoted, but he was still a member of the Politburo and a Vice-Premier, with strong support among the lower reaches of the Party. Zhivkov, the Party leader, was still intent on building up his own support and consolidating his power. Yugov, the new Premier, was also eager to broaden the base of his support. The Party that Chervenkov had effectively paralyzed was now open to an uneasy factionalism. In its internal policy, it remained dogmatic and orthodox. Externally, it was a model of loyalty to the Soviet Union.

Then followed a phenomenon still not easy to explain. Since 1945, the regime's economic policy had hinged on rapid industrialization and the collectivization of agriculture. In industry, where the starting base had been next to nothing, a great deal of progress had been made, but the results had been disappointing in terms of the targets fixed. Largely because of the collectivization drive, agricultural failures had been serious. In 1958, therefore, economic rationalism pointed to moderation in quantitative planning and to emphasis on quality, low costs, and other hallmarks of efficiency. What occurred was just the opposite. An ambitious Five-Year Plan approved at the Seventh Party Congress in June, 1958, was almost immediately set aside and replaced by the so-called Zhivkov Theses, which aimed to fulfill the Five-Year Plan in three years and set astronomic targets for the national income, industry, and especially agriculture. The venture, which became known as Bulgaria's "great leap forward," probably had both economic and political motivations. Despite the progress it had made, Bulgaria was still virtually undeveloped, there was a great deal of "slack" in the economy (especially in agriculture), and labor was overabundant. Politically, the aim evidently was to shake the Communist Party and nation out of their malaise and galvanize both into action. The venture was both robust and daring and, for once, it was not modeled on anything that was happening in the Soviet Union. Yet, it was not independent but essentially imitative, because its inspiration and even some of its terminology came from China.

There was some Chinese influence in Bulgaria at the end of 1958. Bulgaria's "great leap forward" is proof that there was a fascination with Peking's dazzling boldness. Chinese policy may have appealed to the traditional romanticism that still lingered in the Bulgarian Party despite the discouraging experiences of its years in power. The Chinese short cut to industrialization and to Communism certainly evoked some response. Bulgaria's kolkhozes were amalgamated into about 1,000 giant farms with an average size much larger than in any other East European satellite. The term "communes" actually appeared in the Party's main newspaper. But in the last analysis, the Bulgarian Party manifested its lack of confidence. It had allowed itself temporarily to be fascinated with China because it did not seem to be aware of the Soviet Union's intense disapproval of the Chinese experiments and especially of the ideological pretensions behind the commune system. Once the Soviet opinion became known, the Bulgarian leaders strove to dispel the unfortunate impression they had created, and they reverted to type with increased intensity.[13]

Whatever may have been the reasons behind the Bulgarian "great leap forward," there seems little doubt as to its effects. The regime's claim of success, its contention that the Five-Year Plan had actually been fulfilled by the end of 1960—that is, after three years—deceived nobody. The whole project hurt the Bulgarian economy much more than it helped, and caused damage that still needs repair. The regime neglected all considerations of efficiency in its frantic efforts to meet the targets of the plan.[14] But most serious of all, the plan had the opposite effect on morale from what had been intended. It shattered what was left of Party pride and confidence and led the regime to cling more closely to what was greater than itself, i.e., the Soviet Union.

More important even than the growing dependence on the U.S.S.R. was the growing dissension within the Party leadership. Although this dissension was a struggle for power among rival groups, policy issues also played a part. For example, in the first half of 1959, the first year of Bulgaria's "great leap forward," Boris Taskov, a

Politburo member and Minister of Foreign Trade, was disgraced, apparently for opposing the new economic policy, and shortly afterward the Party had to issue severe warnings against indiscipline and the creation of centers of opposition. As the new policy plunged more deeply into difficulties, disillusionment became more marked and Party dissatisfaction increased. In many cases, the various factions used different issues indiscriminately and opportunistically for partisan reasons.

Generally speaking, there were three main Party groups. First, there was the Todor Zhivkov "official" group. As First Party Secretary, Zhivkov controlled the power of patronage. By 1960, after six years as Party leader, he had grown in experience, and had considerable support from men materially indebted to him. His group was pro-Khrushchev, more out of self-interest than conviction, and hence enjoyed Kremlin support. Second there was the Chervenkov group, which was perhaps the most numerous. Despite his demotion in April, 1956, Chervenkov remained a powerful figure with much rank-and-file support. His group was anti-Khrushchev and anti-Tito. It probably had little genuine sympathy with China, but Peking was the center to which it could gravitate, simply because it did not like Khrushchev. Finally, there was the group of the Premier Anton Yugov, an ambitious man ready to capitalize on any issue. Yugov may well have toyed with the idea of "national Communism" or, at least, with a more independent "Bulgarian road to socialism" as a means of gaining more influence. Such a policy, ably presented by the right man, would have had strong support. Yugov, however, despite his "home" Communist background, his "association" with Traicho Kostov, and a certain personal appeal, carried neither the respect nor the weight to become a rallying point for nationalist sentiment.

Naturally, the man in office, the man with the Kremlin's support, won the battle for supremacy. In his struggle against Chervenkov, Zhivkov used the Twenty-second Congress of the CPSU. He returned from Moscow in October, 1961, a fervent exponent of "de-Stalinization," an issue on which his opponent was particularly vulnerable. Chervenkov was stripped of his Politburo and governmental positions and remained only nominally a member of the Central Committee. In the year between the CPSU Congress and the Bulgarian Party's own Eighth Congress in November, 1962, it became clear however, despite all the protestations of unity, that Party dissension had increased rather than diminished. The Soviet dispute with China and the internal de-Stalinization issue had caused great confusion and doubt. The old "Stalinists," despite their leader's disgrace, were still strong. Zhivkov's pro-Khrushchev group tried to use the momentum that the Twenty-second Congress had given it to press home its advantage. On the right, a small group of "revisionists" was pushing Zhivkov to go much farther than he was prepared to. Another source of confusion and doubt was Khrushchev's new policy of *rapprochement* with Yugoslavia. This was a particularly sensitive issue in Bulgaria because of the Macedonian problem, and it was one of the main reasons for the Soviet leader's visit to Bulgaria in May, 1962. He was preceded by Ilychev and followed by Kirilenko. All three came to give the faithful Zhivkov the support he needed in the struggle for power. As a result, Zhivkov felt confident enough, not only to complete the disgrace of Chervenkov and expel him from the Party, but also to remove Yugov from all his Party and government posts. This he did at the Eighth Congress itself, where Yugov began the proceedings as Premier and ended as a pariah against whom almost every charge in the Communist lexicon was leveled. It is probable that Yugov's fate was finally sealed only shortly before the Congress, but there had been earlier indications that his position was insecure.[15] He had represented a threat to Zhivkov and may have urged a more independent road for Bulgaria as an instrument against his Party leader.

The Eighth Congress of the Communist Party in November, 1962, looked like the beginning of a new era for Bulgaria. The cases of Chervenkov, Yugov, and Tsankov,[16] the former Minister of the Interior, were used to spotlight the illegal methods and abuses of the past and to stress that they would never happen again. The Congress seemed to be guaranteeing the favorable developments of the year since the Soviet Congress and mapping out a brighter future. But it flattered only to deceive: Within six months, it became evident that the de-Stalinization process had ground to a halt in Bulgaria. The regime had raised hopes only to leave them unfulfilled.

There are three possible explanations. The first is that Zhivkov was never really interested in de-Stalinization and merely used it as a weapon with which to batter his opponents in the struggle for power. Once the struggle had been won, he gladly laid aside the double-edged weapon. The second is that, though Zhivkov may have won the struggle for power, he has yet to win the struggle for the successful implementation of his policy. He is faced by a strong wall of opposition in the lower ranks of his Party, especially in the provinces, and he has neither the strength nor the will to break it down. (In Hungary, Kadar has also been faced with strong opposition from his own *apparatchiks* against his "New Deal," but he has shown firmness and resolution in getting his way and has won considerable popular support for his efforts. Zhivkov, though having support from Moscow, has not had the same inclination or strength.) A third possible explanation is that the ever-deepening economic crisis in Bulgaria has called a halt to the process of relaxation. A symptom of this crisis has been the shortage of food and consumer goods. Both the Communist Party and the public took advantage of the new atmosphere to criticize the regime's failures, and Zhivkov found he had made the error of allowing people to complain at precisely the time they had the most to complain about. He then signified his insecurity by a series of repressive measures. For example, he made great efforts in 1963 to crush the intellectual ferment that had resumed in the country after the Twenty-second Congress of the CPSU, and—always a sign of a weak dictatorship— he began, in the same year, to punish severely those who criticized the regime through jokes or "antisocialist slanders." All three explanations are plausible, but probably a combination of the second and third provides the best key to Zhivkov's conduct.[17]

So impotent a leadership, whose support from Moscow is its very life line, could hardly have been expected to take an independent attitude in something so important to the Soviet Union as the dispute with China. All-out support was the only course open to Bulgaria. Albania was driven by pressing reasons to take the extreme step of siding with China. Romania saw her best interests served by a "ruling party neutralism" that played one side off against the other. Bulgaria ostentatiously supported the Soviet Union and was quite handsomely rewarded for it. But her action was not the result of a calculating decision on the part of her leaders. It was prompted by the weakness that comes from failure and lack of confidence.

Apart from the fact that he has been maintained in power, Zhivkov's chief rewards have been economic. Here the contrast between Soviet policy toward Romania and Bulgaria has been striking. Moscow objected to the Bulgarian policy of comprehensive industrialization, which is as ambitious for Bulgaria as the Romanian policy is for Romania, and yet, not only has it shown no obvious signs of opposition but has recently given Bulgaria a large credit to help her carry through this policy.

Why is it that, in dealing with two countries which, relatively speaking, were at about the same economic level, the Soviet Union has shown two different faces? Why approve of Kremikovtsi[18] when you disapprove of Galati? A possible explanation is that Kremikovtsi was conceived in 1958, before Khrushchev's ideas on the "socialist international division of labor" began to change, and he therefore allowed the Bulgarians to proceed without objection. But this would hardly explain the fact that at the Eighth Congress in November, *1962,* the Bulgarians were allowed to pass their twenty-year economic program, which is their real charter of industrialization. A more plausible explanation would be that this was a reward for loyalty, and a slight to the Romanians, whose differences with the Soviet Union may have begun on economic issues but soon acquired a political significance and hence became more challenging and dangerous. The difference in the Soviet Union's treatment of the two countries and of her relations with them was shown in February, 1964, when a new Soviet-Bulgarian agreement on economic cooperation was signed involving still more "intimate cooperation" and a new 300 million ruble loan for Sofia.

"Intimate cooperation" is, of course, a euphemism for utter dependence, and one should perhaps end this essay on a note of skepticism as to how long this unenviable status can continue. Like Romania, Bulgaria may be approaching the crossroads in her relations with the Soviet Union, even if the two countries have approached the crossroads by very different routes. Too much independence has produced Romania's peculiar situation; in Bulgaria's case, it may have been too much dependence. With the Sino-Soviet dispute in its present phase, the Kremlin prefers Zhivkovs to Gheorghiu-Dejs. But the Kremlin has demanded not only loyalty but also stability and efficiency. It has no assurance that, despite constant Soviet aid and supervision, the Zhivkov regime will ever be able to stand on its own feet. In the long term, it needs a viable, dynamic satellite system. Zhivkov is desperately trying to halt Bulgaria's economic decline by introducing new, more flexible methods of industrial planning and management. Through these means and through Soviet help, he may halt this decline. If he does not, and if he fails to imprint his political mastery more firmly on the country, he may find that devotion alone is no longer enough. As for the Bulgarian people, they have suffered too many disappointments under Zhivkov to feel that they can continue giving him the benefit of the doubt. After the Eighth Party Congress, they would have responded to a positive appeal for genuine change. Now they must realize that a genuine change of policy can come only from a genuine change of leadership.

7. East Germany

MELVIN CROAN

At ONCE inherently vulnerable and yet superficially stable, the Communist regime in East Germany has long impressed observers in the West as a major political paradox. Neither the official protestations of irrevocable Soviet commitment to the German Democratic Republic, nor the apparently entrenched power of the dominant Socialist Unity Party (SED), has contributed very much to a normalization of the situation. If anything, the East German paradox has been even more striking in recent years than ever before. For no sooner had the SED regime thrown up the Berlin Wall against the West, than its internal stability was challenged anew by an unexpected second wave of de-Stalinization from the East. And while still coping with the dilemmas of de-Stalinization, the East German Communists were confronted by another distasteful development—the disintegration of the international Communist monolith—as the result of the Sino-Soviet dispute and its attendant consequences.

That both these unwelcome challenges had wrought considerable political damage upon the East German regime was unmistakable by early 1964. Under the leadership of its long-time First Secretary, Walter Ulbricht, the SED had limited the inroads of de-Stalinization —at least for the time being. But it had done so at a rather heavy price. Almost alone among the East Central European Communist regimes, East Germany stood out as a conspicuous relic of the bygone era of Stalinism. Yet, unlike Stalinist Albania, the East German regime had not defiantly sided with the Chinese against the Russians; nor had it attempted to approximate the feat of the Romanian Communist leadership in exploiting the Sino-Soviet conflict for limited purposes of its own. On the contrary, the SED had aligned itself promptly and uncompromisingly with Khrushchev. But by so doing, it had also furnished fresh evidence of its subservience to Moscow. Small wonder that Western observers have been struck by the novel paradox of a Stalinist Ulbricht regime so closely allied with post-Stalinist Russia or that they should have questioned the long-range viability of such an arrangement.

In view of certain early signs of sympathy for the Chinese on the part of the East German Communists, the speed with which the Socialist Unity Party fell into line behind Khrushchev and the spirit of its participation in the march toward the final break are especially instructive. From late 1958 until mid-1960, certain ranking figures in the SED leadership and a segment of its more ideologically convinced cadres seemed genuinely enthusiastic about Chinese domestic practices and the revolutionary *élan* of the CCP. They also appeared to warm to Chinese militancy on questions of international strategy, on the plausible basis of a special affinity between the German Democratic Republic and the Chinese People's Republic, each of which occupied a forward post on an exposed periphery of the socialist camp. While such sentiments never developed into anything like a full-scale public campaign of support for China to the neglect of the Soviet Union, on the occasion of the tenth anniversary of the establishment of the People's Republic of China in 1959, Ulbricht himself seemed to be exceptionally generous with his words of praise for the CCP and its leader, Mao Tse-tung. Indeed, at that time, some students of international Communist affairs began to speculate about the emergence of a "Peking-Pankow axis." Their speculation, however, was not only premature but also ill-founded. Before long, all manifestations of Pankow's flirtation with Peking came to an abrupt end. During June, 1960, the month of the Sino-Soviet clash at Bucharest, the SED explicitly rejected the Chinese communes as a model worthy of imitation in East Germany and ruled out further recourse to the distinctive Chinese idiom on world affairs.

From that point to the present, the East German Communists

have given full public support to Khrushchev. Indeed, on occasion, they have been almost a step ahead of the Soviet leadership in escalating the dispute with the Chinese. Thus, for example, following the Bucharest meeting, an editorial in *Neues Deutschland,* the SED's official organ, hinted at the conflict that had occurred there, even though the dispute had not yet been revealed elsewhere in the Communist world. And, in the wake of the Moscow meeting of the eighty-one Communist parties (November, 1960), it was Ulbricht who first publicly attacked the Albanians for harboring "sectarian conceptions." The following year, immediately after the Twenty-second Congress of the CPSU, Ulbricht castigated the Albanians in much the same language that Khrushchev had employed and followed the Soviet lead in publicly chastising the Chinese for their failure to help bring the Albanians to their senses. Again, on the occasion of their own Sixth Party Congress in January, 1963, the East German Communists gave another demonstration of the zealousness of their support for the Russians against the Chinese. In his report to the Congress, Ulbricht not only rebuked the "dogmatists," but also added the previously unpreferred charge that the Chinese had violated "the agreed policy of peaceful coexistence . . . in dealing with frontier questions with India."[1] At the same Congress, the remarks of the Chinese delegate were greeted with some thirty minutes of stamping, booing, and cries of "Pfui!"—a contrived display of political hysteria which the Chinese will not soon forgive.

During the course of 1963, the pace and pitch of the East German anti-Chinese polemics closely followed those of Moscow. On July 15, *Neues Deutschland* published the open letter of the Central Committee of the CPSU together with the text of the provocative twenty-five Chinese theses of the previous month to which the Soviet letter was a rejoinder. At the end of July, following the suspension of the Sino-Soviet ideological meetings in Moscow, Kurt Hager, Chairman of the SED's Ideological Commission, delivered a comprehensive, scathing indictment of the Chinese to the Central Committee Plenum. Although the full text of Hager's speech was not immediately carried, the published communiqué on the plenary discussion condemned the Chinese in no uncertain terms. In October, 1963, *Einheit,* the SED's theoretical journal, published a series of major articles whose anti-Chinese invective surpassed anything that had previously appeared in print. It denounced the Chinese as nationalists, chauvinists, racists, anti-Marxists, primitive collectivists, unreconstructed Trotskyites, empty phrase mongers, and arrogant windbags.[2] Toward the end of the year, however, when Moscow sought to de-emphasize the polemics, the SED did the same. Thus, the Politburo report delivered by Albert Norden to the Central Committee Plenum in November, 1963, stressed that "public discussion should be stopped . . . so that these controversies will not be brought to the state level," and cautioned that a "continuation of public polemics would be welcomed only by the enemies of the socialist states and of the world Communist movement."[3] Nonetheless, in February, 1964, when the Chinese renewed their challenge to Khrushchev by publishing the seventh installment of their reply to the Soviet open letter of the previous July, the SED was the very first party to defend the Russians. Addressing the Central Committee in behalf of the Politburo, Horst Sindermann labeled the Chinese article the "vilest to date," and his attacks on the Chinese were promptly published in *Neues Deutschland*.

Such consistent East German partisanship for the Russians against the Chinese is noteworthy on another count. Unlike the more circumspect anti-Chinese position of, say, the Polish United Workers' Party, the SED's opposition to Peking has always been linked with an explicit endorsement of the "leading role of the CPSU." As a result, official East German wrath has also extended to other parties that, even though they may be basically pro-Soviet, have sought—and in many cases obtained—a measure of authentic independence for themselves. At the special Central Committee Plenum convoked immediately after the Twenty-second Congress of the CPSU, for example, Hermann Axen, Editor of *Neues Deutschland,* indicted the Italian Communist Party for having reawakened visions of polycentrism, which he denounced as being "even more miserable today than in 1956."[4] To give even more permanent expression to the SED's unconditional rejection of polycentrism, the Preamble to the new Party Statutes, adopted at the Sixth Congress, describes the East German Party as an integral component of the international Communist movement and refers to the CPSU as its established "advanced guard."

How does one account for the uncompromisingly pro-Soviet stance taken by the Ulbricht leadership of the SED? Are there no issues that have divided East Berlin from Moscow?

Clearly, the Chinese do not believe that Ulbricht's interests were in complete alignment with those of Khrushchev. They seem to understand the extent to which the Ulbricht regime has sought to counter disaffection at home through a dynamic, aggressive policy toward the West. Accordingly, the Chinese have raised the issue of

Berlin and the larger question of Germany as a whole. They did this indirectly, as early as 1961, after the Twenty-second Congress of the CPSU, at which Khrushchev—to the evident disappointment of Ulbricht—rescinded an earlier deadline for the acceptance of Soviet terms on Berlin. At the time, Enver Hoxha, China's Albanian mouthpiece, accused Khrushchev of irresolution and downright cowardice. By the summer of 1963, however, Chinese commentary on the German situation was more direct and forceful. In return for a limited nuclear test-ban agreement with the West, the Russians, as the Chinese now saw it, had deliberately sold out the German Democratic Republic. They based this conclusion on Soviet willingness to accept the Western stipulation that East Germany's accession to the test-ban agreement did not imply recognition of the German Democratic Republic by any signatory that had not previously recognized East Germany. This Soviet acceptance, according to the Chinese, represented an act of "common treason," one that was "seriously damaging to the interests of the German Democratic Republic."[5]

In making these charges, the Chinese doubtless had more in mind than merely to warn that if the Russians "sell out the interests of the German Democratic Republic today, who can say that they will not bargain away the interests of another state tomorrow?"[6] Most likely, the Chinese expected to employ this line of criticism to embarrass the Ulbricht leadership and perhaps even to win over adherents within the SED. Although Ulbricht and his closest associates were not likely to embarrass easily, the SED leadership's earlier militancy over Berlin provided the Chinese with plausible grounds for the belief that they had fastened upon a sensitive issue. The Chinese were not alone in this assessment. In fact, many Western observers had been postulating a divergence of interest between Ulbricht and Khrushchev on the same issues—Berlin and the German question as a whole. Indeed, a prominent American student of Communist affairs had speculated that Ulbricht's support for Moscow actually amounted to an attempt to "exercise leverage on the Russians to take a stronger stand over Berlin" and suggested that there were "limits to the Soviet ability to force him into line."[7]

Recent events leave no doubt that such an assessment was nothing more than fanciful conjecture. Ulbricht's support of the Russians against the Chinese never constituted a lever to force the Soviet Union to take a stronger stand against the West. On the contrary, Ulbricht's support for the Russians has meant acceptance of Khrushchev's version of peaceful coexistence, up to and including the Soviet post-Cuban missile crisis program for a relaxation of tensions within Germany and over Berlin itself. Significantly, Ulbricht himself made the first public announcement of the shift in Moscow's German strategy, in a speech in early December, 1962—a speech that evoked widespread comment in the West as "a remarkable backdown."[8] The following month, at the Sixth Congress of the SED, Khrushchev bluntly informed the East German Communists that the construction of the Berlin Wall had given them all that they could expect to get in the immediate future and that they would do well to concentrate their energies on domestic economic tasks. These developments offered striking proof—if proof were still needed—not merely that Ulbricht had failed to impress his presumably distinctive personal strategic views on the Soviet leadership but also that he had never really been in a position to do so. How could it be otherwise when basic geopolitical constants deprive the East German Communists of the power to defy Soviet wishes?

These factors are so elementary that they are often overlooked in the quest for a more sophisticated explanation of SED behavior. The first of them, the massive Soviet military presence, is of special significance because, more than a decade after the Soviet Army put down the popular uprising of June, 1953, the twenty or more Soviet divisions stationed on East German soil still constitute the ultimate guarantee of the Communist regime's survival. This is so, of course, because of the one overriding political weakness of the German Democratic Republic—its lack of a national base.

The East German Communist regime is the unfortunate legatee of the bipolarization of international power that, in the aftermath of World War II, produced the division of Germany along unnatural geographical as well as novel ideological lines. Confronted by a more prosperous and more popular rival, the Federal Republic to the west, the regime's hold over its subjects has always been precarious. The construction of the Berlin Wall may well have been useful to the regime in arresting the outpouring of refugees; by no means, however, did it relieve East Germany of its basic political anomaly. On the contrary, by bottling up dissidence, it implied an additional long-range threat. More immediately, it deepened popular rejection of the regime as little more than an alien authority. These popular sentiments of unrequited nationalism, which also penetrate the rank-and-file membership of the ruling SED, perpetuate the regime's dependence upon its Soviet sponsors and confer an important political role on the Soviet military power that sits heavily if unobstrusively in its midst.

In addition to the massive continued presence of Soviet power, reckoned in terms of Stalin's favorite criterion of "the number of divisions," a recent proliferation of economic ties has bound East Germany to the Soviet Union along the lines prescribed by Khrushchevian norms for international Communist integration. Ever since 1954 and the termination of the first postwar phase of Soviet economic exploitation, the East German economy has received continual Soviet aid. Coupled with the traditional industriousness of the Germans, this Soviet help has produced notable results. Despite an uneven industrial base, the shortcomings of the Communist planning bureaucracy, and the near chaos of its economic administration—which have contributed to East Germany's recurrent economic crises—the German Democratic Republic is the sixth largest industrial power in Europe and the most highly industrialized Communist country. East Germany has become a major producer of capital goods, excelling not only in machinery and machine tools, but also in electronic equipment, precision instruments, high quality optical goods, and a wide variety of chemical products. Since 1960, the German Democratic Republic has been the Soviet Union's leading foreign trade partner. More than fifty per cent of East Germany's foreign trade is directly with the Soviet Union, which in recent years has provided most of her imports of oil, iron ore, and grain. The dependent economic relationship thus fashioned between the two countries has been well attested to by the many revisions in East German economic plans undertaken to accommodate changing Soviet domestic priorities.

All of these basic factors may help to clarify the East German regime's subservience to Moscow. That very subservience, however, raises other important questions. How can one explain Khrushchev's unqualified endorsement of Ulbricht personally and the unstinting Soviet backing for the distinctively repressive brand of Communist dictatorship, so unmistakably tarred with the brush of Stalinism in both its personalities and policies, over which Ulbricht has presided within East Germany? While it would be mistaken to exaggerate Ulbricht's personal dictatorship to the neglect of its social function, the conundrum is inextricably bound up with the man's remarkably long survival in power.

It is fairly well established that at the time of the June, 1953, uprising, Moscow was preparing Ulbricht's downfall. Ulbricht's Stalinist record was a less pressing consideration than the mere convenience of sacrificing him as a scapegoat for the economic disasters of Stalin's own policies in East Germany, which, of course, Ulbricht had put into effect. After the June uprising, however, Moscow was no longer willing to risk tinkering with the top leadership of the SED. Indeed, Ulbricht was allowed to move against his opponents, the Zaisser-Herrnstadt group. This group had been in contact with Beria, whom both Ulbricht and Khrushchev were subsequently to charge with willingness to sacrifice the German Democratic Republic and its "socialist achievements" in exchange for a negotiated settlement with the West concerning Germany as a whole. Whether or not these charges are valid need not detain us here. The important point is that the June uprising marked a decisive turning point in respect to Ulbricht's position, as in so many other respects. Its naked exposure of the total bankruptcy of East German Communism must have come as an unwelcome shock to the entire Soviet leadership and, as such, obliterated whatever initial differences may have existed among the post-Stalinists on the German question.

Ulbricht's position, however, was not immune from further challenge. A second challenge occurred during the period of Khrushchev's first anti-Stalin campaign in 1956. Its only consequence, however, was the purge of the Schirdewan-Wollweber-Oelssner group. This was carried out, after some delay, in early 1958.

The politics of this second wave of opposition to Ulbricht is particularly revealing, if only because of its circumspect character. From the start, Ulbricht's inner-Party critics were deprived of a moral issue, comparable, say, to that which existed in Hungary. (Not without reason has Ulbricht thought it appropriate to stress on many subsequent occasions that, even during the height of Stalinism, East Germany had been spared the travesties of the Rajk and Kostov trials and a blood purge of the Communist faithful.) Those SED leaders who had been victims of the earlier Stalinist purge were still alive. The fact that Ulbricht himself had presided over their rehabilitation served to enchain the most likely leaders of the Party opposition, notably Dahlem and Ackermann, to Ulbricht's own cause. More important yet, deprived of a moral issue, none of the new "factionalists" dared to associate himself with the discontents of the SED rank and file, much less with popular dissidence. To have done so, they all seemed to have realized, would have jeopardized the very survival of the SED regime itself and thus their own chances for power. As a result of such well-advised concealment within the SED central *apparat,* the regime's revisionist intellectual critics of 1956 were denied access to the leaders of the Party opposition and found themselves, in effect, politically disarmed from the start. This, in turn, enabled Ulbricht to control the intellectual ferment and to render a major service to the Soviet leadership by sparing Moscow another revolutionary outbreak in East Germany at precisely the time when it had to deal with the Polish October and the Hungarian Revolution.

Having narrowly averted a major disaster in 1956 throughout East Central Europe, Khrushchev was content subsequently to allow Ulbricht to consolidate his personal power and to grant him virtual *carte blanche* to follow the tough domestic course that he deemed necessary. This decision was greatly facilitated by Ulbricht's own astuteness as a Communist politician. Although presumably out of sympathy with de-Stalinization from the outset and probably distrustful of Khrushchev, Ulbricht never ventured to oppose the post-Stalinist Soviet leadership. On the contrary, fully conscious of the liability of his own Stalinist record and fearful lest it give Moscow cause to oust him, Ulbricht's participation in the drive to dispose of the Stalinist legacy has always been impeccable. In 1956, upon his return to Berlin from attendance at the Twentieth Congress of the CPSU, Ulbricht spoke out immediately and openly against Stalin. Much to the shock of Party functionaries, Ulbricht decreed that the late Soviet dictator could no longer be considered a "classicist of Marxism." Again, in the wake of the Twenty-second CPSU Congress in 1961, Ulbricht ordered the swift enactment of all the necessary measures of "cartographic de-Stalinization"—that is, the renaming of streets, squares, and towns, and the dismantling of monuments, to expunge all references to Stalin from the East German landscape.

Ulbricht coupled these tangible manifestations of endorsement for successive Soviet campaigns against Stalin with an attempt to present himself as a consistent anti-Stalinist. No doubt, some of these exercises of apology have been a nuisance for Ulbricht, for they have required, among other things, that he go back over the history of the old German Communist Party (KPD) in order to "prove" that he had opposed the Comintern's self-defeating strategy and tactics during the last years of the Weimar Republic. No doubt, also, others have fallen quite short of the intended mark. (How else can one interpret Ulbricht's remarks to the Sixth Congress of the SED to the effect that East Germany had been immune to Stalinism because the Soviet Military Administration had been comprised of only Leninists or that the East German Communists themselves had run the risk of acting "undemocratically" in order to keep out "certain agents of Beria"—and the spontaneous but brief outburst of delegates' laughter occasioned by these incredible assertions?)[9] Still, whether or not Ulbricht's attempts at self-justification have been persuasive is perhaps less important than the equanimity with which he has made them. Whatever the nature of Ulbricht's own political preferences, he has never allowed them to interfere with more personal objectives. And he has pursued the quest for the preservation of his own position with an uncanny and almost infallible knack for anticipating Moscow's own thinking on the major issues of the day. The same instinct for personal survival that Ulbricht so successfully practiced for three decades under Stalin has continued to serve him in good stead throughout the post-Stalinist period. Finally, the same readiness to "learn from Soviet experience" which Ulbricht so naturally displayed under Stalin outlasted the demise of the Soviet dictator and, indeed, persists to the present day. Among other things, it has been exemplified by the speed with which the SED was revamped to correspond to the latest reorganization of the CPSU along "productive lines," and by the introduction into the East German economy of various incentive schemes in accordance with the Liberman-Khrushchev proposals in the U.S.S.R. In short, while eager to make his formal break with Stalin's memory, Ulbricht has remained a "proletarian internationalist" of the old Soviet school— something of an anachronism in the era of polycentric Communism, perhaps, but precisely as such, a deservedly prized asset for Khrushchev.

Given this kind of leadership at the helm of the SED, Khrushchev's decision to grant the East German Communists a measure of internal autonomy may not have been at all troublesome. What is more, all the available evidence suggests that Khrushchev's own evaluation of the East German situation was exceptionally realistic. The Soviet leader apparently fully appreciated that although he always had the necessary power to remove Ulbricht, the East German boss's mastery of Party and state apparatuses was such that Khrushchev could not have removed him without running the risk of undermining the potentially shaky East German political structure. Add to this the fact that Khrushchev seemed completely to have shared Ulbricht's own view of East Germany's "specially complicated circumstances" (to use the official jargon with which the SED has denoted the hostile popular environment in which it has been condemned by circumstances to function). On this basis, the Soviet leader has acknowledged the necessity of the Ulbricht regime's oppressive domestic policies. Speaking to the Sixth Congress of the SED, in January, 1963, Khrushchev commented with understanding sympathy on the "difficulties of socialist construction" in East Germany. Since "the country is divided into two states with different social systems," he observed, "the class struggle in your republic frequently assumes acute forms." Indeed, in this connection, Khrushchev even went so far as to admonish East German writers and artists to "observe vigilance" and never to forget the exposed position of the German Democratic Republic, "so close," as he put it, "to the world of suppression, speculation, and profits."[10] By so speaking, Khrushchev was offering an explicit personal endorsement of Ulbricht's obscurantist policies in the cultural and intellectual fields—that is, in precisely those areas of East German domestic policy in which Stalinism has persisted in its most undiluted form.

As a consequence of all of this, the recent East German domestic scene has been a curiously mixed one. On the one hand, in economic affairs, the SED leadership and Ulbricht himself have recommended theories and practices that were castigated as "revisionist" not so many years ago. The "law of value"—or, more conventionally put, the principle of supply and demand—seems finally to have subdued more orthodox Stalinist ideological criteria. Ideological functionaries have had to make room for technical experts in all of the major agencies of state planning and economic administration. In the interest of unfolding productive energies on a more spontaneous basis, Ulbricht has relaxed the notorious crackdown on labor and some of the more vicious practices of law enforcement that were introduced immediately after the construction of the Wall in 1961. On the other hand, however, both narrow Stalinist ideological standards and tight Party control persist without letup in the ever-sensitive intellectual realm. Among the many recent examples of the perpetuation of Stalinist "Party-mindedness," none is more symptomatic than the case of Robert Havemann. Professor of Physical Chemistry at the Humboldt University in East Berlin and a long-time Communist, Havemann also has lectured on philosophy. In this capacity, he presumed to declare war on dogmatism and Stalinism and to do battle on the platform of the need for greater freedom of opinion, information, and criticism in East Germany. This immediately brought down upon him the wrath of the Party. While the personal fate of Professor Havemann has not yet been decided, the SED leadership has made it clear that it cannot tolerate such a recrudescence of "revisionism" and that the Party is prepared to combat it, as before, by whatever "administrative measures" may be necessary.

Its perpetuation of Stalinism in the intellectual realm has set the German Democratic Republic strikingly apart from its Communist neighbors. Not only is East German cultural and intellectual life much more sterile than that of Poland, Hungary, or, for that matter, the Soviet Union, but, even more to the point, the SED has excluded intellectual influences from a number of these ostensibly fraternal socialist states. Surprisingly, the East German Communists' determination to preserve Stalinist orthodoxy has even resulted in recent measures directed against the Soviet Union itself. This development began in the wake of the Twenty-second Congress of the CPSU. In early 1962, Alfred Kurella, then Chairman of the Cultural Commission of the SED Politburo, took issue with a Soviet literary historian and former cultural officer attached to the Soviet Military Administration in Germany, Ilya Fradkin, who had advocated increased liberalization in literature and art.[11] Since then, Soviet movies have been cut and Soviet articles censored so as to distort their message. Some Soviet books, such as Solzhenitsyn's *One Day in the Life of Ivan Denisovich,* have been banned entirely, on the grounds that such literary portrayals of the excesses of Stalinism could only do harm to the German Democratic Republic. As Ulbricht himself expressed it: "Certain works of this kind may be effective in relation to the Soviet internal situation, but there is absolutely no reason for us to publish them."[12] More recently, the rigidities of East German cultural policy have all but destroyed East Germany's previously intimate political relations with Czechoslovakia. The East German Communists have been compelled to throw up additional dams against the belated Czech thaw. They have done so with determination and indignation. Both these qualities were manifested in the official Politburo condemnation of Havemann which included a sustained, detailed attack against the trend of developments in Czechoslovakia and made a point of "the connection between [Havemann's] own [opinions] and certain revisionist theories that are pushing their way toward us from Prague."[13]

Despite these concerted efforts, the German Democratic Republic cannot—and indeed does not—function in isolation from developments elsewhere in the Communist world, or even, despite the Wall, from the West. On the one hand, judging by the tone and content of complaints recently carried in the East German press, the population remains fully conscious of its imprisonment and contemptuous of its warders. On the other hand, the Sino-Soviet dispute has seriously demoralized the warders themselves. The ideologically militant Communist cadres, who naturally constitute the Ulbricht regime's most energetic supporters, have in fact been badly shaken by the international split. Striking proof is provided by the fact that *Einheit* felt obliged to publish a chance reader's letter which expressed bewilderment and betrayed distress that the Chinese, whom the East German Party faithful had long been taught to admire for their revolutionary heroism, should now turn out to be guilty of so many unforgivable deviations.[14] This is not really a question of the existence of a pro-Chinese faction within the SED. It is much more serious. With the fabric of Communist internationalism rent asunder to reveal its underlying strands of nationalist particularism, the basic anomaly of the East German regime, its lack of a national base, now stands out more forcibly than ever before. And this, in turn, fosters disillusionment and threatens skepticism precisely where the regime can least afford it, within the ranks of the ruling Communist Party itself.

What future, then, can one predict for the East German regime? Some circles look for major changes once Ulbricht departs from the scene. Although his personal power is presently secure, Ulbricht is in his seventy-first year, and the days of his active leadership are numbered. Those who follow him are sure to lack his experience and perhaps also his purposefulness. Yet it would be unwarranted to expect Ulbricht's successors to venture a major reversal of the over-all direction of his policies. However much the regime may seek genuine popular acceptance, the risks of a genuine liberalization remain far too great. Even a limited step in that direction, a restoration to the population at large of the right to travel to the West, could bring politically embarrassing and economically damaging consequences. The likely results of tearing down the Wall need no comment. A comprehensive program of de-Stalinization behind the Wall would be no less menacing. An enlargement of the areas of free discussion and open criticism, even one as modest as that proposed by Professor Havemann, would inevitably unloose long-suppressed currents of nationalism and thus threaten the survival of this still eminently artificial "second German state." For the present—and for the foreseeable future—genuine internal liberalization remains inseparably linked to the cause of national reunification and thus necessarily evokes the specter of the liquidation of the Communist dictatorship in East Germany.

The Ulbricht regime may well constitute both a source of embarrassment and a cause for concern to the Soviet Union. Yet, the unmistakable risks involved in any meaningful change cannot fail to distress Moscow even more. Given the Soviet strategic and economic stakes, the range of options open to Moscow is sharply circumscribed. On many occasions in recent years, Khrushchev referred to Germany as "problem number one" in international politics. Let us grant him the point, for if the present phase of international politics is one of East-West *détente,* the "search for areas of agreement" seems destined to falter in Germany—largely, it must be said, on account of the accumulated commitments of Soviet policy. And that is the larger significance of the East German paradox.

8. Outer Mongolia, North Korea, North Viet-Nam

PAUL F. LANGER

OUTER MONGOLIA

To APPRECIATE the role of the Mongolian People's Republic (M.P.R.)—better known as Outer Mongolia—in the Communist world and the impact the Sino-Soviet conflict is having on that country's policies, one must keep in mind certain basic facts of geography and history.

As conquerors of China and Russia, the Mongols, centuries ago, played a brief but important role in history. Today, the descendants of Genghis Khan live for the most part under Chinese and Soviet rule. Outer Mongolia, with its capital of Ulan Bator, remains the only Mongol-ruled independent state. This vast country, however, is landlocked, underdeveloped, and militarily weak. Its population of a mere million thus lives uneasily in the threatening shadow of two giant empires that encircle the M.P.R.'s territory: the U.S.S.R. with 220 million inhabitants in the north and Communist China with 700 million people in the south.

Of the two neighbors, China is viewed by the Outer Mongolians as the principal menace to their independence, not only because China has traditionally been the enemy of Mongolian national aspirations, but because the fate of the Mongolians in neighboring Inner Mongolia constitutes a clear warning of a Chinese ethnic threat. Here in Chinese Inner Mongolia—Ulan Bator's *irredenta*—during the past several decades, a veritable flood of Chinese immigrants has engulfed the 1.5 million Mongolians who are by now a minority in their own country.

The Russian threat appears much less grave. Soviet armed intervention in Outer Mongolia during the early 1920's destroyed any hope of real independence, and the Soviet-sponsored Mongolian People's Republic was soon reduced to the status of a Soviet satellite, hermetically sealed off from international contacts. But the Outer Mongolians, in contrast to their brothers in Inner Mongolia, were allowed at least nominal independence, and there has never been any fear of Russian colonization. Under Soviet tutelage, the M.P.R. has generally enjoyed a good measure of cultural autonomy, and the Mongolians have at least materially benefited from incorporation into the Soviet sphere of influence. On the whole, what the frequent visitors to Ulan Bator from the neighboring Buryat A.S.S.R. have reported about the transformation of their environment has been more reassuring than Mongolian accounts of Chinese policy in Inner Mongolia.

By 1964, the Outer Mongolians had been exposed to Soviet influence continuously for four decades. The small elite of the M.P.R. —there are some 40,000 members in the Mongolian People's Revolutionary Party—owes its preferred status to the Soviet-sponsored regime. Government and Party officials, teachers, engineers, and scientists have absorbed a Russian education, often in the U.S.S.R. itself. They are familiar with Soviet institutions, and they speak, read, and write the Russian language, which has opened up to them the world of the twentieth century. Somewhat like French civilization in Africa, Russian civilization is identified in the minds of the Outer Mongolians with material and cultural progress and with intellectual sophistication. China, on the other hand, not only seems more threatening, but also more alien: Few Outer Mongolians have traveled to Peking, and very few know the Chinese language. Outer Mongolia today is facing West rather than East.

At least since the death of Stalin, early in 1953, there has been evidence of Chinese Communist efforts to bring Outer Mongolia out of its Soviet-imposed isolation and to break the monopoly of Soviet influence there. In 1954, during Khrushchev's visit to Peking, Mao Tse-tung raised the Mongolian issue in his talks with the Soviet leader.

By the mid-1950's, the Chinese had made some inroads into the Soviet position: Chinese aid programs were being implemented in Outer Mongolia; thousands of Chinese laborers appeared on Mongolian construction sites; a railroad linking Peking and Ulan Bator had been pushed to completion; and a Chinese cultural offensive sought to bring China to the attention of the Russia-oriented Mongolians. Since this period also coincides with the withdrawal of Soviet forces from the M.P.R., it seems plausible that the leaders of the M.P.R. were beginning to feel some uneasiness about Chinese intentions despite the existence of the Soviet-Mongolian military alliance of 1946. This would explain why two lengthy Soviet-Mongolian policy statements were signed on May 14 and 15, 1957, in the Kremlin between, respectively, Khrushchev and D. Damba, then First Secretary of the Mongolian People's Revolutionary Party, and Premiers Bulganin and Yumjagiin Tsedenbal of the M.P.R., and why they were given considerable attention in Moscow and Ulan Bator.

These statements underlined the continuing Soviet interest in Outer Mongolia, promised an increase of Soviet aid to the Mongolian economy, and touched repeatedly on the role of the Chinese People's Republic. There was frequent mention of the "fraternal friendship" linking the M.P.R. with the U.S.S.R. and the C.P.R. and recognition of the importance of the Chinese Communist victory for the future of the Far East. Particularly significant was this passage in the Bulganin-Tsedenbal statement: "The two great fraternal neighboring states guarantee the peace and tranquility of the borders of the M.P.R."[1] After having been shut out of Outer Mongolia for four decades, the Chinese appeared to have regained a foothold in the area by 1957.

In the 1960's, the continued Chinese offensive in Outer Mongolia has brought forth vigorous Soviet counteractions. So far, the advantage in this developing politico-ideological, economic, and cultural competition has been on the Soviet side.

Confronted with the superior Soviet position in the M.P.R., the Chinese have avoided an open challenge and pursued a consistently soft line in dealing with Outer Mongolia throughout the late 1950's and early 1960's. While the exchanges between Moscow and Peking have gained in bitterness, and the Outer Mongolians have backed the Russians in this conflict, Chinese criticism of Mongolian policies has remained rather mild. The Chinese leaders have even tolerated Outer Mongolian attitudes that could be interpreted as provocative.

A striking example was provided in December, 1962, when Premier Tsedenbal visited Peking to sign an agreement for a settlement of the 2,600-mile border with China, essentially on Mongolian terms.[2] Despite this tangible evidence of Chinese reasonableness, Tsedenbal apparently felt the need to make clear his continued support for the Soviet ally. Addressing a large festive crowd, he shocked his Chinese hosts by praising "peaceful coexistence" and other favorite notions of Soviet foreign policy that the Chinese leaders particularly oppose.

Material Chinese assistance to the M.P.R. has continued, despite China's economic difficulties and the lack of tangible appreciation in Ulan Bator. But new Soviet and East European offers, combined, amount on the average to three or four times Peking's economic aid.[3] Outer Mongolia had long been an area of low priority in Soviet economic planning, but Chinese competition has left the Russians little choice but to respond more positively to Mongolian requests for assistance. How this situation has benefited the M.P.R. is illustrated by the development of the Darkhan industrial complex in the north. The idea for the project originally came from the Chinese, but they have been completely excluded from participation in the development. Soviet, Czech, and Polish contributions include the construction of a thermal power plant,[4] tanneries, cement plants, agricultural machinery manufacturing facilities, a brick factory, coal mines, and grain elevators.

For several years, Peking enjoyed some leverage in the M.P.R. through its supply of labor forces. Chinese laborers were needed, since the Mongolians preferred nomadic life or more stimulating tasks to construction work. Since 1962, however, the number of Chinese workers in the M.P.R. has rapidly dwindled and now appears to be insignificant. It is not certain if this withdrawal is the result of a Mongolian request, of Soviet pressure, or of Chinese policy.[5] At any rate, the gap left by the departure of the Chinese is now apparently being filled, if reluctantly, by the Mongolians themselves and by Soviet labor, probably imported from the Buryat A.S.S.R.

The Chinese cultural offensive has been even less successful. Countering Peking's efforts to bring the area back into the Chinese orbit, the Russians have intensified their own propaganda drive. In 1964, the resident of Ulan Bator reads his daily *Unen,* which in

Mongolian means "truth" just as *Pravda* does in Russian. Comparing the two papers, he will find that key articles are often the same. If not fluent in Russian, he is likely to study the language in an evening course under the stepped-up Russian-language drive launched in 1963. His children learn Russian in school and acquire their education from texts that are mostly translations from the Russian. The brighter Mongolian students enter Soviet universities. (Very few find their way to China.) Meanwhile, an enormous Soviet propaganda effort, carried on largely under the auspices of the Soviet-Mongolian Friendship Association, is affecting all facets of Mongolian life in the 1960's: Books, periodicals, radio, motion pictures, photo exhibits, lectures, study groups, and mass meetings constantly keep the image of the Soviet Union before the eye of the Outer Mongolian citizen. During the annual Soviet-Mongolian Friendship Month, which precedes the celebrations of the Russian October Revolution, these activities reach their high point.[6]

Contacts between individual Russians and Outer Mongolians have increased substantially during the past few years through the growing number of visiting Soviet delegations. These delegations have included scientists, writers, artists, architects, archeologists, engineers, and technicians, as well as veterinarians and agronomists. Particularly close cultural relations between the Asiatic territories of the Soviet Union and the M.P.R. are facilitated by their common use of the Cyrillic script, whereas, in an attempt to keep out Soviet influence, Mongolians living in Inner Mongolia have been instructed by Peking to use the Latin script.

Chinese advances are also rendered difficult by the fact that the M.P.R.'s social, cultural, and economic policies have long imitated those of the Soviet Union and that the M.P.R.'s administrative and party apparatus is modeled after that of the U.S.S.R. and maintains close relations with its Soviet counterparts. Thus, Outer Mongolia has its People's Great Khural, which corresponds to the Supreme Soviet in Moscow and, after the Soviet fashion, elected in 1963 as Vice-President an "honored milkmaid." While Stalin was alive, the M.P.R. had its "little Stalin," Marshal Choibalsan, who passed away a year before his Soviet idol, and now that Khrushchev is in control in the U.S.S.R., Outer Mongolia is ruled by his Mongolian counterpart, Tsedenbal, who, like the Soviet leader, is his country's Premier and First Secretary of the Mongolian People's Revolutionary Party. That Party is in turn patterned after the CPSU and maintains intimate ties with its Soviet counterpart: Many of its cadres are trained in the U.S.S.R. and spend prolonged periods in the Soviet Union to acquaint themselves with the "ideological work" of the CPSU. In the spring of 1964, for example, at the time that Suslov bitterly attacked the CCP before the Soviet Party's Central Committee, a high-level Mongolian People's Revolutionary Party delegation stayed three weeks in the Soviet Union.

Peking's competitive position in Ulan Bator remains weak, and since the beginning of the Sino-Soviet conflict, the M.P.R. leaders have consistently backed the Soviet stand on all major issues dividing the two great Communist powers.

The decisions of the historic Twentieth, Twenty-first, and Twenty-second Congresses of the CPSU have invariably been endorsed in Ulan Bator and have been reflected in Outer Mongolia's domestic and foreign policies. Occasionally, however, when Soviet policy changes impinge on Mongolian nationalist feelings, the M.P.R. leaders have hesitated to follow the Soviet lead or have gone only part of the way in the required *Gleichschaltung*. This was particularly true with respect to de-Stalinization. The late Marshal Choibalsan, a dedicated practitioner of the "cult of personality," was lowered from his pedestal after Khrushchev launched his attack against Marshal Stalin, and the Mongolian Party eventually also pressed the attack against Stalinism at home; but Choibalsan was not dragged out of his Ulan Bator mausoleum, where he rests as Stalin once was allowed to do in the Kremlin until removed by Khrushchev.

From the Moscow Conference in November, 1960, down to the present day, the Mongolian leaders have aligned themselves without reservation with their Soviet teachers on all major international issues, even when this meant a clash with the Chinese. At the Twenty-second Party Congress and thereafter, they bitterly criticized the Albanian foes of the Soviet Union. They have lashed out against dogmatism and ultraleftism—that is, against the Chinese— but they have had only kind words for Tito.

Like Khrushchev, Tsedenbal and his government disavowed the Chinese attack against India. An Ulan Bator broadcast of January 27, 1964, quoted the Mongolian leader as having sent a message to Prime Minister Nehru that contained the following passage, which must have angered the Chinese:

> The Mongolian people rejoice at the successes achieved by the Indian people in strengthening their independence and developing their country's economy and culture. We are convinced that the friendly relations between the Mongolian and Indian peoples will

develop and widen to the benefit of peace in Asia and throughout the world. I take this opportunity to wish you good health and all the best, Your Excellency, and growth and prosperity to the friendly Indian people.

On the issue of the Soviet handling of the Cuban missile crisis, Khrushchev enjoyed complete Mongolian support. An *Unen* editorial of November 23, 1963, for example, asserted that "the dangerous crisis in the Caribbean region was peacefully resolved through the calm and wise policy of the Soviet Union." And the man responsible for these policies, Premier Khrushchev, continued to be described in the Ulan Bator press as a "wise and tested Marxist-Leninist"—terms never applied to his rival Mao Tse-tung, whose name rarely figures in official documents emanating from Outer Mongolia.

On the crucial issue of war and nuclear weapons, Moscow finds in Outer Mongolia a stanch ally. Tsedenbal and his colleagues have time and again emphasized the need for peaceful coexistence and pointed to the menace of nuclear war. To underline its support for Soviet policy, the M.P.R. hastened to sign the partial nuclear test-ban only three days after the United States, Britain, and the U.S.S.R. had affixed their signatures to the pact. How the Mongolian leaders feel about the issues involved is evidenced in the *Unen* editorial of December 6, 1963, which contains this significant passage:

> The basic political problem at the present stage is the dilemma of war or peaceful coexistence. The Moscow Statement says that at the present time, when the world is divided into two systems, the only correct principle in international relations is the principle of peaceful coexistence between states with different social systems advanced by V. I. Lenin and reflected in the Moscow Statement, in the decisions of the 20th and 21st CPSU congresses, and in the documents of other Communist and workers parties. The MPRP has always been guided and will continue to be guided by this principle. The principle of peaceful coexistence between states with different social systems is in no way an obstacle to revolution and national liberation movements . . . the Moscow partial test ban agreement is a great victory for the policy of peaceful coexistence and a step toward the prevention of world war. The "general line" which the leaders of the Chinese People's Republic have advanced in opposition to the general line of the international Communist movement . . . is a leftist-opportunist line . . . a position of empty theorizing . . .

On the whole, the Mongolian treatment of the Chinese problem has closely paralleled Soviet procedure. During 1963 and 1964, the anti-Chinese tone gained in virulence in Ulan Bator,[7] and the M.P.R. press faithfully reproduced the major Soviet attacks against Peking. When, early in April, 1964, *Pravda* released the hitherto secret report Suslov had made on February 14 before the Central Committee of the CPSU, *Unen,* only a few days later (April 8), followed suit, despite the severe accusations against the Chinese neighbor that the report contained.

With the sharpening of the Sino-Soviet conflict, it has become essential for Moscow to assure itself of Outer Mongolia's allegiance. Outer Mongolians can do useful work in frustrating Peking's efforts to drown out Moscow's voice in the Communist front organizations of the Afro-Asian world. At a time when most Asian Communist parties line up behind Peking, and when almost all the others waver, the M.P.R. plays an important role in preventing Peking from claiming that Moscow represents no more than the fat white race of Europe. By building a showcase of Moscow-style Communism in the M.P.R., the Soviet Union can at least attempt to prove to Asians that Moscow's prescriptions apply also to Asia and that they are more effective than those advocated by Peking.[8] From a neglected, backward Asian satellite of the Soviet Union, Outer Mongolia is thus changing on the chessboard of Soviet strategy into an important piece.

For some time to come, the Soviet Union has the military power to discourage Chinese aggression against the M.P.R. It also commands sufficient organizational control to prevent, or at least to reverse, an attempted Chinese-sponsored or supported coup in Ulan Bator. Any outright Chinese challenge against the predominant Soviet position in Outer Mongolia thus seems unlikely. But the strong Soviet position is by no means immune to slow erosion resulting from the effects of the Sino-Soviet conflict and from the Soviet policies to which this conflict has given rise.

Outer Mongolia has not remained unaffected by the world-wide trend of nationalism in the lesser developed countries. The country's enhanced importance in recent years, the growing Sino-Soviet competition over its allegiance, as well as the loosening of Moscow's controls within the Soviet sphere of influence, have provided new opportunities and stimulation for Mongolian nationalist sentiments to assert themselves. These sentiments—essentially aspirations for genuine national independence—have survived, despite Soviet efforts at assimilation, and are likely to grow with time. While such aspirations may not directly benefit the Chinese in their struggle with Moscow, they are bound to be directed not only against Chinese control over Inner Mongolia but also against the position of the Soviet Union in the M.P.R.

Indications of this can be found in the series of purges that have taken place among the top leadership in Ulan Bator during the past several years. It is an established fact, for example, that, as the result of Russian pressure, Politburo member Tomor-Ochir was purged in September, 1962, and that he was accused of chauvinist proclivities in connection with his attempted glorification of the great Mongol ruler Genghis Khan—a logical rallying point for Pan-Mongolian nationalism. Similar reasons seem to be responsible for the sudden fall from grace of Second Secretary and Politburo member Laibuzyn Tsend in December, 1963.[9]

The Soviet hold over its former satellite is also likely to be weakened by the growing diversification of the M.P.R.'s international contacts. Soviet stress on "international socialist division of labor" and attempts to prevent economic self-reliance among the Communist states brought about Outer Mongolia's full-fledged membership, in 1962, in the Soviet-dominated Committee for Economic Mutual Assistance (CEMA). In turn, this has led the M.P.R. into a greater involvement with the Communist nations of Europe. Both the economic and the political effects of such involvement will, no doubt, encourage independent thinking and policies in Ulan Bator.

The M.P.R. has also finally succeeded in breaking out of its isolation from the non-Communist world. Its membership in the United Nations (1961) has gained it recognition by many nations, among them Great Britain. And Outer Mongolia now trades with such capitalist countries as Japan, Britain, Austria, and Switzerland.

Given a continuation of the present trend of Soviet policy and of the Sino-Soviet conflict, the M.P.R.'s freedom of action and its bargaining power vis-à-vis the Soviet Union are likely to grow further during the 1960's. Outer Mongolia does not share Communist China's world outlook; it lacks Peking's militant mood, and Chinese rather than U.S. "imperialism" is of relevance to the M.P.R.'s foreign policy. It seems improbable, therefore, that Outer Mongolia should wish to forego entirely the protection that the Soviet alliance now provides. One may anticipate, however, that, in the years to come, Ulan Bator's government will bargain determinedly with Moscow to gain a more genuinely independent status, and that in this bargaining process the M.P.R. may be tempted at times to play the Chinese card to broaden its freedom in dealing with the Soviet Union.

NORTH KOREA

The Democratic People's Republic of Korea (D.P.R.K.), which occupies the northern half of divided Korea, is ruled from Pyongyang, the capital, by a tough Communist regime in which the Korean Workers' Party holds the monopoly of power. The Party's chief, Kim Il-sung, is also the leader of the North Korean Government and Commander-in-Chief of the Republic's armed forces.

Kim's earlier career is lost in the haze of Communist mythology. It is certain, however, that he is Korean-born, lived for years in the Soviet Union, and operated as an anti-Japanese guerrilla in Manchuria during the prewar period. Kim returned with the Red Army to his native country after World War II, reportedly wearing the uniform of a Soviet major. Ever since, he has displayed a combination of ruthlessness and skillful intrigue in eliminating his rivals that reminds one of Stalin.

For a decade, Kim pursued the goal of making himself the wielder of all power in North Korea. By 1958, he had succeeded in eradicating all his identifiable rivals: the returnees from China, known as the Yenan faction; the Soviet faction, composed of Korean Communist returnees from the U.S.S.R.; and the various groups of Communists and non-Communists who made up the several "domestic factions."[10] Despite the pronounced Korean inclination toward internecine struggle and factionalism, Kim's control over the 11 million North Koreans seems secure for the time being.

North Korea borders on the U.S.S.R. in its northeast corner and shares a long frontier with Communist China. The support of one or preferably both of these powers will remain essential as long as Communist and anti-Communist armed forces confront each other across the 38th Parallel. This division of the peninsula suggests the third dominant factor shaping the D.P.R.K.'s policy. As long as U.S. forces are stationed in South Korea and there is a clear U.S. commitment to defend the Republic of Korea against internal and external Communist aggression, Pyongyang cannot expect a reunification of the country on Communist terms. Moreover, the U.S. presence in northeast Asia is not only an obstacle to Communist objectives; in the North Korean capital, it is viewed as a potential threat to the Communist regime's very existence.

In many respects, therefore, Communist North Korea shares problems and concerns with North Viet-Nam and with Communist China. All three must contend with rival governments that have the backing of the United States. All three are not fully recognized internationally and are unable to gain admission to the United Nations. All three see their desires to unify their divided nations under Communist governments frustrated by resistance from the non-Communist world and particularly from the United States. Concern with "U.S. imperialism" therefore plays a central role in the policies of Communist China, North Korea, and North Viet-Nam, but not in Communist Outer Mongolia, where the issue of U.S. power in Asia is not one that impinges directly on the Communist regime's aspirations.

Until the outbreak of the Korean War in 1950, North Korea and Kim Il-sung were under strong Soviet control, and Korean domestic policies tended to be inspired by the Soviet example. But during the 1950's, a number of factors tended to reduce Soviet and enhance Chinese influence in Communist North Korea—Mao Tse-tung's successful seizure of power in 1949; the massive intervention of Chinese "volunteers" on the side of the North Koreans in the Korean War; the presence of Chinese armed forces in North Korea even after the armistice of 1953; the internal struggle within the Soviet leadership after Stalin's death that same year; the subsequent Soviet difficulties in controlling events in Eastern Europe; the less militantly anti-U.S. line of Khrushchev's regime and his insistence on de-Stalinization (which was obviously distasteful to the Stalinist Kim Il-sung). By 1956, Soviet and Chinese influence on North Korean decisions apparently had reached a state of equilibrium that permitted Kim increased freedom of action to choose at will among Soviet and Chinese models and policies. Significantly, when Kim's position was threatened by the last important round of factional struggle in 1956, both Communist neighbors sent (or were requested to send) high-level arbitrators to Pyongyang—Marshal P'eng Teh-huai and Deputy Premier Anastas Mikoyan, respectively.

By 1960, the pro-Chinese orientation of Kim Il-sung's regime had become a matter of public record. In the post-Stalin world of Communism, however, it has become possible for a Communist regime to embrace the ideological and foreign-policy positions of either Moscow or Peking without necessarily submitting to its dictates and without imitating its domestic policies. This would seem to be evidenced by the case of North Korea in the 1960's.

Since the Bucharest Conference of Representatives of Communist Parties of June, 1960, and throughout the subsequent international gatherings where Moscow and Peking have clashed, the Korean Workers' Party has given increasingly overt support to Chinese policy positions. At home, however, Kim Il-sung has displayed a growing tendency toward self-glorification—he is the expert on guerrilla warfare,[11] the wise planner, and the theorist—and has placed increasingly heavy stress on the need for a "self-reliant" course. This may, in part, reflect Kim's response to economic pressures exerted by Moscow in an attempt to enforce Kim's compliance with Soviet policy. But under Kim Il-sung, the Korean Communists seem to chart their own course: "Kim-ism"—which is neither Maoism nor Khrushchevism.

North Korea did not follow Mao Tse-tung in his "Hundred Flowers" liberalization campaign. It did not adopt Khrushchev's de-Stalinization policy. That North Korea's *Chollima* ("Flying Horse") movement—aimed at tremendously accelerating the development of the Korean economy—was inspired by China's "Great Leap Forward" of 1958 is doubtful. (The North Koreans insist that their movement was launched in December, 1956,[12] at a time when the Chinese were not yet considering such bold economic experimentation.) North Korea's agricultural policy is more than a mere replica of the Chinese model, and so is its industrialization program; both are vastly more successful than those of China. Even today, when Kim has aligned himself with Mao on key ideological issues, North Korean domestic policies give the impression of having been conceived independently of Peking's advice. Thus, a letter sent by the Korean Workers' Party Central Committee to Party members, in the fall of 1963, advocates that the "firepower of the Party" should henceforth be concentrated on the production of consumer goods, "to make an epochal improvement in the standards of living within one or two years." This letter speaks in tones reminiscent of consumer-goods-minded Khrushchev rather than of austerity-bent Mao:

> The Party intends to completely materialize the century-old cherished desire of the people who want to live in tile-roofed houses, who want to wear silken clothes, who want to eat rice and broth, and who want to live a cultural existence. We must solve everything so that our people can live an affluent and cultural life as do other peoples . . .[13]

The Chinese Communists are enjoying a much better press in Pyongyang than are the Russians. In the fall of 1963, for example, the North Korean press criticized the Soviet Academy of Sciences'

History of the World for minimizing the Korean historical contribution and for playing down the role of Kim's guerrillas as "extremely regrettable" and "unbearable."[14] Korean newspapers describe Soviet contributions to the Korean postwar effort as "spiritual and material assistance for our rehabilitation after the war," but praise Communist China in language charged with emotion: ". . . the Chinese People's Volunteers demonstrated their true moral character as fighters of internationalism. They defended each tree and blade of grass as if their own and shared the joy and grief of the Korean people during the fierce battle."[15]

From the very beginnings of the Sino-Soviet conflict, North Korea sympathized with Chinese ideological and foreign-policy positions, but during the late 1950's and early 1960's, its sympathy turned into support. At first, however, this support, while unequivocal, was still couched in terms allowing for a reconciliation between Moscow and Peking, along the lines of a militantly anti-u.s. policy. At the Twenty-second Congress of the cpsu, Kim joined the Chinese in backing Albania against Khrushchev's charges. In his subsequent report to the Central Committee of the Korean Workers' Party, in November, 1961, he praised the Soviet Union as the vanguard of international Communism, but did not endorse Khrushchev's condemnation of Stalin. Kim's line was that the whole affair was an internal Soviet matter, without relevance to the Korean Workers' Party, and that individual Communist parties, being completely equal and independent, should be free to decide whether they wished to draw on one another's experience. He hinted that he saw no reason why he would want to draw on Khrushchev's advice.[16] In fact, soon thereafter he sent friendly greetings to the Albanians;[17] vilified the Yugoslav revisionists; refused to do anything about de-Stalinization at home; and supported the Chinese rather than the Soviet interpretation of the Sino-Indian border dispute.

As yet, there had been no direct North Korean attacks against Khrushchev and the Soviet "modern revisionists." One of the reasons for Kim's comparative restraint may have been Chung-hee Park's *coup d'état* of May, 1961, in South Korea, which seems to have aroused in Pyongyang a fear of invasion from the south. Kim apparently felt the need for military guarantees from both the u.s.s.r. and China. He visited the Soviet capital on July 6, and Peking five days later, for the signing of bilateral military pacts, acknowledging by his itinerary the continued importance of Soviet backing against any external threat.

As the Sino-Soviet conflict again flared up after the Cuban missile crisis of July, 1962, and as it continued to sharpen throughout 1963 and 1964, Kim Il-sung was compelled to state his position clearly, even at the risk of incurring Soviet antagonism. While his decision had already been suggested by his actions in 1961, his pronouncements during 1962, and later, gave an idea of the lengths to which he was willing to go in order to bring pressure against Khrushchev's "peaceful coexistence" policy.

Kim criticized Khrushchev's policy on Cuba as appeasement of "U.S. imperialism." He refused to participate in CEMA's "socialist division of labor," and stressed at home the need for economic self-reliance. In 1963, the Korean edition of the Soviet-sponsored theoretical journal *Problems of Peace and Socialism* was discontinued. In June of that year, Choi Yong-kun, the President of the D.P.R.K., and Chinese Chairman Liu Shao-chi issued a joint statement reviewing "with satisfaction" their "increasing unity in the common struggle against imperialism and modern revisionism."[18] Then in August, the official *Nodong Sinmun* (*Labor News*) and Radio Pyongyang attacked the partial nuclear test ban as "practically meaningless"; but, unlike the Chinese, they did not accuse Khrushchev of intending to prevent China from acquiring nuclear weapons.[19]

The conclusions reached by North Korea on the principal issues dividing China and the Soviet Union were expounded during 1963 and 1964 in a number of policy statements. Particularly significant was *Nodong Sinmun's* lengthy editorial of January 27, 1964, which was widely quoted in Chinese and Japanese Communist publications. In sum, the official voice of North Korea accused the "modern revisionists" and "certain people" (meaning Khrushchev), by their insistent advocacy of a "peaceful coexistence" strategy, of dissuading the Afro-Asian and Latin American peoples from waging national liberation struggles. This strategy, it was said, produced a "peace malady," and would lead to the "ideological disarmament" of revolutionary movements, especially in the Afro-Asian–Latin American area, the "main area" of the all-important struggle against "U.S. imperialism." The North Koreans denied, as Mao had, that the emergence of nuclear weapons had changed the nature of war and that, in a nuclear age, local revolutionary wars and insurrections posed a serious problem of escalation to atomic war. Finally, the editorial stated that the differences that had arisen in the international Communist movement had now developed into questions of principles and that "Marxist-Leninists unjustly expelled from certain parties" would be justified in building up their own (rival) party organizations.

This policy statement accurately reflected Communist China's philosophy. With its militant nationalistic, anti-Western tone, its emphasis on Asia and on attempts to change the *status quo,* this philosophy better fitted the mood of Pyongyang's young, revolutionary, and highly nationalistic regime than did Khrushchev's long-range, Western-oriented, and seemingly compromising policy. And, even more importantly, the Chinese strategy held hope that, within the foreseeable future, Kim Il-sung might rule over a unified Communist Korea.

In pursuit of this primary objective, Kim is following a policy that seeks to undermine the U.S. position in South Korea—a necessary prelude to Communist seizure of power—by action on two fronts. In the world arena, the North Koreans lend vociferous and (within their modest capabilities) tangible support to all movements, regimes, organizations, projects, and individuals who oppose the United States or might be able to tie down its forces or resources. Any international organization that advocates opposition to "U.S. imperialism," any propaganda campaign directed against the United States, whether in Panama or in Africa, is assured of strong North Korean support. Kim has mobilized the several hundred thousand pro-Pyongyang Korean residents in Japan, has paid much attention to building up close ties with the Japanese Communists and left-wing socialists, and has consistently sought to push them in the direction of anti-U.S. radicalism. Castro's challenge to the United States greatly boosted morale in Pyongyang and is receiving all-out North Korean support. Thus, far-away Cuba has become the recipient of Korean aid, technicians have been dispatched from Pyongyang to Havana, and delegations travel back and forth between North Korea and the Caribbean. At the same time, relations between the North Koreans and the North Vietnamese are becoming increasingly intimate, as they face the same opponent and, to some extent, the same problem in their divided countries. The rationale behind this strategy is clear from Kim Il-sung's significant statement of 1955 (reproduced in his *Selected Works*): "Whereas it would be difficult for us to fight all alone against American imperialism, under conditions where they must disperse their forces on a global scale it will be comparatively easy for us to defeat them."[20]

In view of the militant international and ideological positions taken by Kim Il-sung, his assault on South Korea, the main front, seems to lack aggressive vigor. But Kim, like Mao, has not forgotten the lessons of the Korean War, and weighs the risks of militant action.

To take over South Korea, through essentially political means or by insurrection, Kim Il-sung must first remove the U.S. presence from the area. Like the North Vietnamese, therefore, he advocates the development in South Korea of an anti-American "liberation front" that could mobilize Korean nationalist feelings while promoting Communist objectives. While Kim's attempts to create an effective "liberation front" in South Korea have so far been quite unsuccessful, largely because of the strongly anti-Communist sentiments of the people, the North Korean Communists have given no indication of having abandoned such a plan. Meanwhile, they have approached the South Koreans with proposals for a confederation that would be created "after the removal of foreign troops and influence" and after the mutual reduction of the indigenous military apparatus. In such a confederation, the Communists would, of course, expect to dominate their opponents, especially since they have specified that, until complete unification, "the existing social and political systems" in the two Koreas would be left to continue. Such an arrangement could create the socio-political conditions for Communist insurrection and a final takeover.

Should the Sino-Soviet conflict continue to provide Pyongyang with two policy choices, Kim Il-sung must be expected to go on favoring China, since Peking's militant strategy reflects a world outlook very much like that prevailing in Pyongyang and, more than the Kremlin's strategy of "peaceful coexistence," seems to accord with the North Korean Communist regime's objectives. This is all the more true, for their geopolitical position would allow the North Koreans to obtain Soviet support at any time, should Peking's influence become too strong in Pyongyang.

NORTH VIET-NAM

The Vietnamese Workers Party, which rules the Democratic Republic of Viet-Nam (D.R.V.)—North Viet-Nam—presents a problem to the political analyst. At one time or another during the past several years, its orientation could have been called, with some justification, "pro-Peking," "pro-Moscow," or "neutral." Its vacillating course, which stands in such contrast to that of the Outer Mongolian or North Korean Party, reflects the dilemma that the North Vietnamese Communists face as a result of the Sino-Soviet confrontation, and points to the severe restraints imposed upon their policies by North Viet-Nam's precarious internal and external position.

Like Outer Mongolia and North Korea, the D.R.V. shares a long border with China. Unlike the other two Asian Communist states, however, North Viet-Nam does not enjoy the reassuring backing of a common frontier with the U.S.S.R. Soviet aid to the Hanoi regime must cross the vast expanse of China or take the long, expensive sea route.

Much like Korea and, in more recent times, Mongolia, Viet-Nam has been part of the Chinese sphere of influence. Whenever China was strong it was also expansionist. During long periods of its history, Viet-Nam was thus a colony of its northern neighbor or subject to its suzerainty. In contrast to the Koreans and Mongolians, the Vietnamese always strongly resisted such inferior status. Their history is therefore punctuated by frequent and violent clashes with Chinese invaders. More recently, the North Vietnamese people saw their traditional distrust and fear of the Chinese confirmed, when, after World War II, Chinese occupation forces pillaged the country and manhandled the population. Even today, when there is much talk of Sino-Vietnamese friendship, the North Vietnamese regime continues to abolish geographic names that are of Chinese origin or that are reminders of Viet-Nam's Chinese past.[21] Distrust of China is therefore no doubt more deeply ingrained in Viet-Nam than in Korea.

There are, of course, important parallels between Viet-Nam and Korea. Each is a divided country, where the Communist regime in the north seeks to extend its power southward and finds its way barred by U.S.-backed indigenous resistance. But while the North Korean regime may at times fear an invasion from the south, the situation has been relatively stable since the end of the Korean War, and no fighting has taken place on the peninsula for over a decade. The North Vietnamese Communist regime, however, is deeply involved in military and subversive operations outside its borders. The ties between the Viet-Cong in South Viet-Nam and their Communist allies in the north are well known. And even if the Hanoi government prefers to disclaim responsibility for the Viet-Cong guerrillas' political arm, the National Front for the Liberation of South Viet-Nam, that organization continues presumably to operate under Hanoi's direction. In view of the U.S. presence in South Viet-Nam and the growing scale of the insurgency and counterinsurgency operations there, the Hanoi regime, more than its Pyongyang counterpart, must be anxious to assure itself the backing of the two big Communist powers.

This need for Chinese and Soviet support is especially great because of the chronically catastrophic economic situation in the D.R.V. If North Korea today is not prosperous, it is at least fairly advanced and economically rather stable. North Viet-Nam, however, continues to face the problems of a small country that lacks not only an industrial base but also sufficient food for its population. Since food imports will remain necessary for some time to come, and since the long-run solution of North Viet-Nam's problems must await a higher degree of industrialization, dependence on outside help will continue to be a factor in Hanoi's policy. North Viet-Nam must extract maximum economic support from China and the Soviet Union, if a rapid pace of industrialization is to be sustained. In the past, China has provided greater quantities of aid, but the Soviet Union has furnished the more sophisticated industrial and military equipment North Viet-Nam needs.

Even under these conditions, the D.R.V. has been existing in a state of quasi-permanent economic crisis. Hanoi officially declared 1963 a year of "innumerable difficulties." Food rationing continues. The Hanoi regime cannot afford to alienate either China or the U.S.S.R. The former's significance is obvious, but only the U.S.S.R. can supply the industrial machinery that China cannot produce or spare and that is so desperately needed in North Viet-Nam. Only reunification with South Viet-Nam or the reopening of trade channels, allowing food from the rich agricultural south to flow north, could produce a solution to the D.R.V.'s acute food problem and assure internal stability. This may account in large part for (1) the strong support that the Hanoi regime lends the guerrilla effort in the south, despite the obvious risks involved, (2) the proposals of the National Front for the Liberation of South Viet-Nam for a neutral South Viet-Nam,[22] and (3) Ho Chi Minh's suggestion (presented at the special political conference of March 27, 1964) that the two zones—i.e., North and South Viet-Nam—enter into economic exchanges pending reunification.

The D.R.V.'s difficult situation is further complicated by internal political pressures accentuated by the Sino-Soviet rift.

Since its inception in 1954 as a result of the Geneva armistice agreements, the D.R.V. has been led by Ho Chi Minh, the grand old man of international Communism. His career goes back to the early days of the Comintern[23] and has spanned France, the U.S.S.R., China, and most of Asia. As a veteran with much international experience, a participant in (or planner of) many an Asian revolution, and one of the most skillful practitioners of both "peaceful" and violent seizure of power, Ho enjoys great prestige throughout the Communist world and is the object of much adulation: "His rosy face, his kind eyes, his fresh smile radiate so much love into our heart and spread so much enthusiasm and confidence throughout the country . . . brilliant leader of our Party . . . we attentively listen to Uncle Ho's advice . . . the most perfect and complete model of socialist and communist man in our country."[24]

For more than three decades, Ho led a Southeast Asian Communist organization, once known as the Indochinese Communist Party, that had jurisdiction over Viet-Nam, Laos, Cambodia, and, to some extent, also over Thailand and Burma, and of which the present Vietnamese Workers Party is a direct descendant.[25] Even today, Ho's interests and ambitions reach well beyond the borders of Viet-Nam.

Unfortunately for Ho, his North Vietnamese power base is not commensurate with his prestige. Although, like Tito, he managed to come to power essentially through his own strength, he needs Chinese (and, preferably, also Soviet) backing if he is to attain his goals—an economically stable North Viet-Nam, reunification of the divided country under Communism, and Communist control over the neighboring non-Vietnamese areas. Since Peking probably views Southeast Asia as being in the Chinese sphere of influence, and since the insurrectionary wars in South Viet-Nam and Laos impinge not only on local but also on great power interests and have world-wide implications, Ho's task is a difficult one, for he must reconcile his own interests with those of the two great Communist powers. As the interests and strategies of China and the Soviet Union have been diverging increasingly during the late 1950's, Ho has been compelled to engage in a delicate balancing act—pleasing Moscow on one issue without displeasing Peking, or the reverse, or, if necessary, taking a middle position without falling.

Under such conditions, and despite Ho's authority and prestige, pro-Chinese and pro-Soviet factions have sprung up in Viet-Nam— to an extent quite unknown in Outer Mongolia or North Korea. (Or, perhaps one should say that elements banded together who believed that it would be to North Viet-Nam's advantage to lean more clearly toward one or the other Communist big power.) Such genuine tactical disagreements are intertwined with long-standing bitter personal antagonisms among many of the Party leaders, who are only barely held in check by the prestigious, shrewd, but aging Ho.[26]

It is not Ho's style to resort to party purges, and no potential rival is likely to challenge him. However, he has been unable to avoid the fierce jockeying for position among his deputies and potential successors who have gathered in contending factions. The pro-Moscow faction is headed by General Vo Nguyên Giap (the old guerrilla strategist and victor at Dien Bien Phu), who continues to command the very powerful armed forces of the D.R.V., and the pro-Peking faction by Truong Chinh, a China-trained Party leader of much ability and a great admirer of Mao Tse-tung.

It is clear that Ho Chi Minh, his Vietnamese Workers Party, and the cause of Communist North Viet-Nam can only lose by Sino-Soviet disagreements and that a complete Moscow-Peking rupture might produce severe discord within his Party. During the past several years, Ho and his delegates have therefore used their influence and diplomatic skills to prevent just such an eventuality.

By steering a middle course between Moscow and Peking, at least until the middle of 1963, Ho had succeeded in assuring himself of aid from both powers and in maintaining their good will. Up to that time, in Hanoi, both Chinese and Russians were carefully given equal billing in all matters. Whenever a Chinese economic, political, military, or cultural mission appeared in Hanoi, a similar Soviet delegation was generally not far behind. Thus, President Novotny of Czechoslovakia, a leading exponent of the soft Khrushchevian peaceful coexistence line, was welcomed in Hanoi in January, 1963, and was followed in May by the Chinese Chairman Liu Shao-chi, a prominent spokesman of the hard anti-imperialist philosophy.[27] Whenever Vietnamese delegations went to Moscow, they always stopped also in Peking, and upon their return to Hanoi their praise for both sides was measured out carefully and diplomatically.

In June, 1960, when the Soviet Union clashed with the Chinese-Albanian coalition at the Bucharest Conference, the Vietnamese acted as mediators. They did so again in November at the Moscow Conference. At the Twenty-second Congress of the CPSU in October, 1961, Ho avoided any direct reference to the controversial Albanian issue.[28] He pleased Chou En-lai by disappearing from the Congress, but ingratiated himself with his Soviet hosts by remaining for some time in the Soviet Union. Significantly, at the end of the year, when a Chinese military mission came to Hanoi and offered a military pact, Ho seemed less than enthusiastic, and the matter was dropped for the time being. When China criticized Khrushchev's handling of the missile crisis, North Vietnamese commentators preferred to dwell on Castro's successful challenge to "U.S. imperialism." When the Chinese attacked India, Hanoi granted that China was "correct," but otherwise appeared more interested in discussing, as usual, the "nefarious role" that "U.S. imperialism" had supposedly played in the regrettable affair.

In its domestic program, the Hanoi regime selected among Chinese and Soviet policies those deemed most suitable for Viet-Nam.[29] In the mid-1950's, Chinese models seem to have prevailed, but after a disastrous agricultural crisis in 1956 (for which pro-Chinese Truong Chinh was blamed), and after a Chinese-inspired "Hundred Flowers" liberalization program revealed serious antigovernment sentiments among North Viet-Nam's intellectuals, the D.R.V. turned increasingly away from the Chinese example. There was no "Great Leap Forward" in North Viet-Nam, and no mention was made of Chinese-style communes.

Like any Communist Party that is working aggressively for a change in the *status quo,* Ho's Vietnamese Workers Party never accepted Yugoslav theories. Especially since 1958, Tito has been anathema and revisionism has been a bad word in Hanoi. In keeping with this ideological outlook, Albania has consistently been included in Vietnamese listings of "socialist states," and Albania has exchanged friendly greetings with North Vietnamese leaders.

Yet, as the gap between the Chinese and the Russians widened, and as they insisted that the Communist parties must stand up and be counted, Ho probably began to fear that in following the difficult middle course he might alienate both powers and be engulfed in a chasm. There are indications that during 1963 the respective merits of Chinese and Soviet policies were being heatedly discussed among the Communists in Hanoi. There is also evidence that Moscow and Peking put considerable pressure on the North Vietnamese to clarify their position. Finally, in August, 1963, it became almost impossible for Ho to walk the tightrope when the Soviet Union signed a partial nuclear-test-ban treaty with the Western nuclear powers. Ho lined up with China and refused to sign the pact.

While Ho's refusal to sign the nuclear-test-ban treaty would seem to have constituted the turning point in North Viet-Nam's policy toward Moscow and Peking, the sharp modification of Hanoi's orientation may already have occurred in May, 1963, when Liu Shao-chi visited Viet-Nam and made it clear that a reconciliation between

China and Russia was unthinkable as long as Khrushchev held to his views. Perhaps a defensive alliance between the two countries was secretly concluded upon that occasion.

During the remainder of 1963 and in early 1964, there were many new indications of a closer alignment of the Vietnamese Workers Party with Peking. On December 27, 1963, a North Vietnamese publication stated that one should not speak of any "U.S. imperialist" as "displaying good will" (as Khrushchev had done in speaking of the U.S. President); that the South Vietnamese people would never "beg the U.S. imperialists for peace at any price"; and that the South Vietnamese revolutionaries were being strongly supported by the Afro-Asian and Latin American peoples (no mention of the Soviets!). The statement concluded with these words, suggesting a growing emphasis on the insurrectionary struggle in South Viet-Nam:

> Whether a person supports the South (i.e., South Vietnamese insurgents) thoroughly or to some extent or does not support it at all is a positive yardstick to measure his attitude toward U.S. imperialism, the national liberation movement, the movement for democracy and peace, and the Marxist-Leninist doctrine. In a sense, one's attitude toward the revolution in the southern part of our country can be said to be the line between a revolutionary and a non-revolutionary.[30]

This statement was preceded by an article in the official *Nhan Dan* that managed to celebrate the Russian October Revolution without ever mentioning either the CPSU or its leader Khrushchev. Subsequent articles and policy statements stressed the important role of violence in carrying out revolution, minimized the significance of nuclear weapons and the danger of escalation to nuclear war, and emphasized that the Afro-Asian–Latin American countries constituted the main area of the struggle for Communism (contrary to Soviet contentions). Finally, First Secretary Le Duan paid homage to Mao Tse-tung in the February, 1964, issue of the Party journal *Hoc Tap* (*Study*): "It is the CCP headed by Comrade Mao Tse-tung that has carried out most satisfactorily the instructions of the great Lenin."

Had Ho Chi Minh thus aligned himself irrevocably and completely with Peking? Certainly it would seem so. Yet, in view of the considerations stated in discussing the North Vietnamese dilemma, and in the light of the many past zigzags in Ho's strategy, perhaps one ought not to draw rash conclusions. One must not forget that even early in 1964, and in contrast to the Chinese and the Koreans, the Vietnamese refrained from direct attacks against Khrushchev and his policies. Moreover, the communiqué issued by the Central Committee of the Vietnamese Workers Party regarding its session of December, 1963, continued to mention (even if parenthetically) dogmatism and sectarianism (of which the Soviets accuse the Chinese) as enemies, and emphasized that the Party made a clear distinction between the "Tito revisionist clique, lackey of imperialism," and "people within the international Communist movement who commit the error of revisionism or right-wing opportunism" (i.e., Khrushchev)—a distinction that the Chinese had long abandoned. It is also significant that, in reporting in *Hoc Tap* of February, 1964, on the Central Committee meeting of December, 1963, Le Duan defined the attitude of the Vietnamese Workers Party as one of "unmasking modern revisionism" and of "endeavoring to maintain the solidarity of the world Communist movement and the Socialist camp, especially solidarity between the u.s.s.r. and China." Also, there was talk of "right-wing elements" among the Party cadres. As of early 1964, the Soviet wing of the Vietnamese Workers Party remained intact.

It would be surprising if the North Vietnamese did not continue to seek to keep the door open to the balancing influence of the Soviet Union, since only Soviet power might be able to prevent North Viet-Nam from becoming Communist China's satellite.

In conclusion, it appears that the three Asian Communist states, all of them in territory that belongs traditionally to the Chinese sphere of influence, have reacted quite differently to the Sino-Soviet conflict.

Outer Mongolia, firmly aligned with Moscow, has benefited from the effects of the Sino-Soviet split. Its economic development has been accelerated as a result; it has been able to broaden its international contacts, and has gained greater freedom from direct Soviet controls and greater bargaining power in dealing with the Soviet Union, while continuing to enjoy Soviet protection against Chinese expansionism.

North Korea is in a position where it can play its great Communist neighbors against each other without jeopardizing its security. Temporarily at least, it has thrown in its lot with China, whose militant strategy seems to hold out better hope for the attainment of Kim Il-sung's objectives than does the Kremlin's peaceful coexistence policy. It is true that North Korea is paying a price for its alignment with Peking, for Soviet aid is being cut back, but this aid is no longer the powerful weapon that it might have been a few years ago; and Pyongyang may hope that its alliance with Peking may eventually lead Moscow to support a policy that could change the *status quo* in the divided country.

North Viet-Nam has been the most seriously affected by the Sino-Soviet split. It needs Soviet economic, political, and military support. Yet Moscow's policies seem increasingly unpalatable in Hanoi. From necessity rather than from choice, the Hanoi regime has thus lent support to Chinese policy positions. But it seems likely that Hanoi will do its utmost in working for a Sino-Soviet reconciliation or at least for the formulation of a unified Moscow-Peking strategy in Southeast Asia. North Viet-Nam can hardly fail to realize that protracted and exclusive reliance on Peking may lead to the incorporation of the D.R.V. into the Chinese orbit and eventually to satellite status.

9. Cuba

C. IAN LUMSDEN

EVEN BY THE STANDARDS of the postwar era, the Cuba of Fidel Castro is a strange phenomenon. The revolution that swept the Fidelistas into power on January 1, 1959, has had a traumatic effect on the Western Hemisphere, and its consequences have to a greater or lesser extent affected the entire world. Cuba's proximity to the United States has inflated the importance of the revolution out of all proportion. The values of Western liberal democracy have been rejected on the threshold of their greatest advocate, the United States, and replaced by the alien ideology of the Soviet Union situated 6,000 miles away.

Interest in Cuba is not derived solely from this fact. The Communist states, historically, have had Marxism-Leninism imposed upon them either by Soviet military might or by a Communist revolution that had fought for this from the outset. The Castro regime, however, is the first government to have successively withdrawn from a Western alliance, rejected neutralism, and then voluntarily sought membership in the Communist bloc. No other member of the Communist bloc has achieved this status similarly. Moreover, Cuba's independent road to Communism was eased because the initial suc-

164

cess of the Castro revolution owed nothing to the Cuban Communists or to Soviet aid. This factor alone probably insured that Cuban Communism would develop a character setting it apart from the ideological mainstream whose fountainhead lay in Moscow. Additionally, the polycentric developments in the world Communist movement since Stalin's death permitted Castro to seek membership in the Sino-Soviet bloc without having to modify greatly Cuba's own revolutionary ideology according to the rigid demands once made by Moscow.

Finally, Cuba's entry into the Communist bloc has been conditioned by the Sino-Soviet dispute, enabling Castro to attract and be courted by two suitors simultaneously. In the circumstances, both the nature of the Cuban Communist state and its relations to the outside world have developed in a manner that sets it apart from the other Communist states. Likewise, the future of Cuba remains more problematical than that of any other Communist state.

Cuba's geographic position may hold the key to a fuller understanding of the events that have taken place there during recent years. Its location, within easy reach of the United States, partly accounts for Fidel Castro's foreign policy. In fact, President Kennedy himself is reputed to have said that ". . . there is no country in the world, including all the African regions, including any and all the countries under colonial domination, where economic colonization, humiliation and exploitation were worse than in Cuba, in part owing to my country's policies during the Batista regime."[1] And almost from the outset, as the *New York Times* has noted, the Cuban revolutionaries have sincerely believed "in the danger of an armed attack some day or other from the United States."[2] The continuing fear of American intervention is conditioned by Cuba's historical experience, and until very recently by the facility with which such intervention could be repeated.

It would be both inaccurate and naive to place on the United States the entire blame for the emergence of a Soviet-oriented regime in Cuba. A spate of recent publications has given many and varied explanations for the origins and course of the Cuban revolution.[3] But, whatever stress may be placed on other causal factors—be they the semicolonial sugar economy, the betrayal of a once middle-class revolution, a conspiracy masterminded from the Kremlin, or the paranoic delusions of a Latin *caudillo*—one cannot avoid giving some consideration to the historical relationship between Cuba and the United States.

Although the Spanish-American War marked the beginning of active American intervention in Cuba, the United States had exerted considerable influence on the island throughout the nineteeth century. The U.S. decision to intervene in Cuba's revolt against Spain deprived Cuba, in effect, of the independence for which it had fought at a greater cost in lives and for a longer period than any other Latin American republic. As an object of the Monroe Doctrine, Cuba has taken second place to no other state in the Western Hemisphere. Its independence after 1902 was limited by the terms of the notorious Platt Amendment. Cuba experienced military intervention by the United States in 1906, 1912, and 1917, and American intervention was threatened again in 1933. Finally, the United States has given active support in Cuba to two of the most bloody tyrants in Latin American history, Gerardo Machado and Fulgencio Batista.

The American contribution to the development of the Cuban economy must also be recognized. It was in large part owing to American trade and investments that, before the advent of the Castro regime, the Cuban people had attained one of the highest per capita incomes in Latin America. Cuba, however, is not the first place, nor will it be the last, where the native people have resented foreign investments, even when these have been to their own advantage.

Over a long period of time, a store of resentment was built up in Cuba against the United States. It was not always manifest, and it was not always justified. The initial failure in U.S. policy lay in not taking Castro's demands seriously, and in not recognizing that the United States would have to go far more than halfway in meeting these demands if old scores were to be forgotten. Castro thereupon decided that he must choose between the revolution that he wanted and the continuation of close relations between the United States and Cuba. He chose the former. The latent resentment toward America was then converted into a wave of anti-Yankeeism, without parallel in the Hemisphere, which sustained the revolution throughout its initial phase.

Cuba's relations with the United States thus deteriorated rapidly. In mid-1960, the Anglo-American oil companies were nationalized, the U.S. sugar quota was cut off, and Cuba began to expropriate the remaining business interests. In October, the United States proclaimed an embargo on all exports to Cuba, except for some foodstuffs and medical supplies, and on January 3, 1961, diplomatic relations between the two countries were severed.

Whatever factors may have been responsible for the events leading to Cuba's final break with the United States, the consequences were clear. Castro was forced to find alternative markets for Cuban exports (principally sugar) and alternative sources of imports to sustain the Cuban economy, which had previously been geared to the needs of the United States and based on u.s. capital goods. The United States, for its part, had also given notice that it intended to overthrow the Castro regime and that, given its reluctance to intervene openly as in the past, it would attempt to do so by a process of economic attrition and isolation of Cuba from the rest of the Hemisphere. In addition, there was good reason to believe that the u.s. Central Intelligence Agency was already training and financing a counterrevolutionary force manned by Cuban exiles.[4]

There is little evidence to indicate that Cuba's rejection of the United States and its adhesion to the Soviet bloc were the direct outcome of any long-term Soviet policy in Latin America directed to that purpose. On the contrary, the facts would suggest that neither the local Communists in Cuba nor their overlords in Moscow were prepared for the success of Fidel Castro's revolution or the rapidity with which it embraced the Communist ideology. Soviet experience in Latin America had not prepared them for such a contingency.

The inability of the Soviet Union to exploit the seemingly ideal conditions for Communism in Latin America can be explained on two grounds. Historically, Russia has sought to expand into Europe, the Far East, and the Middle East. Latin America is far away from the sphere of its immediate interests, and it was only when the United States emerged as the bastion of the Western alliance after World War II that the Soviet Union turned its attention to the rest of the Western Hemisphere. Stalin, for his part, was not in the least concerned with Latin America. It would have been quite out of character for him to have actively encouraged the emergence of a Latin American Communist state, and thereby to have created a situation that he might not be able to control in its entirety.

In the years following Stalin's death in 1953, the Soviet Union began to revise its policies toward Latin America. The first few exploratory steps were taken to see if the latent anti-Americanism and revolutionary conditions in the Hemisphere could be better exploited. The most obvious example of this new policy took place in Guatemala, where the Communist involvement in local politics entered its most militantly anti-American phase in 1953. In the same year, the first major Soviet loan to a Latin country was extended to Argentina as part of a $150 million trade agreement.

Two main factors may be said to have influenced Khrushchev's Latin American policy. On one hand, the Soviet Union could be strengthened by depriving the United States of the support of its Latin allies, while on the other hand, the thermonuclear implications of a direct confrontation with the United States could not be ignored. The policy was in accord with the Soviet line adopted at the Twentieth Congress of the cpsu in 1956 and the Moscow Declaration of 1957, where neutralism and national liberation movements were first recognized as forces for peace.

Relations between the Soviet Union and Latin America reached a turning point in 1960. The rapid deterioration in Cuban-American relations and the virtual termination of u.s. trade with Cuba provided Khrushchev with an excellent opportunity to expand Soviet influence in the area. The Cuban revolution could be exploited as the vindication of his belief that underdeveloped nations would gravitate toward the Soviet bloc, since it was able to outbid the West in supplying their economic and ideological needs. The association with Fidelismo, moreover, was expected to further the Soviet cause in Latin America.

The Cuban revolution not only provided Khrushchev with an excellent opportunity; it also constituted a grave test of his policy of peaceful coexistence. The abortive Paris summit meeting in May, 1960, had exposed Khrushchev to greatly increased pressure from within the Sino-Soviet bloc. He had failed to achieve an understanding with President Eisenhower that would lessen the risk of a nuclear war and that would yet allow the Soviet Union freedom to expand its sphere of influence in the Afro-Asian regions and Latin America. Cuba would demonstrate how much support the Soviet Union was prepared to give the national liberation movements. It would also show whether or not the fear of nuclear war had so paralyzed Khrushchev, as the Chinese contended, that he now feared to support wars of national liberation.

The Soviet offer of rocket protection for Cuba on July 9, 1960, demonstrated the dilemma in which Khrushchev found himself. His desire to appear as champion of the revolutionary movements in underdeveloped countries was counterbalanced by his respect for American military power. Accordingly, his rocket threat was couched in highly ambiguous terms. He declared that ". . . figuratively speaking, in case of necessity, Soviet artillerymen can support the Cuban people with their rocket fire, if aggressive forces in the Pentagon dare to start an intervention against Cuba."[5]

The key words in Khrushchev's declaration, as the Cuban leaders understood, were "figuratively speaking, in case of necessity." Within arm's reach of a hostile United States, and faced with the possibility of a counterrevolutionary coup, Castro was in desperate need of military protection to guarantee the revolution against possible American intervention. The Cuban Premier immediately thanked Khrushchev for his offer of rocket protection, making no mention of the fact that the offer was never intended to be interpreted literally. The Cuban strategy would henceforth consist in persuading Khrushchev to remove this qualification, and to interpret the "necessity" in Cuban and not Soviet terms. Though Khrushchev repeated the offer of rocket protection on several occasions thereafter, the Cubans were conspicuously unsuccessful in getting the original element of ambiguity removed from the rocket offer. Khrushchev did not interpret the April, 1961, assault on the Bay of Pigs or the 1962 crisis as cases of necessity.

Although Castro may have counted on Russian economic and military aid from the outset, such aid was not a foregone conclusion in 1960, as the subsequent history of Soviet-Cuban relations has borne out. The credit of $100 million that the Soviet Union extended to Cuba at the conclusion of Mikoyan's visit in February, 1960, had, of course, encouraged Castro to believe that trade could be expanded with the Communist bloc. The February trade agreement, by which the Soviet Union undertook to purchase one million tons of sugar annually, might be the forerunner of further trade enabling Cuba to escape from its humiliating relationship with the United States.

Cuba had little to offer the Soviet Union in exchange for a major commitment. The new ideological orientation of the Cuban regime, and the increasing Fidelista ties to the Cuban Communist Party, the Partido Socialista Popular (Popular Socialist Party), did not obscure the fact that Castro, his brother Raúl, and Ernesto "Che" Guevara were still in sole control of the revolution. Their aggressive policy toward the United States and its President-elect ran counter to those of the Soviet Premier, who still believed that a *détente* was possible in the Cold War. Furthermore, any substantial investment in Cuba might prove worthless if, as Khrushchev may have feared, the Castro regime were to be overthrown by the counterrevolution that was then in the offing.

Though Castro could not be certain of receiving all the economic aid and military protection that he was seeking from the U.S.S.R., the embargo on U.S. exports and elimination of the sugar quota virtually made Cuba completely dependent on the Communist bloc for trade and aid. There were no viable alternatives. Even if America's NATO partners had had the technical and economic capacity to replace the United States, they obviously could not do so on military and political grounds. Castro's early hopes of sponsoring allied Fidelista regimes in the Hemisphere which would rescue Cuba from its political and economic isolation also did not materialize.

There was no *via media* for Castro to follow in 1961. Having ended Cuba's semicolonial relationship with the United States, he was now forced to bind Cuba to its only possible replacement if he was to secure the aid he needed. Throughout that year, Castro's ties with the world Communist movement were strengthened. Prior to the April invasion he described his regime as "socialist," and on December 2, 1961, declared that he was a Marxist-Leninist, and would be for the rest of his life.[6]

Castro's policy of aligning Cuba with the Soviet bloc was so successful that by March 26, 1962, he felt strong enough to execute a double coup. He first restated the Marxist-Leninist nature of the Cuban revolution, and then removed the "old" Communist Anibal Escalante from his position as organizing secretary of the official Party organization, Organizaciones Revolucionarias Integradas. Henceforth, the original leaders of the Cuban revolution would be firmly in control of the regime. Any thoughts that the "old" Communists in Cuba or in Moscow might have had about displacing Castro in Cuba would have to be set aside. "Old" Communists such as Carlos Rafael Rodriguez and Blas Roca would still retain prominent positions but would have to abide by Castro's definition of Marxism-Leninism as applied to Cuba.

Khrushchev acceded to these domestic developments in Cuba, for they were very much in the nature of a *fait accompli* as far as the Soviet Union was concerned. Furthermore, the Soviet Union agreed to continue subsidizing the Cuban economy, which by this time was in dire straits. Following the decision to install rocket bases in Cuba, it appeared that Castro had succeeded in obtaining both the military and economic guarantees from the Soviet Union that he had consistently been seeking.

Although the missile crisis developed and was finally resolved in terms of classic power politics, there is good reason to believe that the Cubans played a considerable role in influencing Khrushchev to install the rocket bases in the first place.[7] The existence of the missile bases, supported by large Soviet ground forces, would have effectively guaranteed Cuba against any attempt by the United

States to intervene in support of an uprising against the increasingly unpopular Castro regime.

There was a fair possibility of such an uprising taking place in 1962, for economic conditions in Cuba had deteriorated greatly during the year. The sugar harvest, for example, dropped from 6,875,000 tons in 1961 to 4,882,000 tons in 1962.[8] In July, Castro once more declared that Cuba would eventually have to face an American invasion. There may well have been good reason for Cuba to fear intervention on this occasion,[9] for although President Kennedy had declared that he was "not for invading Cuba at this time,"[10] the United States was nevertheless in the grip of a war fever reminiscent of that of 1898.

The revelation of the clandestine Soviet attempt to install missile bases in Cuba almost brought about the U.S. intervention that Castro so feared. However, the American ultimatum compelled the Soviet Union to withdraw the rockets, and the Soviet Premier suffered a total defeat. Castro, for his part, had been thwarted but not entirely defeated. By the terms of the agreement on dismantling the missile bases, President Kennedy had implicitly agreed not to invade Cuba. Furthermore, Castro's humiliation at not being consulted by Khrushchev during the crisis was partly repaired when he conjured up his Five Points as the basis of any permanent solution to the Caribbean crisis. These included the cessation of the economic blockade, of all subversive activities, of all "piratical attacks," and of all violations of Cuban air space and territorial waters, and the return of the Guantanamo base to Cuba. The lesson of the missile crisis was driven home to the Castro regime. Cuba could not depend on Soviet rocket protection, nor could it be certain, in the circumstances, of receiving economic aid indefinitely. Soviet aid might well be reconsidered in the event of a wider settlement of the outstanding issues involving the United States and Russia.

Nevertheless, the Soviet Union has continued to underwrite the Cuban revolution. It has continued to aid a regime that has almost brought about its destruction in a nuclear holocaust, and that continues to represent a major security risk for the Soviet Union; and it continues to support a state whose Communist credentials, as the Escalante affair indicated, may be suspect. Cuba may have once represented the vindication of Khrushchev's policies in the underdeveloped world, but it also came to represent a threat to his policy of peaceful coexistence.

It is Castro's good fortune that Cuba's irrevocable break with the United States coincided with the maturation of the Sino-Soviet dispute. This factor, as much as any other, accounts for the support given to Castro by the Soviet Union. Cuba's position within the Communist bloc has been fortified by several factors. In the first place, Fidel Castro's revolution was home grown, and owed nothing to the Soviet Union or to the local Communists for its original success. It occurred on an island that, from the viewpoint of geopolitics, was both equidistant and far from Moscow and Peking. Moreover Fidelismo as an ideology separate from Marxism-Leninism had become a magnet to the Latin American masses long before Cuba's adhesion to the Soviet bloc. Castro had addressed his message to the entire Hemisphere, for he visualized himself as a liberator in the tradition of San Martín, Bolívar, and Martí.

At the outset, the Cuban revolutionaries sought aid and trade throughout the Communist bloc irrespective of ideological considerations. It seems unlikely that they consciously set out to play off China against the Soviet Union or vice versa. Late in 1960, Guevara visited Russia and China. Russia's offer to purchase up to 2.7 million tons of sugar in 1961 was supplemented by a Chinese credit of $60 million attached to a trade agreement whereby China would purchase a million tons of sugar annually. The latter proved to be the only major aid that China has been able to offer Castro, whereas the Soviet Union has continued to finance the Cuban revolution. The Chinese credit, which coincided with the Moscow Declaration of eighty-one parties, was a substantial sum for the Chinese. It was, in any event, a considerable reward for Cuba's recognition of Communist China on September 2, 1960, and a suitable acknowledgment of the latter's first recognition by a Latin American republic.

By the end of 1960, then, Cuba had succeeded in obtaining considerable aid from both the Soviet Union and China without having associated itself with the ideological stand of either country. During the following eighteen months, Castro's military and economic links with the Soviet Union were strengthened. At the same time, however, it became apparent that Castro's foreign policy was more akin to China's than to that of the Soviet Union. The Second Declaration of Havana, issued in February, 1962, and addressed to the whole of Latin America, was a revolutionary call to arms which Cuban theorists considered the correct application of Marxism-Leninism to Latin American conditions.[11]

The "certain differences"[12] that had arisen between the Soviet

Union and Cuba over the missile crisis were immediately exploited by the Chinese. They upheld Castro's Five Points,[13] and later accused the Russians of "adventurism" and "gross capitulation" in the face of the American paper tiger. The Cubans publicized the Chinese support, but otherwise refrained from commenting on the Sino-Soviet dispute which had flared up once more over China's border clashes with India. They were aware that, in the last resort, only the Russians could provide the economic aid that Cuba so desperately needed. Nevertheless, in January, 1963, Castro injected Cuba into the dispute. In a rally celebrating the fourth anniversary of the Cuban revolution, he declared that the Cubans "see very clearly how great the need is to overcome these differences, how much need there is for unity, how much need there is for unity of all the forces of the entire socialist camp in order to face the enemy."[14] Two weeks later, in a speech to the Congress of Women of America, Castro once more called for unity in the socialist camp. Cuba, he said, faced "a difficult situation derived from two circumstances. In the first place, it is the fundamental immediate target of Yankee imperialism. In the second place, there are divisions, or differences, or whatever one wants to call them in a more or less optimistic fashion, that have arisen within the socialist camp."[15]

He also resuscitated the Second Declaration of Havana, accused "hackneyed theoreticians" of denying the existence of objective conditions for revolution in the majority of Latin American countries, and charged "some revolutionary organizations" with having ignored the Declaration.

For much of 1963, Cuba oscillated between an ideological posture that tacitly endorsed the Chinese position and a pragmatic one that recognized Cuba's dependence on the Soviet Union for economic aid. Castro's primary reliance on the Soviet Union was emphasized by his first visit to Moscow in the spring. At the conclusion of the visit, a joint statement was issued which mollified the Cubans by paying lip service to the Five Points and promised thermonuclear rocket protection to Cuba in the event of U.S. intervention.[16] In return, Castro supported the Soviet attitude to the nuclear test-ban issue, and agreed that "the principles of peaceful coexistence were the only correct and rational bases for the settlement of international problems involving states with different sociopolitical characters." He also retreated from his militant attitude toward the objective conditions for revolution throughout Latin America, agreeing that "the peaceful or non-peaceful ways to socialism in one country or another will be resolved in the final analysis by the struggling people themselves, according to the actual correlation of class forces and the degree of resistance offered by the exploiting classes."

The rapport established in Moscow was endangered by the July, 1963, test-ban treaty to which Castro objected despite favorable reference to such a possibility in the Soviet-Cuban statement. The "differences" that had arisen over the decision to withdraw the missiles were once more in evidence. The Cuban leaders have been consistently opposed to Cuba's ratification of the treaty, although Castro has indicated his support for its general aims. The reason is clear. A permanent settlement of the Caribbean crisis could be solely at Cuba's expense. Any normalization of the situation in the Caribbean, for which Khrushchev again declared himself in favor early in 1964, would have to involve concessions from both the United States and Cuba; consequently, Castro once more echoed Peking in his annual July 26 speech. "In Latin America, the pre-revolutionary conditions are incomparably superior to those that existed in Cuba," he proclaimed, adding that the duty of Latin American revolutionaries was not to wait for a miracle to produce social revolutions but to make revolutions themselves.[17]

In September, "Che" Guevara, the theoretician of the Cuban revolution, published an article which stressed that the objective conditions for revolution existed throughout the Western Hemisphere and that consequently guerrilla warfare must be the "principle means of struggle in America." The Chinese imprimatur was given to the article, originally appearing in *Cuba Socialista,* on its publication in the *Peking Review.*[18] In December, Guevara again stressed the need for violent revolution in Latin America, adding that fighting should not be limited to those countries in which it was already taking place—Nicaragua, Honduras, Guatemala, the Dominican Republic, Colombia, Venezuela, and Paraguay.[19]

In spite of the independent line that Castro has taken, no irreparable breaches have appeared in the Soviet-Cuban alliance. On the contrary, Castro's relations with Moscow appear, outwardly at least, to be closer than ever. At the conclusion of his second visit to the Soviet Union in January, 1964, a joint statement was issued in which the Cuban Premier gave his support to the measures adopted by the Central Committee of the CPSU to end the "existing divisions, and strengthen the unity and solidarity of the ranks of the international Communist movement."[20] In return, the Soviet Union signed a major long-term trade agreement to increase its purchases of sugar at a fixed price of 6 cents a pound. A peak will be reached in 1968, by which time the Soviet Union will be committed to purchasing 5 million tons annually.

It is foolhardy to forecast the course of Cuba's future relations with the other Communist countries, when even their own relations are becoming increasingly uncertain. Since 1960, when the first trade agreements were signed and diplomatic relations were established with the Soviet Union and China, Cuba has pursued policies that cannot be accounted for purely in terms of conscious ideological alignment with either Moscow or Peking. Nor can they be explained solely in terms of Cuba's dependence on Russia for economic aid, for Castro certainly appeared to follow a Latin American policy inimical to the u.s.s.r.'s own immediate interests. Khrushchev cleverly exploited the 1964 rioting in the Panama Canal Zone and the unrest elsewhere in the Hemisphere. But though he brandished his rockets as faithfully as ever, there is considerable evidence to indicate that he did not want to become embroiled again in an explosive crisis in Latin America.

The ideological stand taken by the Latin American Communist parties is indicative of Khrushchev's policy toward that area. Since late 1962, a series of statements by leading Latin American Communists has appeared in the *World Marxist Review,* denying, in effect, that guerrilla warfare must be the "principle means of struggle in America." Luiz Carlos Prestes, the General Secretary of the Brazilian Communist Party, has criticized the leading Brazilian Fidelista, Francisco Julião, for not understanding "the present situation in the country." He added in the May, 1963, issue that the Party was "fighting most vigorously . . . the manifestations of sectarianism and dogmatism" that had done incalculable harm to the revolutionary movement.[21] "Trotskyite provocations," "reckless adventurers," and "ultra-'left' adventurism" have been rejected by spokesmen for the Peruvian, Uruguayan, and Colombian parties.[22] Victorio Codovilla, once possibly the most influential "old" Communist in Latin America, has stressed that the line taken by the Argentine Communist Party "even before the Twentieth Congress of the cpsu was to create favorable conditions for taking over power by peaceful means."[23] Luis Corvalan, the General Secretary of the Chilean Communist Party, scornfully referred to "political adventurers and dogmatists" in December, 1962, and again returned to the subject in a lengthy article in December, 1963. "The Latin American democratic movement," he wrote, "is following political developments in Chile with great interest," because of the real possibility of bringing about revolutionary changes by peaceful means. He attacked the "dogmatists" and "Trotskyites" for denouncing this policy as "revisionism" and for claiming that it was "tantamount to renouncing revolution."[24]

Although these remarks should be interpreted within the general context of the Sino-Soviet dispute, they are clearly addressed to Peking's ideological counterpart in Latin America, Havana. They indicate that Khrushchev may have acquired an Achilles' heel in Cuba instead of the Trojan horse that he had once expected. Cuba, then, is not so much the pawn that it has been portrayed. Nevertheless, the Kremlin will still hold the whip hand over Castro as long as the United States, by its policy of economic blockade, forces Cuba to remain almost entirely dependent on Soviet trade and aid for its continued existence as a socialist state.

There is, therefore, reason to believe that the Kremlin would welcome more permanent settlement of the Caribbean crisis. Cuba has been a heavy investment in terms of the total Soviet economic aid program, and the outlook for Cuba's economy still appears uncertain. Whatever may be the revolutionary potential of Latin America, Moscow obviously does not relish the prospect of another Caribbean-style crisis in the area. The prime target of Castro's foreign policy throughout the early 1960's has been Venezuela. The Russians must know that the emergence of a revolutionary regime in that country could precipitate, at the worst, a thermonuclear confrontation with the United States, and, at the best, a Soviet commitment to subsidize the Venezuelan economy, which already has the highest per capita income in Latin America—an income derived very largely from its exports of oil. The Soviet Union, with its own surplus of oil, would find it extremely expensive to underwrite a Venezuelan revolution.

Since Cuba is still heavily dependent on Soviet economic aid and sugar purchases for its survival as a Communist state in the Western Hemisphere, one would expect the Kremlin to exert considerable economic pressure to get Castro to modify his Latin American policy. The Soviet Union apparently began such a policy in mid-1963. The Cubans were compelled to rationalize the Cuban economy and to admit that a fundamental error had been made in ignoring the primary role of sugar in their country's economy. Within five years of decrying "the tragic ties of our national economy to the fluctuations of the sugar industry,"[25] the Cuban revolutionaries were planning to produce sugar harvests of 10 million tons by 1970. The net effect would be to integrate the Cuban economy within that of the CEMA countries. There would be a dual aspect to the "advantages of the international division of labor,"[26] for, henceforth, the Soviet Union would have a considerable lever with which to exert pressure on Castro.

It is not certain that Castro would be amenable to a tripartite agreement as a solution to the Cuban problem. However, in spite of his claims to continental leadership in Latin America, the Cuban Premier is a realist and a very skillful leader of his country. Surely no better evidence of this is needed than the way he reacted to the missile crisis. As a leader of a small and isolated island, his claims to leadership of the hemispheric revolutionary movement are, at best, weak; deprived of Russian support, they would be insignificant. It is not inconceivable that he could be made to accept a diminished status for Cuba. But Castro has consistently claimed that the Cubans could not consider themselves at peace with an imperialist power that has attempted to strangle them at every turn, and that this situation has determined their international policy. Any genuine solution to the Cuban problem thus must first involve some form of accommodation between the United States and Cuba.

The United States has made no serious attempt to negotiate its differences with the Castro regime. Its economic blockade of Cuba has been a failure. It has succeeded neither in toppling the Castro regime nor in curbing Castro's revolutionary message to Latin America. One doubts if it has yet given up its "frivolous assumption that the mere overthrow of the Cuban regime will finish the struggle"[27] for the mind of America. The Alliance for Progress, for its part, has met with little success. The road facing it, according to President Kennedy, appeared "longer and longer."[28] The United States is handicapped by its policy of attempting to bring about revolutions without actually having them, and in the final analysis will be forced to come to terms with those that are *sui generis*.

The United States, as has been noted earlier, has historically limited Cuban independence. Indirectly, it still does so today, and it has the capacity to do so in the future. Cuba's relations with the United States will largely determine its position within the Soviet bloc in the foreseeable future. The United States has indicated that, in certain defined circumstances, it will support a genuine social revolution, and it appears likely that it will eventually recognize a socialist regime in the Western Hemisphere. In Bolivia, it has financially underwritten a social revolution that was possibly more extreme than that in Cuba and that has had considerable influence on the other Andean states, which are largely populated by Indians living outside the bounds of the national economies. A reappraisal of U.S. policy toward Latin America could make room for non-aligned socialist states in the Western Hemisphere, as elsewhere. Although Cuba may never completely revert to a status of non-alignment, the adoption of a more flexible policy would allow the United States to associate itself with the irreversible revolutionary movement that is now sweeping Latin America.

In conclusion, it should be emphasized that Fidel Castro's conversion to Communism is but one aspect of the revolution that Cuba is still undergoing. Castro is committed principally to the Cuban revolution, and his involvement in the world Communist movement is incidental to this fact. It is in this light that one should view his various statements on Communist unity. He became a Communist because it was the only way in which he could obtain the aid that he sought. But he will go only so far to obtain this aid. Cuban Communism retains a highly individualistic flavor. Castro has said that he will support Moscow in the Sino-Soviet dispute; but Cuba has not signed the test-ban treaty, it has considerably increased its trade with China, and it has strengthened its diplomatic relations with Albania.

10. Yugoslavia

MILORAD M. DRACHKOVITCH

THE HISTORY of the Yugoslav Communist Party is replete with sharp contrasts and exceptional developments. In 1919–20, the Communist Party of Yugoslavia (CPY) was considered one of the best Comintern sections—indeed, the most promising after those of Russia and Germany. By the middle of the 1930's, it had become one of the worst, and was threatened with official dissolution by the Comintern. In 1945, the Yugoslav Communists emerged as complete masters of the country which they hastened to remodel according to the Soviet blueprint. Three years later, they were expelled from the Cominform as traitors to the cause of Communism.

Of all the Communist parties in the interwar period, the CPY suffered particularly from Stalin's purges of its leaders. Nevertheless, under Tito's leadership, it systematically inculcated its members with the cult of Stalin. (This explains their tendency in the immediate postwar years to outdo Stalin in Communist militancy.) In June, 1945, the CPY was ready for a union between Yugoslavia and the U.S.S.R.[1] At the meeting that established the Cominform, in September, 1947, the CPY representatives, Kardelj and Djilas,

179

vehemently accused the French and Italian Communist parties of being incompetent and timorous, and hailed the radicalism of their own Party as a paragon of revolutionary virtue. They did not realize at the time that their very zeal had displeased Stalin to such an extent that the machinery of the Cominform was built largely in order to clip their overambitious wings. Stalin's remarkable mishandling of Tito's case and the very Stalinist efficiency of Tito's defense, however, had determined the CPY's survival. Western economic aid and promise of protection against an attack from the East did the rest.

The phenomenon of Titoism as the first successful attempt to develop a Communist system different from the Soviet prototype was not the result of Tito's rebellion but of an imposed self-defense. The Tito-Stalin conflict was ferocious, merciless, and total, and could not be halted as long as both protagonists were alive. Nearly five hundred pages of a White Book, which the Yugoslav Ministry of Foreign Affairs published in 1951, were devoted to examples of political and economic forms of aggressive pressure against Yugoslavia by the governments of the Soviet Union and East European countries. Cases of direct espionage and terrorist actions, as well as use of military power on the Yugoslav frontiers, spoke eloquently about the relations between the "fraternal" parties. Thousands of Yugoslav "Cominformists" were arrested and maltreated in Tito's jails (particularly in a concentration camp on a barren Adriatic island), and became mute witnesses of one of the strangest episodes in the entire Communist history.

Yet, behind the Western protective shield, Yugoslav Communism emerged as a challenge and competitor to the Soviet Union. Tito and his leading supporters were eager to emphasize that, contrary to Stalinist dogmatism, they were not only authentic Marxist-Leninists but in fact were the only creative innovators in the field of Communist theory and practice. The Sixth Congress of the CPY turned into a monstrous anti-Stalinist demonstration. In his report to the Congress, Tito accused Stalin of every imaginable crime, and declared that even Hitler would envy the methods Stalin used to liquidate entire ethnic groups in the Soviet Union. Another target of Tito's charges was Soviet imperialism, which had transformed formerly independent East-Central European states into mere colonies of the U.S.S.R. At the Congress, the great villain was the "imperialistic, bureaucratic, anti-socialist" Soviet Union. The Congress itself was an inverse echo of the statement made by Malenkov at the Nineteenth Congress of the CPSU, a few weeks earlier, when he declared that Yugoslavia was already converted into an American colony.

At the time of their severest clash with Stalin, and perhaps in search of hope, if not support, elsewhere, the Yugoslav Communists turned toward Mao Tse-tung's China. In a book published in 1953, a Yugoslav writer contrasted sharply the Chinese "authentic revolution" with the "antirevolutionary and imperialist practice of Stalin's Russia." Regretting, of course, the Chinese alignment with Russia in attacking Tito, he voiced the hope that the internal crisis of the Soviet system, and the germ of the democratic socialist thought which had triumphed in Yugoslavia, would favor China's future move toward an "independent and progressive force in the world."[2]

Among the slogans issued by the CPSU in May, 1953, two months after Stalin's death, there was no reference to Yugoslavia. At the same time, the first diplomatic contacts between the Soviet and Yugoslav governments were established; and in June, the Soviets proposed resumption of normal diplomatic relations between the two countries. The real and conspicuous change took place in the fall of 1954. Within a few weeks, in September-October of that year, the Soviet transmitter "Free Yugoslavia" (the mouthpiece of the emigré Yugoslav Communists) was closed down, and Radio Belgrade ceased to be jammed in the U.S.S.R. At the same time, on the occasion of the tenth anniversary of the entrance into Belgrade by the Russians and partisans, the Soviet press had some friendly words for Yugoslavia.

Following the Soviet lead, the Chinese Communists and the other "people's democracies" resumed diplomatic ties with Belgrade. Two years and three months after Stalin's death, Khrushchev made his "Canossa" trip to Yugoslavia, with a plea to forgive and forget. As a price for reconciliation, Khrushchev subscribed to the basic tenet of Titoism—the concept that "questions of internal organization, or difference in social systems and of different forms of socialist development, are solely the concern of the individual countries."[3] The next year saw a new "honeymoon" in Yugoslav-Soviet and Yugoslav-Chinese relations. In a letter to the Twentieth Congress of the CPSU, Tito praised the "tremendous triumphs" achieved in the U.S.S.R., and hailed the "Leninist consistency, firmness, and tenacity" of the Russian Communists.[4] In response, Khrushchev, in his political report to the Congress, spoke in friendly terms about Yugoslavia as a country "where state power belongs to the working people, and society is founded on public ownership of the means of production," so that the "specific concrete forms of economic management and organization of the state apparatus are arising in the process of socialist construction."[5] The Cominform, Tito's *bête noire*, was dissolved in April, 1956; and two months later, a beaming Tito triumphantly toured the Soviet Union. The words he uttered in a speech at Stalingrad, on June 11, 1956, were the climax of his new feelings and dispositions toward the Soviet Union: "In time of war as well as in time of peace, Yugoslavia marches shoulder to shoulder with the Soviet people toward the same goal—the victory of socialism."[6]

This spectacular improvement was also visible in Yugoslav-Chinese relations. An official invitation to attend the Eighth Congress of the CCP was extended to the League of Yugoslav Communists (LYC) and was enthusiastically accepted. In his political report delivered before the Congress on September 15, 1956, Liu Shao-chi commented on the improvement of relations with Yugoslavia, and emphasized the development of a "friendly intercourse with the Federal People's Republic of Yugoslavia."[7] In a long speech before the Congress, Jovan Veselinov, member of the LYC Executive Committee (Politburo) and head of the Yugoslav delegation, lavishly praised the past and present achievements of Chinese Communists, and explained the way in which socialist construction in Yugoslavia had strengthened the progressive forces in the world. Tito could not have wished for anything better. Khrushchev and Mao Tse-tung seemed to approve the "Yugoslav road to Communism," and Tito, the blackest sheep of Stalin's era, appeared to be one of the recognized leaders of the international Communist movement.

This situation, however, was soon shattered by popular explosions in Eastern Europe. Events that shook the Kremlin, and that afforded the Chinese Communists the opportunity to appear as advisers to the bewildered Soviet leaders, again put Tito in an awkward position vis-à-vis Moscow and Peking. His speech at Pula, on November 11, 1956, in which he recognized the "necessity" of Soviet intervention in Hungary but strongly attacked the still prevailing "Stalinists" in various Communist parties, evoked mixed response in the Soviet and Chinese press. Interestingly, Peking's reaction was calmer and friendlier in tone and substance than that of Moscow. The Chinese objected to Tito's insistence that, after the events in Hungary, the crucial question was whether the Yugoslav course or the Stalinist course would prevail. In the Chinese view, this could only lead to a split in the Communist movement.

Therefore, they offered "our brotherly advice to the Yugoslav comrades" to refrain from creating conditions that the enemy could exploit to cause confusion and division in Communist ranks.[8] The Soviet reaction was more caustic. *Pravda* reproached Tito for making a number of critical remarks about the CPSU, and for having "abused various leaders of the Communist and workers' parties." It contemptuously assailed the "Yugoslav road to socialism" and made disparaging remarks about the "imperialists'" aid to Yugoslavia.[9]

Nevertheless, these recriminations—which took place toward the end of 1956—again seemed to be superseded by a new wave of inter-Communist cordiality. In 1957, and more particularly after the elimination of the "anti-Party" group from power in the U.S.S.R. in June, Tito was extremely busy in three directions—Moscow, Peking, and Warsaw. His closest collaborators, Kardelj and Rankovic, as well as Defense Minister Gosnjak, visited Moscow in July. There they met with leaders of the Albanian and Bulgarian parties. Tito's meeting with Khrushchev in Romania, early in August, although veiled in complete secrecy, seemed to have re-established the good relations that had existed a year earlier. As proof of his good intentions, Tito adopted several foreign policy measures—the most important being the recognition of the Ulbricht regime in East Germany—that brought him closer than ever to Khrushchev's global diplomatic line.

Relations with the Chinese, who were just experiencing the "Hundred Flowers" tactics, unfolded under even more promising auspices. Improvement seemed to reach a climax in September, 1957, during the official visits to China of two Yugoslav delegations headed by members of the LYC Politburo, Svetozar Vukmanovic and Peter Stambolic. They were cordially received—the first by Chou En-lai, the second by Mao Tse-tung himself. In an editorial greeting to the Yugoslav visitors, *Jen Min Jih Pao* stated: "Now the peoples of our countries are advancing along the road to building socialism. We all have the same approach to many international problems. Unity on these fundamental problems furnishes a foundation for friendly cooperation between our countries . . . For cohesion we must, above all, ascertain what we have in common in the approach to the main problems, must respect each other's achievements and each country's experience in building socialism in different historical conditions."[10]

Belgrade had only superlative words for the Gomulka regime. "This is the epoch of the Polish renaissance. Gomulka . . . became its most authentic protagonist, its legend . . . ," wrote a noted Yugoslav commentator during Gomulka's official visit to Yugoslavia in mid-September.[11] It seemed, indeed, in the early fall of 1957, that Tito was finally about to accomplish and even improve that which had misfired a year earlier—a triumvirate with Khrushchev and Mao at the head of a decentralized Communist world, and the establishment of a Belgrade-Warsaw axis as a guarantee against the revival of Stalinist practices. Then, only a few weeks later, the situation changed abruptly. The Communist summit meeting in Moscow, convened to celebrate the fortieth anniversary of the Bolshevik Revolution, instead of putting a final stamp of approval to Tito's endeavors, dealt a harsh blow to his ambitions.

During the few months prior to the Moscow gathering, and with increasing sharpness ever since, the Chinese Communists had begun to change their "liberalism" in both inter-Communist and domestic areas. The Chinese attitude in the late fall of 1957 came as an unpleasant surprise to many East-Central European Communists— particularly Gomulka and Tito[12]—who in 1956–57 had looked upon China as a rising power that would exercise a moderating influence on Russia and lessen the Soviet control over the satellites. It seemed, indeed, as if Khrushchev and Mao had exchanged their previous roles. Khrushchev's successes at home, abroad, and in outer space increased his self-confidence, and he appeared certain that, by combining the psychological effects of his new strength with a more tactful approach to the problems of Eastern Europe (including Yugoslavia), he could nullify the effects of Stalinism. Thus, Khrushchev was again ready to come to terms with Tito. He invited him to attend the Moscow conference and permitted him to take part in drafting its declaration. From the same Soviet successes, however, Mao Tse-tung drew different conclusions. For him, the existence of Soviet intercontinental ballistic missiles and the orbiting of Sputnik were proof that "The East wind was prevailing over the West wind," and that the moment had come for a global offensive against capitalism. He regarded the tightening of inter-Communist screws as a precondition for a successful struggle against the enemy. On Mao's insistence, the original draft of the Moscow declaration was changed to include several positions that were unacceptable to Tito. Among these were an emphasis on the leading role of the Soviet Union and the CPSU, stress on an "even closer unity" between socialist countries "united in a single community," and, in particular, the condemnation of revisionism as the greatest danger to the Com-

munist movement. Although the document made no mention of
Yugoslavia, revisionism obviously implied "Titoism."[13]

The Moscow meeting was a prelude to the second open dispute
between Yugoslavia and the Sino-Soviet bloc. Apparently, it
restored complete unity at the top—with the u.s.s.r. and China as
primi inter pares—strengthened internal discipline, and increased
anti-Western militancy. It was only natural, therefore, that the draft
of the new LYC program, made public a few weeks prior to the
convening of its Seventh Congress in April, 1958, served as a pre-
text for all the invited Communist parties to boycott the Congress.
Even the Poles, who were inclined to attend, did not go, and, by
espousing bloc discipline, proved how ephemeral was the *rapprochement* with Tito.[14]

During the months that followed, the air was filled with shrill
denunciations of Titoist revisionism. This time, the Chinese were
particularly adamant and uncompromising. *Jen Min Jih Pao* (*People's Daily*) not only abandoned its recent friendliness toward Tito,
but announced a new anti-Titoist trend, which, to this day, has not
changed in substance. The Chinese, who were on the eve of their
economic "Great Leap Forward," easily associated with Titoism
their own domestic nonconformists, who had given them so many
unpleasant surprises during the short-lived "Hundred Flowers" period. By endorsing, as "basically correct," the Cominform's 1948
indictment of Yugoslav Communism, the Chinese were in a position
to denounce the "anti-Marxist-Leninist out-and-out revisionist program" of the League of Yugoslav Communists and to condemn "the
program put forward by the Yugoslav revisionists [that] fits in
exactly with what the imperialists, and particularly the American
imperialists, need."[15]

The Soviet reaction to the Yugoslav program was more varied.
Three days before the beginning of the Seventh Congress of the
LYC, *Kommunist* moderately criticized the Yugoslav draft program
and concluded that "comradely Party criticism must not be an obstacle to further development of friendly relations between our
parties and countries."[16] Less than three weeks later, *Pravda* considerably sharpened this "friendly criticism," and affirmed that the
LYC had "departed from the principles of Marxism-Leninism on a
number of major issues."[17] Then, at the end of May—as if to show
that the Russians still considered questions of theory and practice
as a unit—the promised Soviet credits to Yugoslavia (amounting to
$285 million) were postponed for five years. Finally, on June 3,
speaking in Sofia at the Seventh Congress of the Bulgarian Commu-

nist Party, Khrushchev formulated his own approach to Tito. Like
the Chinese, Khrushchev assailed the Yugoslavs as "revisionists, the
lackeys of the imperialist camp." He asserted that "present-day revisionism is in its way a Trojan horse" striving to "corrupt the
revolutionary parties from within and to disrupt the unity of
Marxist-Leninist theory." He also stated that the Cominform had
been "fundamentally correct" in 1948 but that it had committed
later "mistakes and rigidities" in handling Tito's case. Khrushchev
indicated that he would not repeat the earlier mistakes. He acknowledged that the Yugoslav Communists "have considerable revolutionary experience and have achieved great merits in the struggle
against our common class enemies." For that reason, and despite
the Yugoslav ideological errors, he argued that the CPSU would
strive to reach mutual understanding and cooperation with the
League of Yugoslav Communists. And even if cooperation on the
Party level could not succeed, "we shall support and develop normal
relations with Yugoslavia on the state plane."[18] Khrushchev was
obviously unwilling to use Stalinist methods in his second dispute
with Yugoslavia. His greater flexibility did not appear, at first, to be
at variance with the Chinese position.

Subjected to this heavy barrage of Chinese-Soviet fire, Tito was
again forced to defend his isolated course. In a speech at Labin on
June 15, he declared that the "Chinese leadership stands firmly on
Stalinist positions," which he identified with those of the "most reactionary warmongering elements in the West." Replying to the Chinese in their own polemical style, Tito adopted a different, less
violent tone when answering the "unprincipled campaign of Khrushchev, and other Communists against socialist Yugoslavia." He insisted that the LYC did not want a new conflict, that he did not in
any way attack the Soviet Union, and that Yugoslavia did not make
"any concession to the United States, political or otherwise." Stating
regretfully that the "old methods of 1948 are again appearing on the
scene of the anti-Yugoslav campaign," Tito argued as he did six
years earlier when defending his Party from Cominform accusations. "It appears to us," he exclaimed, "that history bestowed on
us this hard road to preserve the development of socialism from
degeneration and to enable socialism to emerge from the chaos
which today prevails in the world with such moral strength that it
will hew a victorious road in its further development . . ."[19]

Despite the heated exchanges that took place in the spring of
1958, the estrangement of the LYC from other Communist parties
never assumed the character of the 1948–53 Tito-Cominform feud.

For the following two years, the Chinese were too preoccupied with domestic problems to be concerned specifically with Tito, whom they had so unequivocally condemned. Relations between Khrushchev and Tito unfolded according to the pattern outlined in Khrushchev's Sofia speech. The "Yugoslav revisionists" continued to be verbally abused in the Soviet and satellite press—most characteristically in Khrushchev's report to the Twenty-first Congress of the CPSU—while interstate relations, especially the cultural and economic exchanges between Yugoslavia and the Soviet bloc, continued normally.[20] Moreover, the Soviet Union was satisfied with Yugoslavia's foreign policy. Thus the resolution of the Twenty-first Congress, while reiterating the Moscow declaration's condemnation of Yugoslavia's "revisionist program," stated that the "Soviet Union will continue to work for cooperation with Yugoslavia in all questions of the struggle against imperialism for peace in which our positions will coincide."

Tito was not happy with this treatment,[21] but he realized that Khrushchev did not intend to subvert and unseat him as Stalin had tried to do. If Tito had to pay for his security by aligning Yugoslav diplomacy more closely with that of the Kremlin, the price must not have seemed exorbitant. Thus, the second Soviet-Yugoslav dispute evolved differently from the first, and began to change its original character with the gathering of a greater storm within the Sino-Soviet bloc.

The Moscow meeting of November, 1957, represented a genuine effort by both sides, Russians and Chinese, to establish complete unity within the Communist bloc. A few months later, however, that unity was impaired by unprecedented Chinese domestic policies. The establishment of the first "people's commune" in China, in April, 1958 (at the same time that Yugoslavia's "revisionist" program was adopted) was in fact "the most serious political challenge [for the Soviet Union] since Tito dared to defy Stalin and claim for Yugoslavia its own separate road ten years earlier. And the challenge of 1958 was far more serious than that of 1948, if only because China was infinitely more important than Yugoslavia."[22] Peking's insistence that the communes were emerging as "the best organizational form for the gradual transition from socialism to Communism," and that the "people's commune will become the basic unit of future Communist society," displeased the Kremlin. During a long conversation with U.S. Senator Hubert Humphrey on December 1, 1958, Khrushchev denounced the Chinese communes as "old-fashioned and reactionary."[23] At the Twenty-first Congress of the CPSU, however, he attacked the "Yugoslav revisionists" for "compiling all sorts of inventions about differences of opinion that allegedly exist between our Party and the Communist Party of China."[24]

Although the issue of the communes was temporarily settled by a Chinese retreat, other problems in Sino-Soviet relations soon developed. In April, 1960, a violent attack on the "Tito clique" appeared in an article in *Red Flag*, the CCP's theoretical journal.[25] This article ("Long Live Leninism!"), one of a series written to commemorate the ninetieth anniversary of Lenin's birth, both in form and substance was the bluntest expression of Chinese radicalism. It contended that atomic war would destroy only capitalism, and that "on the debris of a dead imperialism, the victorious people would create very swiftly a civilization thousands of times higher than the capitalist system and a truly beautiful future for themselves." It stated further that the capitalist-imperialist system would not crumble of itself but must be "overthrown by the proletarian revolution within the imperialist country concerned, and the national revolution in the colonies and semicolonies." It defined "peaceful coexistence" as inferior and subject to the imperative of "people's revolution." Although the article attacked only Tito by name, and hailed the "leadership of the Central Committee of the Communist Party of the Soviet Union and the Soviet government headed by Comrade Khrushchev," it referred (in the plural) to "modern revisionists," hammered systematically at Yugoslavia when reviewing the basic problems of Marxism-Leninism and international relations. (Three years later, *Jen Min Jih Pao*[26] informed its readers that in the "Long Live Leninism!" article, the Yugoslav revisionists had been used as the sole target in order to preserve Communist unity, while the real purpose of the article was to warn and criticize "other comrades"—obviously Khrushchev and his Western European followers—whose "erroneous views . . . contravened the Moscow Declaration.")[27]

Reaction to the Chinese attack came in a series of doctrinal and polemical articles written by Edvard Kardelj, the chief ideologist of Titoism. His first article appeared on August 12, 1960, in *Borba*, the LYC's official organ, and the entire series was later published in book form. Kardelj's articles—written in an orthodox Marxist style (full of quotations from the holy trinity of Yugoslav Communism, Marx, Lenin, and Tito)—aimed to prove Chinese betrayal and deviation from genuine Communism. They represented a systematic investigation of Chinese "pseudorevolutionary ultraradicalism," which Kardelj equated with the "worst kind of opportunism." These articles not only attacked China but also praised the Russians, to the embarrassment of the Soviet Union. They expressed Kardelj's confidence that the u.s.s.r., "the greatest socialist force," would prevent the implementation of the "adventurist" Chinese line.

Kardelj knew that Moscow shared many of his views but that, at that stage of Sino-Soviet relations, Khrushchev could not allow Kardelj to serve as his mouthpiece. Thus, in the November, 1960, issue of the *World Marxist Review,* a Soviet polemicist, A. Rumyantsev, attacked Kardelj's "vulgar, mechanistic, quantitative, evolutionistic methodology," but did not deal with the crux of Kardelj's writings—namely, his denunciation of the Chinese ideas. Soon after the publication of Kardelj's articles, while in New York attending the U.N. General Assembly, Tito and Khrushchev displayed a conspicuous mutual cordiality and seemed eager to herald full agreement on international problems.[28]

In the fall of 1960, after several weeks of secret deliberations, the Moscow conference of representatives of eighty-one Communist parties issued a long statement. Although it represented a victory for the Soviet theses, the Chinese had their way on the issue of Titoism. The 1960 statement was a reinforcement of the 1957 Moscow declaration, but this time the Communist parties "unanimously condemned the Yugoslav variety of international opportunism." The "Yugoslav revisionists" were called traitors of Marxism-Leninism and were indicted for their "subversive work against the socialist camp and the world Communist movement." In consequence, and most significantly, the statement required that "further exposure of the leaders of Yugoslav revisionists and active struggle to safeguard the Communist movement and the working-class movement from the anti-Leninist ideas of the Yugoslav revisionists, remain an essential task of the Marxist-Leninist parties."

The harshness of the Moscow statement did not seem to worry the LYC leadership. On February 10, 1961, an enlarged session of its Executive Committee quickly rejected the charges as totally unfounded. On the same occasion, in a report entitled "A Step Backward," Veljko Vlahovic, a prominent member of the Executive Committee, singled out the Chinese and Albanian Communists for a full-fledged counterattack. He contended that the Moscow conference "was called in connection with completely different problems which have no direct connection with socialist Yugoslavia," and predicted that "life will continue along its own path and not along the path which has been paved with verbal compromises, formulated in the Statement."[29] Vlahovic was right. The "unanimity" of the 1960 manifesto was extremely short-lived. The Russians' endorsement of the antirevisionism statement became a source of trouble in their later verbal battles with the Chinese.

During the first half of 1961, with the single exception of the Yugoslav outcasts, an outward appearance of restored Communist unity was preserved. But the draft of the CPSU's new program, published on July 30, presented everything Russian in glowing colors and reduced the role of Chinese Communism to eleven words: "The victory of the revolution in China was of special importance." This was a complete retreat from the 1960 Moscow statement, which had mentioned the Chinese Communists in the most complimentary terms (emphasizing that their revolution "exerted tremendous influence on the peoples, especially those of Asia, Africa, and Latin America"). Moreover, as the CPSU program reduced the merits of the Chinese, so it softened the harshness of the 1960 Moscow statement about Yugoslav Communism. This time it was stated that the "Yugoslav leaders by their revisionist policy contraposed Yugoslavia to the socialist camp and the international Communist movement, thus threatening the loss of the revolutionary gains of the Yugoslav people." Although at the Twenty-second Congress of the CPSU, Khrushchev strongly criticized the "revisionist ideas that pervade both the theory and practice of the leadership of the League of Yugoslav Communists," his attack on the Albanian Communists was incomparably rougher. In his concluding speech, he not only exposed every kind of Albanian ideological and political deviation, but also accused the Albanians of being "utterly brutal," worse even than the Czarist police![30] At this Congress—and at the congresses that took place during the next two years—the Russians made vituperative statements against the Albanian "dogmatists" and against others in the Communist world who were said to share the views of the Albanians. At the same time, the Chinese inveighed against the Yugoslav "revisionists" and against other Communists whom they accused of sharing the views of the Yugoslavs.

The period immediately after the Twenty-second Congress of the CPSU resembled the short period following the Moscow meeting, when the Sino-Soviet feud had apparently subsided. The Cuban crisis in the fall of 1962, the Chinese attack on India, and the series of congresses of the Communist parties in Eastern Europe and Italy, from November, 1962, to January, 1963, all contributed to a new, higher-pitched exchange of inter-Communist recriminations, in which both Albania and Yugoslavia served as covers for the Communist giants' settlement of accounts. From the middle of 1963, and progressively thereafter, the Yugoslav and Albanian pretexts were abandoned. A direct, open, and violent confrontation of the two centers of world Communism was now visible to everyone. At the same time, relations between Yugoslavia and the Soviet Union underwent a metamorphosis.

A few months after the Moscow statement of 1960 was issued, relations between the Soviet Union and Yugoslavia began to improve in all areas. At first, diplomatic contacts increased. In the middle of July, 1961, Koca Popovic, Yugoslav Foreign Minister, had talks in Moscow. A communiqué following these talks emphasized that the views of the two governments on the "most important international questions were similar or even identical." At the Belgrade Conference of nonaligned nations in September, Tito's "almost blanket endorsement of Soviet positions" contributed heavily to the general pro-Soviet bias of the entire conference.[31]

This trend was accelerated and extended in 1962. In April, Soviet Foreign Minister Andrei Gromyko paid an official visit to Yugoslavia. A few weeks later, on May 16, in a speech in Varna, Bulgaria, Khrushchev had only friendly words for Yugoslavia. "As a country that builds Communism," he declared, "we will do everything to have good collaboration with Yugoslavia, and thus help her peoples entrench themselves in positions of socialism." The ten-day visit to Yugoslavia at the end of September by President Brezhnev of the U.S.S.R. paved the way for Tito's visit to the Soviet Union in December. As in 1956, Tito was greeted as a friend, and was granted the privilege of addressing a session of the Supreme Soviet. In a speech before that body, on December 12, with Tito in attendance, Khrushchev gave Tito a clean bill of political health and concluded a formal Marxist-Leninist analysis by describing Yugoslavia as an authentic socialist country.[32] He said that all troubles and difficulties that existed between the CPSU and the LYC were not yet eliminated, particularly because of a "number of ideological questions reflected in the program" of the LYC, but he did not refer to these questions as "revisionist." On the contrary, he complimented the Yugoslav leaders for having "eliminated many things that we considered erroneous and harmful to the cause of building socialism in Yugoslavia," and for having taken concrete steps "toward *rapprochement* and unity with the whole international Communist movement."

Khrushchev's display of good will toward Yugoslavia was surpassed during his visit to Tito, in August, 1963. On his arrival at Belgrade, Khrushchev declared that the Soviet Union regarded Yugoslavia as a "socialist and fraternal" country. A day later, during his visit to a factory, he praised the Yugoslav system of "workers' councils," which for many years had been denounced throughout the Communist bloc as symbols of Titoist "revisionism." He hinted that this system could perhaps be adopted in the Soviet Union. "Our country is now ripe," he said, "for a democratization of the management of enterprises. We are looking for forms that would not violate the Leninist principle of unity of leadership, and this is why we are interested in the Yugoslav experience. In this connection we are planning to send a delegation of Party workers, trade union leaders, and members of regional economic councils to study conditions here." Naturally, Khrushchev's friendliness toward Yugoslavia infuriated the Chinese Communists. Shortly after Khrushchev's visit to Yugoslavia, they launched their most violent personal attack on him.

The Soviet-Yugoslav *rapprochement* had many other facets. It extended to practically all fields of interstate and inter-Party relations—economic, cultural, and, to a limited extent, military. Contacts between the Party schools were reopened in January, 1963, for the first time since the break in 1948. Other Communist parties and governments, with the obvious exception of China and Albania, and with greater or lesser degree of genuine satisfaction, followed the Soviet example. Thus, in the winter of 1962–63, official LYC delegations attended various congresses of the Communist parties, and were defended against the constant attacks of the Chinese representative who, with impeccable logic and total futility, pointed to the mandatory anti-Titoist clauses in the texts of Moscow declarations of 1957 and 1960.

Admission of the LYC into the family of the "fraternal" parties led by the CPSU does not mean that the Yugoslav Communists have simply re-entered the Soviet bloc from which they had been expelled. Since their first meeting in 1955, and despite their subsequent exchanges of invective and mutually hostile gestures, both Khrushchev and Tito seem determined not to overstrain their relations and not to permit the emergence of anything like the former Stalinist pattern of conflict. Khrushchev apparently never lost confidence in his ability to make a satisfactory deal with Tito. His increasingly bitter feud with the Chinese forced Khrushchev to avoid a fight on two inter-Communist fronts and to try to reach a truce with the revisionists, since the dogmatists were now regarded as the principal enemy. For Tito, with his memory of Stalin's enmity, Khrushchev was the chief artisan of de-Stalinization, and therefore was a sort of potential "Titoist" himself. We have seen the enthusiasm with which Tito greeted the Twentieth Congress of the CPSU. Even later, at the Seventh Congress of the LYC, in April, 1958, when a new conflict with the Soviet bloc seemed near, Tito remained confident that Khrushchev's Russia would never adopt an aggressive scheme against Yugoslavia. Still later, in 1959, when the early Sino-Soviet disagreements indicated that the monolithic anti-Titoist front was a delusion, Tito and his associates did their best to achieve a *modus vivendi* with Moscow. As the stages of the 1961–63 *rapprochement* amply proved, their persistence and their confidence in Khrushchev finally were repaid.

A recent example demonstrates to what extent Tito pleaded for increased intimacy with the Soviet Union. In his report of May 18, 1963, before the plenary session of the LYC, he developed his theme that since the Twentieth Congress of the CPSU, and owing primarily to Khrushchev, the Soviet Union was rapidly going through a process of progressive social evolution. He attacked those Yugoslav Communists who, because of unpleasant experiences in the past, still distrusted the Soviet Union. On this issue, said Tito, divergent views could not exist in the LYC ranks.[33]

The present *rapprochement* with the Kremlin, which is characterized by the absence of any organic ties or hierarchical subordination, suits the LYC leaders perfectly. It corresponds to their ideological tenets of decentralization and bilateralism in inter-Communist relations, and it guarantees their power base at home. Their preoccupation with maintaining an unchallenged domestic rule and of playing a prominent role in world affairs is manifested in the following three instances: First, the LYC leaders want to be recognized as equal partners by other Communist parties. In this respect, they may point with particular satisfaction to their remarkably close relations with the Italian Communist Party, which is also a specific target of Chinese antirevisionist vigilance. On January 21, 1964, in Belgrade, after a week of high level deliberations, representatives of the two parties, headed by Tito and Palmiro Togliatti, issued a communiqué that reads like an authentic Titoist document. It suggested that the strongest Communist Party in the Western world found in Titoist theory and practice a potent stimulus for its own revised doctrinal and strategic concepts. Thus, the two old Comintern professionals, Togliatti and Tito, carried the flag of modernizing Communism.

Second, the LYC leaders are striving to achieve a *rapprochement* with Moscow, at the same time that they maintain close relations with the Western world. The West, and particularly the United States, represents both an invaluable source of supplies and benefits and, in case of emergency, a protective shield. The paradox that the economic and military aid of the capitalist West has been instrumental first in their remaining in power after 1948, and then in facilitating their economic experiments, has not troubled the conscience of Yugoslav Communists, although it has complicated their relations with Moscow. But they have convinced the Kremlin that increased economic relations with the West, if established without political conditions and concessions, can help overcome domestic shortcomings.

If contacts with the West represent a two-way street—economic advantages versus dangers of ideological contamination—the Yugoslav Communists have discovered a third and ideal field for their proselytizing—the world of the new, emerging, and nonaligned nations. Even as self-appointed mentors of that shapeless third world bloc, they can reap the advantages of securing more friends, while promoting a basic ideological postulate of their program— that "inexorably and in a variety of ways, humanity is moving deep into the era of socialism."

The Khrushchev-Tito *rapprochement* and, in its wake, the LYC's relations with other pro-Soviet Communist parties, the Western world, and the nonaligned states, induced the Chinese Communists to attack Khrushchev violently for his alleged "collusion with the Tito clique in opposition to the fraternal parties which uphold Marxism-Leninism." These words are taken from "Is Yugoslavia a Socialist Country?" a long article published jointly on September 26, 1963, by *Jen Min Jih Pao* and the *Red Flag*. The question was answered unequivocally. In its combination of arguments and invective, the indictment of Tito's regime was strongly reminiscent of the Cominform charges in 1948 and 1949, when the Yugoslav Communist Party and Government were accused both of betraying Marxism-Leninism and of serving American imperialism. The Chinese contended that capitalism was progressively restored in Yugoslavia; that private capital and private enterprise prevail there on a large scale; that the countryside is swamped by capitalism; and that, since economic planning by the state was abandoned, the socialist economy has degenerated into capitalism. As a corollary to such assertions, the Chinese affirmed that Yugoslavia has become a "counterrevolutionary special detachment of u.s. imperialism." Nikita Khrushchev, however, was the real target of this effort to diagnose the lethal disease of Yugoslav revisionism. The Chinese accused him of "following in Tito's footsteps," and listed his twelve irredeemable sins. Lumping together the Soviet and Yugoslav leaders, the Chinese—like the Cominform when accusing Tito in the late 1940's—appealed to Russian Communists to get rid of their supreme leader, who had become a renegade. "Khrushchev has abandoned Marxism-Leninism, scrapped the 1960 statement, and wallowed in the mire with the renegade Tito clique, in complete violation of the interests of the Soviet Union, the Soviet people, and the people of the whole world. This will not be tolerated by the great Soviet people, the overwhelming majority of the cpsu members, and cadres at various levels, all of whom have a glorious revolutionary tradition." This indictment, like those hurled at Tito during the 1948–53 period, indicated at least that as long as Khrushchev and Mao led their respective parties, a reconciliation between them was as unlikely as was the reconciliation between Stalin and Tito.

Now that the two Communist superpowers confront each other directly and openly, Yugoslavia exists only as an epiphenomenon of a much more important world contest. Here, indeed, is one of Titoism's multiple paradoxes. It was born as the result of one of Stalin's major miscalculations, and continued to oppose the Soviet "great-power chauvinism" down to Stalin's death in 1953. Later, and to this very day, it has patiently and successfully tried to achieve an accommodation with Stalin's successors. Many of its earlier anti-Soviet barbs have now been adopted by the Chinese Communists. Instead of becoming "Titoists," however, the Chinese have made anti-Titoism an essential war cry in their contest with the Russians for the leadership of the world Communist movement. Thus, the widening of the Sino-Soviet breach has had as its corollary the betterment of Soviet-Yugoslav relations.

The formulas of Marxism-Leninism have constituted a particularly unreliable guide through the jungle of Communist policies. Tito, Khrushchev, and Mao swore in the name of Marx and Lenin, but drew arguments for mutual vilification from the founding fathers' writings. Consequently, one must look behind the ideology for the forces that are shaping Communist global history. In this era of Sino-Soviet tensions, general inter-Communist diversification, and new signs of popular unrest in East-Central Europe, it is difficult to penetrate the future. Instead, one should examine some of the basic problems of Titoism in the remaining years of the 1960's.

Several problems remain unsolved in the Soviet-Yugoslav relations, and they could flare up at any time. Yugoslavia's formal ties with the Warsaw Treaty Organization and the CEMA are still undefined, and the LYC program has yet to receive an official stamp of approval in Moscow. Although the "Titoist" Khrushchev and the "Khrushchevite" Tito found a basis of understanding, Khrushchev's successors may find Yugoslavia expendable in an attempt at reconciliation with Peking and Tito's heir may be tempted to alter the Titoist course.

Yugoslavia's ties with other "people's democracies" are also unpredictable. "Titoism," as such, has lost much of its prestige now that the Soviet Union allows its satellites a greater degree of internal freedom. Vestiges of the Stalinist past, the new CEMA integrative schemes, and Yugoslavia's own domestic complications have contributed to the lessening attractions of Titoism in Eastern Europe. Tito's alignment with the Russians in foreign policy and the intensification of relations with the Communist countries and parties (except with Albania) have placed Yugoslavia in a different position than it was when it resisted Stalin or argued with Khrushchev. The East European regimes may try to maneuver in their relations vis-à-vis Moscow and may even be lured into a position closer to Peking. This, in turn, may complicate their relations with Belgrade.

In its dealings with the West, Yugoslavia also faces a series of problems. The United States Congress has persistently shown, and will certainly maintain, a high degree of reluctance to extend economic benefits to a country that favors the basic tenets of Soviet foreign policy and actively supports anti-Western movements throughout the world. But administrations in Washington have constantly maintained a policy of helping Tito, on the assumption that a "national" Communist regime, with an economic system different from the Soviet prototype, and an unorthodox ideological program, represents an element of diversification and mellowing within the Communist world that merits Western encouragement and support.[34]

On the European side of the Atlantic, the increasing strength of the Common Market poses important problems for Yugoslavia. As the Common Market moves toward unified prices and rising trade barriers, Yugoslav exports will be weakened. An imbalance in foreign trade is already a sore point of the Yugoslav economy. Yugoslavia's political relations with Western Europe will certainly not remain the same. Relations with Italy are excellent, but those with Western Germany are increasingly unfriendly (more so than the existing break in diplomatic relations suggests). General de Gaulle's inclusion of Yugoslavia, in his 1964 New Year's message, among the "Communist totalitarian regimes that still constrain the captive peoples" has been adversely received in Belgrade, where the January, 1963, treaty between France and the Federal Republic of Germany also has had a bad press. Depending upon their success or failure, the policies of "Popular Front," militantly pursued today by the Italian and French Communist parties, with the LYC's fervent support, will affect Western European relations with Yugoslavia, as will the progress of the economic and political integration of Western Europe.

Yugoslavia's closeness with the third world of developing nations may also, in the near future, grow more complicated. The recent anti-Titoist articles in the Indonesian press indicate that Communist China's growing influence among the nonaligned states of Asia and Africa may negatively affect the friendly relations between Belgrade and these countries. Here again, the bipolarity of the Moscow-Peking conflict contributes to the diminishing of Yugoslav influence.

Finally, much of Yugoslavia's prestige in the world will depend on the solution of its basic domestic problems. Yugoslavia's economic system, which more than anything else has contributed to the reputation of Titoist inventiveness, still is in the process of experimentation and adjustment. Speaking before the plenary session of the LYC's Central Committee, on March 16, 1964, Tito urged, as so often in the past, a "re-examination of the country's entire economic development, beginning with that which is most essential—accumulation, investments, interior organization of enterprises and used and unused reserves."[35] The magnitude of this task should be viewed against the background "of ideological dilution, disunity, and disintegration of our socialist community,"[36] and the mounting, dangerous, internal conflicts of nationalities. In the years to come, Yugoslav Communism will have to solve what will probably be its most delicate and difficult problem—that of Tito's succession. Tito's leadership has been such an unlimited asset for the LYC's rule over Yugoslavia that his successor (or successors) will face a monumental task in replacing his authority both on the domestic and on the international scene.[37]

Multiple ambitions, multiple achievements, and multiple frustrations have characterized the unusual destiny of Yugoslav Communism. There is no reason to assume that its dynamism and contradictions will subside. The remaining years of the 1960's promise to be as full of surprises as were the years whose political highlights are described on the preceding pages—perhaps even more so, because one cannot predict how Sino-Soviet relations will develop or what will happen to Communism in Yugoslavia after Tito dies.

11. Economic Relations Among the Communist States

PHILIP E. UREN

ECONOMIC RELATIONS among the Communist states in the early 1960's have presented a strange paradox of hope and frustration. *The Basic Principles of the International Socialist Division of Labor,* which were approved in Moscow in June, 1962, represented a new blueprint for Communist economic cooperation. The main import of this document was practical; and it was clearly intended to lay the groundwork for rapid progress toward economic unity. The first paragraph stated the Communist vision in familiar terms: "The world socialist system is a social, economic, and political commonwealth of free, sovereign peoples following the path of socialism and Communism, united by a community of interests and goals and by indestructible ties of international socialist solidarity."[1]

At the same time, however, Sino-Soviet economic relations had been deteriorating rapidly. In mid-1960, Soviet technicians were withdrawn from China, and the Chinese thereafter developed a divergent view of the international division of labor. In early 1964, they wrote:

> In the name of the "international division of labor," the leaders of the Communist Party of the Soviet Union oppose the adoption by fraternal countries of the policy of building socialism by their own efforts and attempt to turn them into economic appendages. They have tried to force those fraternal countries who are comparatively backward economically to abandon industrialization and become their sources of raw materials and markets for surplus products . . . and they have pursued a restrictive and discriminatory trade policy against China.[2]

It is, in a sense, unfair to juxtapose these quotations and to compare aspiration with achievement in such a stark way. In this paradox, however, lies the core of the Communist problem for this and succeeding decades. The gap between the reach of Communist theory and the grasp of Communist statesmen is a large one; and nowhere is this more true than in the realm of economic relations.

Communist governments hold sway over an area of great geographical diversity. Beginning at the 17th Parallel in Viet-Nam, traveling north through China, over the frontiers of Inner Asia, north into Siberia, westward over the Ukraine, and through the countries of the so-called shatterbelt* of Eastern Europe, we pass over regions of enormous physical and cultural diversity. Having done so, we must then cross the Atlantic to subtropical Cuba in order to encompass the whole Communist world. Any "grand design" for this great series of states will be some time in the making, even if it is conceived and guided by the most pragmatic and skillful statesmen.

The economic links from which this design must be fashioned are complex and intertwined. There is not a single Soviet view, far less a single Communist one, but many different views of this complexity. The practical traders, the members of the Communist trading corporations, chafe under the precepts of both theoreticians and politicians. Academic economists, impressed by the technical difficulties of socialist trade, wrestle with exchange coefficients and foreign trade profitability formulas. Ideologists elaborate the notion of a world commonwealth of Communist states, and the politicians

---

* The states that emerged in place of the Austro-Hungarian Empire and the western provinces of Imperial Russia.

look to the survival and growth of the power mechanisms that they manipulate. All these views combine to give form, substance, and direction to Communist foreign economic policies.

The Communists' task is further complicated by the dynamism of their world. The international economic system that pertained under Stalin has been analyzed and the goals for the future have been set. The present pattern, however, is kaleidoscopic, and the ground shifting, as all parts of this great geographic area and all the inhabitants act out their roles in response to local conditions and particular interests.

The international economic problems of the Communist world seem to fall into two broad categories. The first includes those in which the political overtones are dominant and where the difficulties derive from the differing character and objectives of various states. The second category concerns the creation of the necessary mechanisms, such as banks and pricing systems, to service economic cooperation on a broad scale. The interstate problems are doubtless of prime importance, for, given the political will, satisfactory technical modes of operation could eventually be devised. Nevertheless, the technical peculiarities of Communist economic thought and practice present formidable obstacles to progress in the direction of economic integration.

In economic affairs, as in politics, the most critical interstate problem in the Communist world is the Sino-Soviet dispute. In recent years, the serious deterioration in economic relations between the two countries has been reflected in decreasing levels of trade and in the withdrawal of Soviet technical assistance from China. More important, perhaps, than these economic reflections of political differences has been the Chinese criticism of Soviet foreign economic policy and the efforts of the Chinese Government to enlist support for its concept of the "world socialist economy."

In retrospect, 1959 can be seen as a turning point in Sino-Soviet economic relations. In that year, China's trade with its great Communist neighbor exceeded $2.0 billion, and China replaced East Germany as the principal trading partner of the Soviet Union. The U.S.S.R. shipped over $600 million worth of machinery and equipment to China, and large numbers of Soviet technicians were working on more than 200 Chinese projects.

In 1960, Chinese trade with the Soviet Union dropped sharply to $1.7 billion. In the following year, the downward trend continued even more precipitously, and total trade for 1961 reached only

$900 million, the lowest figure since 1952. Soviet shipments of heavy machinery and equipment for complete plants virtually ceased, while Chinese exports of foodstuffs and cotton were severely curtailed. In 1962, Sino-Soviet trade amounted to only $750 million, or about 64 per cent below the 1959 level, and it probably dropped a further 20 per cent in 1963. At the same time, China maintained a large export surplus with the Soviet Union—$283 million in 1962. This reflected the determination of the Chinese Government to pay off its debts to the Soviet Union, a goal which it expected to achieve in 1965.[3]

Chinese economic development during the period 1950–60 was largely dependent on equipment received from the Soviet Union— equipment valued at about $3.3 billion and to be used in the construction of 291 projects. Much of it, however, was paid for out of current Chinese export earnings, and the magnitude of the credit facilities provided by the Soviet Union was surprisingly low, particularly when compared with Soviet aid to other Communist countries and to less developed countries of the non-Communist world. Up to 1955, the Soviet Union provided about $1.3 billion in financial credits, but only a part of this was designated for economic purposes. No other details of economic development assistance are available, but in 1961 the Soviet Government agreed to fund accumulated Chinese trade indebtedness in the amount of $320 million over five years and to provide $40 million worth of sugar on deferred payment terms.[4] Soviet credits to China since 1954 have totaled about $2.0 billion, but probably only a small proportion has gone for economic development projects.[5] This stands in contrast to total Soviet credits of over $3.5 billion to non-Communist less developed countries.[6] For all practical purposes, the Chinese Government has been "going it alone" since the withdrawal of Soviet technicians from China in 1960, but in 1964 Soviet sources asserted that aid was being provided to eighty Chinese industrial enterprises.[7]

Recently, China has been turning increasingly to non-Communist sources of supply. Chinese purchases of wheat from the West have amounted to about 5 million tons per year. The Chinese have also shown an increasing interest in renewed trade with Japan, which they had unceremoniously cut off in 1958, and in the eventual purchase of more capital goods from West European nations. At the present time, the Chinese appear to be conducting more than half of their trade with non-Communist countries.

The pattern of Chinese trade during the remainder of the decade will depend on several factors. First, and by far the most important, will be the extent to which the Chinese are able to reduce their dependence on imports of food and so to release foreign exchange for other purposes. Second, much will depend on the Chinese Government's assessment of the political implications of particular import patterns; here the central question will be whether to trade with the Soviet Union and to what extent. Third, China's decisions will have to be taken within the limits of Chinese foreign exchange earning ability.

All of these things are not precisely predictable. However, it seems reasonable to suppose that China's current emphasis on agricultural improvement will be at least partially successful and that China will be able to reduce imports of food to some extent. It also seems likely that, in the context of the bitter political dispute between the two countries, the Chinese will not wish to return to their former degree of dependence on the Soviet Union for industrial goods. Nevertheless, the extent to which Chinese industry is already equipped with Soviet machines suggests a continuing minimal need for Soviet spare parts. Up to now, Chinese imports of Soviet petroleum products have been important, and China's future may depend a good deal on her success in developing a domestic oil industry or in obtaining petroleum products elsewhere. At any rate, there are some economic advantages for China in continuing the present low level of trade with the u.s.s.r.

The precise level of this trade will depend partly on the ability of the Chinese to direct their large export surplus to other world markets. This option will open to them in 1965, when they have finished paying off their Soviet debt. However, many of the textiles and consumer goods that are now sent to the Soviet Union may not be easily marketed in Western Europe or Japan. Mineral products, however, offer better possibilities, and in the long term the Chinese will have the option of changing their production pattern to make available more goods and commodities that sell readily in the West.

In summary, each of the problems that limits China's freedom of action in its economic relations with the Soviet Union seems amenable to at least partial solution. The most likely pattern for future Sino-Soviet trade, therefore, seems to lie somewhere between the present low level and the cessation of trade that might follow an open and complete political break. A return to the 1959 pattern, however, is most unlikely in this decade.

As Sino-Soviet trade has dwindled and Soviet economic aid to China has been withdrawn, the two states have increasingly engaged in economic competition in the less developed countries—particularly those of the Communist world. Recently, the struggle to acquire influence by economic means has extended into non-Communist areas. Since the Soviet Union has much greater resources with which to engage in such competition, the Chinese have sought to redress the balance by offering advantageous terms and forms of aid, and by exploiting political factors wherever possible. China's emphasis on the virtues of "relying on one's own efforts" has apparently appealed to some Communist countries—for example, North Korea—and the Chinese emphasis on Afro-Asian solidarity may have some effect in non-Communist less developed countries.

A startling development in this connection was the alacrity with which the Chinese, who were faced by serious domestic economic problems, came to the aid of the embattled Albanians in 1961. The Albanian economy had been heavily dependent on Soviet aid and trade as well as on economic links with the other East European nations. This dependence has now been largely transferred to China, which has provided large economic development credits, shipments of food grains, and technical assistance.[8] The primacy of political considerations in Chinese foreign economic policy was demonstrated by the Chinese willingness to divert machinery from their own declining industry, to share their food imports from the West (which had been bought with hard-earned convertible currency), and to send skilled personnel. The acquisition of a European ally, detached from Khrushchev's cherished CEMA, was clearly worth a high price.

On the other side, in June, 1962, Khrushchev was able to bring in the Orient to redress his losses in the West when Mongolia was admitted as a full member of CEMA. Mongolia had been in the fortunate position of receiving economic assistance from both the Soviet Union and China, as well as from the East European states, particularly East Germany and Czechoslovakia. The incorporation of this Asian country into the European Communist economic system was a telling victory, but perhaps the most galling part of it for the Chinese was the designation of Mongolia as a country worthy of receiving aid for economic development and deserving of the cooperation of the developed Communist states.[9] With the virtual cessation of Soviet aid to China and the detachment of Mongolia, China's economic isolation was almost complete. Only the vociferous North Korean endorsement of the Chinese economic line, the rather costly task of supporting Albania, and the reported reduction of the Soviet presence in North Viet-Nam provided continuing comfort to the Chinese.[10]

Thus, Sino-Soviet economic relations clearly do not suggest that the two countries are "united by a community of interests and goals and by indestructible ties of international socialist solidarity." Their trade has dwindled to its lowest point since the beginning of the Chinese Communist regime; Soviet economic aid to China, which was never large, has virtually ceased, and technical assistance has been withdrawn; the two countries are engaged in economic competition in a number of Communist and non-Communist countries; and finally, China challenges the basic principles of Soviet foreign economic policy, characterizing it in terms that until recently have been reserved for the "imperialist exploiters."

The seriousness with which the Soviet Government views the Chinese challenge to its foreign economic policy was demonstrated in Suslov's report to the Soviet Central Committee in February, 1964. Suslov devoted a large part of his statement to refuting Chinese criticism of Soviet actions in this field. He ridiculed China's professed concern about Soviet economic transactions with the West, pointing sarcastically to the number of Western delegations in Peking. He dealt at length with Chinese efforts "to denigrate the economic aid rendered by the u.s.s.r. and other socialist states to the underdeveloped countries." And finally, he attacked the Chinese attitude toward economic relations with other Communist countries. The decline in Sino-Soviet trade, he said, was the result of Chinese and not Soviet initiative, and the withdrawal of Soviet technicians was the natural and inevitable result of Chinese unreasonableness.[11]

The achievement of economic cooperation between a powerful, economically developed country and smaller, less developed states is the second major problem facing the Communist states. In a recent discussion of economic specialization, the Chairman of the Sejm Commission for Foreign Trade in Poland referred to the "differences in approach to the problem between less developed countries, which want to develop production and export of machines, and well developed countries, which also want to preserve and expand the export of machines."[12] Professor Vajda, the Hungarian economist, writes that "differences between the development levels of the different countries create objective stresses" that are "not necessarily clashes of interest, but that may develop into these."[13]

The most dramatic example of this problem has been provided by the opposition of the Romanian Government to Soviet notions of supranational planning and to the idea that Romania should curtail its industrialization plans. The forthrightness of the Romanian stand and its apparent success in modifying Soviet policy have led to a great interest in this particular case. However, the Romanians are not unique in their fear that specialization may injure their national interest. Even the Czechs, with their relatively highly developed industry, have found it necessary to publish articles explaining to the people the need for specialization and allaying their fears of adverse consequences.[14] Nor is the Romanian concern confined to a particular Romanian plan or industry. While the Romanian Government is anxious to complete the Galati steel complex, its quarrel with CEMA, and with the Soviet Union in particular, has been much more broadly based.

The political considerations affecting Romanian policy have been complicated by difficult economic problems deriving from the absence of effective investment criteria. As Vajda has said, "planned integration demands . . . numerically definable advantages for all participants."[15] *The Basic Principles of the International Socialist Division of Labor* provide little help in this regard, and the problem is complicated by the absence of useful data on costs and pricing. As long as integration was to be confined to the bilateral coordination of national plans, the Romanian Government could have some confidence in its ability to defend what it deemed to be vital Romanian economic interests. The trouble came when Khrushchev proposed the erection of a supranational planning authority on the shaky framework of the "basic principles."

It has been said with some reason that Romania's interest in broad industrial development, including considerable emphasis on heavy industry, probably reflected the Stalinist heritage of Gheorghiu-Dej.[16] In addition (as indicated in Chapter 6), Romanian nationalism was an important political force from which the Romanian Government could seek to derive strength. Given the economic objectives that Stalinism and nationalism suggest, the vagueness of CEMA decision-making criteria made the surrender of sovereignty especially dangerous for the Romanians. There were, in short, both strong political forces and cogent economic reasons for the Romanians to resist Khrushchev's proposals.[17]

In addition to these reasons for action, there was the opportunity provided by the Sino-Soviet dispute. The political aspects of the dispute have been amply dealt with elsewhere, and they were, of course, important in creating a favorable atmosphere for Romanian policy. The specifically economic element in the Chinese line, however, was particularly helpful to the Romanian cause. The Chinese had developed a policy of "relying on one's own efforts" and had proclaimed this as the only way to strengthen the might of the whole "socialist camp."[18] As indicated above, they pictured the Soviet Union as seeking to turn other Communist nations into economic appendages. They wrote that, "it would be great power chauvinism . . . in the name of the 'international division of labor' and 'specialization' to impose one's will on others, to infringe or harm the interests of their people."[19] Their line was echoed in North Korean editorials extolling the virtues of economic independence as the foundation of political independence.[20] Thus the Romanians, operating in the lee of a bitter Chinese attack on Soviet economic policies and to the windward of a general apprehension among the smaller Communist countries about the consequences of supranational planning, could pursue their course with some confidence.

In the September, 1962, issue of *Problems of Peace and Socialism* and at the November, 1962, Plenum of the Soviet Central Committee, Khrushchev had proposed the creation of a "unified planning organ, empowered to compile common plans and to decide organizational matters." He also proposed centralized joint investments, certain obligatory criteria for national investment planning, and the joint construction of some enterprises that would be internationally owned. These radical proposals were probably prompted in part by his concern about what he called the "objective trend toward the internationalization of production" in the West and in part by the realization that rapid economic growth in the Communist world was becoming increasingly dependent on large-scale, well-coordinated investment. Trade within the European Common Market had been increasing at the rate of 24 per cent per year in the period 1958–61, while the comparable rate in CEMA had been 14 per cent.[21]

Romanian concern about the possible consequences of specialization, which had been mounting up to this point, developed into alarm, and at the February, 1963, meeting of the CEMA Executive Committee the matter was apparently brought to a head. Immediately thereafter, in early March, the Central Committee of the Romanian Communist Party devoted a plenum exclusively to a discussion of the results of the CEMA meeting and ostentatiously endorsed the performance of the Romanian delegate to CEMA.

Furthermore, the Central Committee asserted that the principal means for achieving a division of labor should be the coordination of national economic plans "in the spirit of the principles proclaimed by the 1960 Moscow Declaration of respect for national sovereignty and independence."[22]

Some efforts were made thereafter to convince Romania of the error of its ways, but they apparently met with no success. The communiqué on the conference of first secretaries and heads of government of the CEMA countries held in July, 1963, seemed to record the *coup de grâce* to the concept of supranational planning. It stated that "bilateral consultations carried out among CEMA countries . . . create the best possible basis for a multilateral coordination of plans within the framework of CEMA."[23] This statement, of course, marks a long retreat from Khrushchev's September, 1962, concept of "a unified planning organ."[24]

So it seems that the Romanians won their point, but their victory is a precarious one. Perhaps more than any other Communist country, Romania has a vested interest in preventing the excommunication of China, which would leave it, in J. F. Brown's apt phrase, "alone in the room" with the Soviet Union. Romanian economists point out that "the U.S.S.R. is the country that has had and now has the largest share (41 per cent) in our foreign trade" and that Soviet trade with Romania increased by 42 per cent between 1958 and 1962. The role of nonsocialist countries in Romanian trade increased from 22 per cent in 1958 to 33 per cent in 1962, but the Soviet Union still remains the dominant partner.[25] Given the geographical facts, the leverage that Moscow can exert in Romanian economic affairs remains substantial; it could be decisive if political inhibitions were removed. These facts, in large part, may explain the March, 1964, visit of the Romanian delegation to Peking in what was widely interpreted as an effort to persuade the Chinese not to carry their differences with Moscow to the point of a complete break.[26]

It remains to be seen whether, by a policy of defiance, the Romanians will achieve more than Bulgaria, for example, which has recently been rewarded for its subservience by a $333 million loan for economic development. There is reason to believe that it is not the industrialization of Romania that so irks the Russians, but the emphasis on "national" development. A notable article by a Romanian economist states that "the Party has concentrated the main efforts of the people on the creation of the technical and material base of socialism, by the steady accomplishment of the Leninist policy of industrialization, by developing, in the first place, the heavy industry with its pivot—the machine-building industry." Later, the same writer castigates the "apologists of contemporary capitalism" who "claim that the industrialization of our country has negative repercussions on the development of international exchanges." This, he writes, is "the apology of the colonialist system, of perpetuation of backwardness of poorly developed countries from an economic point of view."[27] This invocation of Lenin and the simultaneous association of the critics of Romanian industrial plans with "colonialism" must cut close to the Soviet quick.

In any event, the problem of the underdeveloped countries within CEMA is likely to be a persistent one. The economic difficulties are substantial, but it is the ebullient nationalism of such societies, with a new sense of power and purpose, that will be most troublesome. The emphasis on "our Fatherland" becoming "a developed industrial country" in the world economy, where it will make "an important contribution" to the socialist world system, must worry Moscow, where the hope is for each country to become an integral part of a "single entity."

The Communists' third politico-economic problem results from the impact of economic developments in the West, particularly the European Common Market, on the Communist world. In an article in *Foreign Affairs,* Zbigniew Brzezinski has noted the ambivalence of the Soviet attitude toward the Common Market and has traced the oscillations in the Soviet reaction since 1957.[28] Although Soviet propaganda paid some attention to the prospects for West European economic integration at an early stage, realization that the Common Market might have a fundamental impact on Communist affairs has been fairly recent. It was not until early 1962 that this concern became fully apparent, and a turning point seems to have been marked by Khrushchev's speech of May 30, in which he attacked the Common Market as an aggressive instrument of NATO designed to intensify the Cold War and to perpetuate the subjugation of colonial peoples.[29]

The reaction of the Communist alliance as a whole was complex. In the Soviet Union in 1962, the response was a combination of a somewhat crude propaganda attack, an appeal for broader international economic groupings, in which the Communist nations would be accepted as equal members, and an effort to revitalize CEMA. Elsewhere in Eastern Europe, concern about the economic impact of the Common Market was much more in evidence, and much of the writing in East European journals represented a sober attempt to assess the technical adjustments that might be necessary in East European trade. The fear that Common Market regulations might endanger commercial ties with the West was most apparent. While the Soviet Union's main concern was political, the other Communist countries of Europe stood to lose more in economic terms.

The smaller Communist nations are still concerned with the development of diversified markets and sources of supply and with the avoidance of too great a dependence on the Soviet Union. Their exports to the West are concentrated to a large extent in agricultural products and foods, which may be more seriously affected by Common Market regulations than the industrial raw materials and fuels that are prominent in Soviet exports. They are much more dependent on trade than is the Soviet Union, where trade as a whole probably contributes only about 5 per cent of the national income. Of their total trade, the portion conducted with the West is also more critical, both in percentage terms and in relation to their national objectives and policies. This has been the case, for example, with Romania, which has been rapidly expanding its trade with Western Europe, and with Poland, which conducts about 35 per cent of its trade with non-Communist countries. These Western connections complicate the task of economic integration for the Soviet Government at a time when the development of common commercial policies in the West makes Communist economic integration most essential.

For the Soviet Union, the Common Market is primarily important as a manifestation of growing Western power. The relatively high rates of economic growth in Western Europe, the rapid expansion of intra-Western European trade, and the broadening economic ties between Western Europe and other parts of the non-Communist world provide some basis for this concern. But the prospect of individual Communist states having to negotiate economic questions with a united Western Europe, perhaps in the next decade, may have been the most worrying facet of the situation for Khrushchev. This would explain, on the one hand, his effort to envelop the Common Market and other purely Western economic groupings in a broader international economic organization, where the Communists might have a political influence quite out of proportion to their role in world trade, and, on the other hand, his attempt to revitalize CEMA by strengthening its executive authority.

Khrushchev's concern about the best form of international economic organization was expressed in his speech of May 30, 1962, and in an article that he wrote later in the year. In the latter he said,

> . . . we take stock of the objective trends toward the internationaliza-
> tion of production operating in the capitalist world and we build our
> policy and economic measures accordingly. In this connection, there
> arises the question of whether economic cooperation and peaceful
> economic competition are possible not only between individual states
> with differing social systems, but also between their economic as-
> sociations.[30]

He called for an international conference on trade, and his appeal was echoed by the members of CEMA in their June, 1962, com-muniqué, which suggested that a new international trade organi-zation should embrace all regions and countries "without any discrimination."[31] At the same time, the CEMA authorities established a new Executive Committee which was to meet more frequently in an effort to give better effect to decisions on integration. A new at-tack was to be made on the old problems of multilateral trade and pricing and, as indicated above, the *Basic Principles* were to serve as a new blueprint for economic integration. These moves were fol-lowed later in the year by Khrushchev's far-reaching proposals for supranational planning.

The new life that this flurry of activity injected into CEMA petered out as the new Executive Committee, meeting every two months, ran into a maze of technical difficulties and was obstructed by the nationalist preoccupations of its members. By July, 1963, when another conference of first secretaries was held in Moscow, it had become clear that the high hopes embodied in the *Basic Prin-ciples* had been disappointed. While the conference was "unanimous in the view that . . . a step forward" had been taken, the specific achievements to which it was able to point made it clear that the step had been both short and halting.

The Kremlin's dilemma derives from the fact that trade with the West is both desirable and dangerous for the Communist alliance. It is torn between the need to develop effective links with the Common Market and the wish to insulate CEMA from its attraction. As Brzezinski suggests, "ideologically, the concept of European unity, with the Common Market as the initial symbol, is proving it-self more captivating as an image of the future than a Europe split into conflicting groups as the Marxist-Leninists hoped."[32] With about 30 per cent of its trade directed toward the West, and with this trade heavily dependent on exports of raw materials and agricultural products, the Communist alliance is not in a strong bargaining position.

The Common Market, however, has had some effect in broadening economic ties of the Soviet Union and other CEMA countries with third nations. This has been particularly true of Yugoslavia, which sent its first observer to a CEMA meeting in December, 1963 —a move that had been preceded by an exchange of visits between Tito and Khrushchev. These visits had resulted partly from Yugoslav apprehension about the possible effects of Common Market regulations on its trade with the West. In economic terms, the *rapprochement* has been limited, however, by Yugoslavia's anxiety not to jeopardize its commercial interests in the West.

It would be foolhardy to attempt a forecast of how the Communist world will adjust itself in detail to the impact of the trend toward economic integration in the West. There are both hopeful and discouraging signs. On the one hand, in the words of Pryor, Communist economists are now "less bound by the fetters of ideology than the older generation."[33] On the other, Communist political leaders continue to emphasize the importance of economic and ideological struggle. Many views and interests must be accommodated in the final outcome; but, if the possibility of a broader economic association between the two Europes is looked upon as an opportunity rather than as a threat, the specter of Stalin's parallel markets may yet be laid.

Underlying these broad political problems is the second main category of difficulties that the Communists face in seeking the economic integration of their alliance. These technical difficulties derive from Communist economic concepts that constantly hamper the creation of flexible mechanisms for economic cooperation. There is, first of all, no Communist theory of trade. The classic works of Marxism-Leninism, especially *Das Kapital,* give only a few hints on trading theory and practice because the adjustment of economic affairs through bargaining was always regarded as much inferior to the imposition of a plan. Secondly, intra-Communist trade is a recent phenomenon, since before World War II there was only one Communist country. It is not surprising, therefore, that the Communists should now be having technical difficulties in ordering their commercial affairs. As late as 1955, the official Soviet economic textbook passed off foreign trade as merely an additional source of aid for the development of production.[34] Only in the past few years have the advantages of an international division of labor been widely discussed in Communist journals.[35]

In short, the Communists are beginners, and their trading system has so far been based on bilaterally balanced clearing accounts. Monetary devices have been used less as instruments for encouraging and facilitating trade than for controlling planned exchanges. It now seems that the inefficiency of this system is clearly recognized, and the CEMA meetings of June, 1962, in Moscow emphasized the need "to introduce gradually the practice of multilateral trade and payments agreements." Perhaps an important factor in the long delay has been the fear that the measures necessary to improve trading flexibility might involve a loss of political control. Commercial bargaining, particularly if it is increasingly decentralized, might make political direction from Moscow even more difficult than it is today. Khrushchev's November, 1962, proposals for supranational planning emphasized the Soviet concern with political control, but the economic and political factors operating in the direction of greater flexibility are strong and are perhaps beginning to have some effect. While the bilateral clearing agreement remains the principal instrument of intra-Communist trade, there is a move in the direction of multilateralism, and the U.S.S.R.'s bid for supranational planning seems to have failed, at least temporarily.

The prospects for the long term, which should become much clearer in the remainder of the decade, will depend a good deal on the work of the newly created CEMA Commission on Foreign Exchange and on the International Bank of Economic Cooperation, which began its operations on January 1, 1964. Their formidable tasks center on the need to relate domestic prices, costs, and international exchange rates in a meaningful way.

A revealing reflection of the earlier Communist attitude to foreign trade is the fact that the Communist countries have no system of foreign trade pricing and must depend on prices in the capitalist world as a guide to bargaining within their own system. The economic literature of the Communist countries is full of discussion of this problem. The Hungarian economist Imre Vajda, who has recently been bitterly critical of the CEMA, regards this problem as one of the most important. Lecturing in late 1963, he said, "I hold the much too slow and far from general effectuation of the consideration of value to be outstanding among the obstacles in the path of progress."[36] Speaking later of the concentration of Hungarian industry in recent years, he said, "International competition must be given unlimited opportunities in this area. But this competition also can only lead to results and lead to progress if it is backed by the whip of the consideration of value."[37] *The Basic Principles of the International Division of Labor* concluded by stating:

> It is necessary to improve constantly the system of price formation on the world socialist market in accordance with the requirements of the planned extension of the international socialist division of labor, the constantly increasing exchange of goods, and the accelerated development of the world socialist economy, while simultaneously creating conditions for gradual transition to an independent price basis.[38]

Yet, in spite of this awareness of the problem and the determination to solve it, price-setting in foreign trade in the Communist world remains to a large extent as Frederic Pryor has characterized it— "a boiling stew of propaganda, ideology, economic forces and self-delusion."[39]

When the principal guide to economic decision-making rests on such a shaky foundation, it is difficult to calculate the profitability of a particular transaction or series of transactions. For this reason, much of the work of Communist economists has recently been focused on the operational problems of foreign trade. As Pryor points out, they are hampered in this endeavor by the lack of any theory adequate to guide them in deciding how "twelve independent decision-making units (i.e. the nations of the Bloc) could coordinate their trade and production decisions through any type of spontaneous process."[40]

The main task of the new International Bank is to operate a multilateral clearing system for the CEMA countries. It is a strange body by Western standards, and in its charter the concern of the smaller countries with their national sovereignty is evident. All countries have equal voting rights, and all decisions of the Bank's Council must be unanimous. Eventually, the Bank is to have a capital of 300 million "transferable" rubles, but only 20 per cent is to be contributed in the first year and, in any case, this represents members' commitments to export rather than convertible currency or gold. It is apparently hoped that, through meetings of CEMA members and the Bank, it will be possible to arrange some multilateral barter, but the volume is likely to be small. The Bank is a clumsy beginning toward flexibility, but it is a beginning, and the experience gained with it may lead to an appreciation of the advantages of even more flexible arrangements.

Despite the mainfest political difficulties that confront CEMA, the growing criticism of its progress by Communist students, and the technical problems that are so apparent to Western observers, there are substantial entries to be made on the credit side. Industrial specialization has made only limited gains amid a welter of bureaucratic resolutions, but some major joint construction projects progressed well. Most notable among these are the Unified Electrical Power System, the Friendship Oil Pipeline, and joint projects for the exploitation of raw materials.

The electric power systems of Czechoslovakia, East Germany, Hungary, and Poland were linked together in 1960. Since then, the western Ukraine has been united with the system, and connections are being made with Romania and Bulgaria to complete the grid. This is undoubtedly an important achievement which makes possible a much more efficient use of power resources. In addition, it can play a part in welding the countries of Eastern Europe more closely together. Although the Central Dispatch Administration has been established in Prague, physical control of the system rests in large measure with the Soviet Union, because the main transmission lines feeding it originate in or pass through Soviet territory.

The Friendship Pipeline is designed to transport oil from the Soviet Union into Hungary, East Germany, Poland, and Czechoslovakia. By 1965, the pipeline was expected to carry 15 million tons of oil to these recipients. The first deliveries were accomplished in 1962, when 3 million tons flowed to Czechoslovakia and Hungary. Each of the participating countries contributes materials and pays for that part of the line passing through its territory, which then becomes its property. Since the line through Poland will carry oil to both Poland and East Germany, the East Germans have granted Poland a ten-year credit to cover the cost of construction. This cooperative achievement is also important and will make a valuable contribution to the fuel supply of the participating countries.

Recently, there has been increasing evidence of multilateral cooperation in the development of the raw materials base of the CEMA countries. For example, the Soviet Union, Czechoslovakia, East Germany, Poland, Bulgaria, and Hungary are cooperating in the construction of a mine and concentration plant in the Soviet Union for the production of phosphate-bearing raw materials. In return for machinery and equipment supplied on credit, the participating countries will receive shipments of phosphates. Another relatively new development is the provision of credits to the Soviet Union by the smaller countries of Eastern Europe for the development of Soviet raw materials. For example, on February 8, 1963, an agreement was signed between the Soviet Union and Poland concerning the extraction and production of potassium fertilizers in the Soviet Union for Polish agriculture. Under the agreement, Poland agreed to extend a credit of about $78 million to cover the supply over five years of Polish machinery and equipment. This credit is to be repaid over ten years by Soviet deliveries of potassium salts to Poland, beginning with 600,000 tons in 1970 and increasing to 1 million tons in 1975. Similar agreements have been made by other CEMA countries with the Soviet Union as well as with one another.

The main criterion of progress, however, is the size and character of intrabloc trade as a whole. Leaving aside the special problem of China, the development of trade among the East European countries is regarded by Communist observers as less than satisfactory in a number of respects. First, the rate of growth of trade has been substantially below that achieved in the European Common Market, and the share of the Communists in world trade has stagnated since 1959.[41] Although intra-Communist trade has approximately doubled since 1955, and now amounts to about $11 billion per year, the comparative lag must be disturbing to statesmen with a vision of a new world system. Secondly, a relatively large proportion, about 30 per cent, of the trade of the Communist countries is conducted with non-Communist states. This attachment to the more dynamic Western trading community, coupled with the recently increased Communist demand for Western food and machinery, also does not augur well for a more tightly integrated Communist trading system. Thirdly, the demand for raw materials, fuels, and agricultural products in the Communist world has exceeded expectations, as well as the ability and willingness of Communist countries to deliver. Particularly anomalous is the large role of the Soviet Union as a supplier of raw materials to Eastern Europe in return for machinery and manufactured goods. Fourthly, intrabloc trade in machinery, which reflects the degree of specialization, has fallen below projected levels, while imports of machinery from the West have been increasing. At the end of 1963, specialization ostensibly involved 1,200 items, but much of this was merely a confirmation of the existing pattern and did not greatly affect trade.

The reasons for this poor performance lie in what Professor Vajda has called "hidden elements of obstruction that must be brought to light in time to make their elimination possible."[42] These elements of obstruction have been characterized above as a complex combination of political and technical factors. The future development of the "world socialist system" will depend upon the degree of success that the Communists achieve in removing these obstacles to progress, and the future of international relations will be affected in no small measure by the methods they employ. Broadly speaking, they must steer a hazardous course between increasing flexibility in economic matters, which might endanger their alliance, and greater rigidity through central planning, which might retard their economic growth.

A number of factors suggest a possible trend in the direction of greater flexibility. First, central planning seems to imply a greater measure of Soviet influence over individual states than is at present possible. Even when it has cut the Gordian knot of the Sino-Soviet dispute, the Soviet Government may find it difficult or inadvisable to re-establish its authority over the smaller Communist states. Secondly, the economic growth of the Communist world must be maintained if its influence in the world at large is to be expanded. Whatever the Stalinist record, rigid economic controls, which would necessarily be accompanied by greater political direction, offer little promise in the present situation. Thirdly, having opened the Pandora's box of foreign trade theory and practice and set off a great deal of study and investigation, the Communist authorities may find it difficult to return to rigid dogma. Having recognized the value, for example, of the international division of labor and the need for more rational pricing, they may not be able to "unrecognize" these things or avoid the logical conclusions. Already there are indications that the Poles would like to overhaul the International Bank and to have its capital deposited in gold or hard currencies, making it, in effect, more like a Western bank.[43] All these things make a retreat difficult but not necessarily impossible.

Several factors could work in the other direction. A deterioration in East-West relations coupled with a decrease in trade could render the smaller Communist nations increasingly dependent on the Soviet Union and thereby oblige them to accept Soviet supranational planning concepts. Secondly, the excommunication of China could lead the Soviet Government to attempt the reassertion of its authority over its "satellites," in spite of the deleterious effects that this might have on economic progress. Finally, the attachment of the Communists, whether theoreticians or statesmen, to Marxist concepts will make it difficult for them to accept the frustrations that will necessarily be encountered on the long, hard road toward a more flexible and rational economic system. They will tend to attribute future difficulties to increasing flexibility and will be repeatedly tempted to return to a greater assertion of central bureaucratic authority. On balance, however, there is a fair chance that the forces now at large will push the Communists toward flexible and pragmatic solutions. But this trend will be resisted by many in the supposed interest of political power. Perhaps all that can be safely said, to paraphrase Galsworthy, is that the *status quo* is the thing most likely to change and the millennium the thing least likely to arrive.

12. The Communist States and the West

ADAM BROMKE[*]

THE CONTEMPORARY WORLD is very complex: it is both compact and divided. On the one side, the dazzling progress in science and technology, overcoming barriers of distance and revolutionizing methods of warfare, is reflected in the close interaction of all events in the international sphere. The emergence in the postwar years of the two main groupings of states—centered around Moscow and Washington respectively—makes the existence of a single world-wide balance of power a tangible reality. On the other side, however, nationalism has remained the strongest single ideological force claiming the loyalties of men. Within each alliance, individual nations continue to pursue their different, and occasionally conflicting, objectives. In doing so, they constantly threaten to subvert the global equilibrium.

* The author is indebted to the Canada Council for a grant in aid of research that enabled him to visit several Communist states in Eastern Europe in the spring of 1964.

219

The existence side by side of the trends toward consolidation and fragmentation makes the mechanism of present world politics a complex one. The close interdependence of all events in the international sphere weighs heavily in favor of the preservation of the *status quo*. When, however, owing to the pressure of conflicting national objectives, a major change occurs in one or the other alliance, its consequences are bound to be far reaching. At first, the change is registered by a shift in the world-wide balance of power. Then, precisely because of the changed nature of the global equilibrium, new national forces are released. These, in turn, bring about still further shifts in the power structure. In short, in the contemporary world, one major change produces a reaction all along the line, tending to breed many other changes.

There is little doubt that the Sino-Soviet schism amounts to a drastic transformation in the Communist alliance. In the words of George Kennan, it represents "a fundamental change in the nature of world communism as a political force on the world scene."[1] As such, the Sino-Soviet split is of profound concern to the West. It affects not only the world-wide balance of power but the Western alliance itself. Indeed, in the end, it might well lead to a major realignment of political forces in the international sphere.

The Sino-Soviet alliance is very much dead. Each side charges the other with malignant and persistent violations of the Treaty of Friendship, Alliance, and Mutual Assistance of 1950, in effect declaring it null and void. Both sides in their open polemics come forward with persuasive and abundant evidence pointing to a disintegration of the alignment between them dating back to the late 1950's. The break is now total—as demonstrated by lack of cooperation between the two countries in political, military, economic, and even cultural spheres.

In the political sphere, since the late 1950's, the U.S.S.R. and the People's Republic of China (P.R.C.) have taken widely divergent paths at several crucial junctions. The Russians refused to back up with their military might various Chinese ventures in Asia. In 1959, they declined active support to the Chinese in their conflict with the United States over Taiwan and the offshore islands. In the same year, and again in 1962, when the Chinese and the Indians became engaged in fierce combat, Moscow refrained from endorsing Peking's stand in its border dispute with New Delhi. The Chinese, in turn, failed to uphold different Soviet schemes in world politics. They objected to Khrushchev's trip to the United States for talks with Eisenhower in 1959, and to his participation in the abortive summit meeting in Paris in 1960. During the Caribbean crisis in 1962, Peking openly came out against the withdrawal of Soviet rockets from Cuba, denouncing this move by Moscow as a surrender to Washington—a "second Munich." In the following year, the Chinese bitterly opposed the conclusion of the nuclear test-ban treaty in Moscow and abstained from signing it. With the deterioration of political relations between the two states, military cooperation between them has also abated. In 1959, the Russians denied nuclear weapons to the Chinese, and soon thereafter they withheld all military assistance to China.

Economic relations between the Soviet Union and China were abruptly broken in 1960. Virtually all Russia's aid to China came to an end: Soviet advisers were withdrawn and agreements were torn up. Trade between the two countries was sharply curtailed: In 1959–62, it declined by two-thirds. In 1962, when plans for expanding economic cooperation among the Communist states were drawn up—Outer Mongolia having been admitted to the Council of Mutual Economic Assistance—China did not take part. Finally, cultural cooperation between the U.S.S.R. and the P.R.C. was also considerably curtailed. The propaganda of Soviet-Chinese friendship was discontinued and periodicals devoted to that end were suspended in both countries. The exchange of students, scientists, and even artists greatly diminished in scope. All in all, after the decline in political cooperation, all other ties between the Soviet Union and China were systematically cut.

In place of the alliance, the Sino-Soviet conflict emerged. Neither side tries to conceal this any longer. Each accuses the other of colluding with its enemies. The Chinese denounce the Soviets for "ganging up with the United States imperialists and the Indian reactionaries."[2] The Russians charge the Chinese with "looking for partners among the monopolist groups in Japan, West Germany, and France" as well as leaguing together with "Pakistan, a member of both SEATO and CENTO."[3] In the course of their diatribes, both sides have provided plentiful, revealing information on the nature of their contest.

The bitterness of the Sino-Soviet quarrel is manifested in many ways. In the early 1960's, diplomatic relations between the U.S.S.R. and the P.R.C. became severely strained. In 1960, and again in 1963, Chinese diplomats were expelled from the Soviet Union for activities unbecoming to their status—and on the second occasion they were accorded a hero's welcome upon their arrival in Peking. Territorial disputes flared up between the two countries, and incidents took place along the Sino-Soviet frontiers, especially along the border in Sinkiang. In 1963, the Chinese brought up the unequal treaties between Russia and China, and claimed a sizable slice of Soviet territory. Posing as the champions of the national minorities across the border in China, the Russians, in turn, hinted at Chinese oppression of these peoples.

Moscow and Peking have tried to meddle in the affairs of the other. The Chinese have accused Khrushchev of giving encouragement to the "anti-Party group" in the CCP ranks. The Russians have never explicitly charged the Chinese with similar activity. Yet, they have persistently linked denunciation of the Chinese stand with condemnation of CPSU "anti-Party" group activities—which suggests that they realize the possibility of such collusion. Propaganda directed at the other country has been disseminated by both the Soviet Union and China. Its objective soon became manifestly subversive: to discredit the leaders of the other state and Party—Khrushchev and Mao in particular—in the eyes of their own people.

In late 1963 and early 1964, each side assumed the mantle of spokesman for the masses in the other country: The Chinese claimed the right to criticize the Soviet Government in the name of the Soviet people, and the Russians claimed the right to criticize the Chinese Government in the name of the Chinese people. Both Moscow and Peking resorted increasingly to open threats. On September 21, 1963, the Russians warned the Chinese that, "if they intend to go on with their hostile actions . . . the most resolute rebuff from the CPSU, from the Soviet people awaits them on this road."[4] In their retort of February 3, 1964, the Chinese ridiculed the Soviet threat. "Do you really believe," they asked the Russians, "that other people are bound docilely to obey your orders and tremble at your roar? To be frank, ever since September 21, we have been eagerly waiting to see what 'the most resolute rebuff' would be."[5] Soon afterward, through V. G. Wilcox, General Secretary of the Communist Party of New Zealand, the Chinese predicted that the Soviet leaders would be thrown into the "dustbin of history."[6]

The removal from power of Khrushchev in October, 1964, eased the conflict somewhat. Both the Russians and the Chinese seemed to be eager to seize this opportunity to avert an ultimate showdown. The Chinese sent their greetings to the new Soviet leaders, and the Russians voiced no objections to the Chinese atmospheric nuclear test. The virulent polemics between them were suspended. With Chou En-lai's visit to Moscow for the celebrations of the anniversary of the Bolshevik Revolution, an outward appearance of unity was restored. Chou's talks with the Soviet leaders, however, apparently did not go well. The restrained tone of the communiqué issued at the end of his stay in Moscow clearly indicated that the sources of friction had not been removed. And in the various statements issued after the talks were completed, both sides reaffirmed their essentially irreconcilable ideological positions.

Is the Sino-Soviet split irreversible? Or will the common allegiance of the leaders of the two countries to Marxism-Leninism ultimately prevail and lead to the restoration of their alliance?

By now, the prospects appear remote for termination of the conflict and a return in relations between the Soviet Union and China to the *status quo ante*. The commitment of both sides to Communist ideology generates rather then moderates the contest.[7] It virtually precludes the possibility of a pragmatic compromise: dividing the Communist world into two zones of influence while preserving the close over-all bonds between Moscow and Peking. The universalist nature of the Marxist-Leninist doctrine—which purports to represent the only true insight into the nature of historical processes—leaves no room for the existence of two Communist centers. As stated in *Problems of Peace and Socialism* early in 1964, "Marxism-Leninism is a universal and integral teaching, and for this reason there cannot be two or several kinds of Marxism either on the international or the national plane."[8] Or conversely, as the same journal asserted on another occasion, "There can be only one international Communist movement . . . just as there can be only one truth."[9]

As long as both the Soviet Union and China continue to adhere to the Communist ideology, the only feasible pattern of harmonious relations between the two would be hierarchical in its nature. Either Moscow or Peking must be the center of the international Communist movement; the other must remain a junior partner. It is inconceivable that, in the near future, the Russians would agree to accepting a status inferior to the Chinese. This would be incompatible with both the position of the U.S.S.R. as one of the two superpowers in the international arena, and the special place of the CPSU as the first party to carry out a successful revolution for the international Communist movement. In this respect, the fall of Khrushchev makes little difference,[10] for it is doubtful if his successors could change their attitude toward China in any essential way. If they should continue along Khrushchev's course, the gap separating them from Maoists would remain impassable. If they should revert to

Stalinism, however, all sources of friction would not be eliminated. In spite of all the militancy of Stalinism, which makes it akin to Maoism, the two ideologies are irreconcilable in at least one critical aspect. Stalinism, as Philip E. Mosely has reminded us, "insisted so far as possible, on the complete subservience of foreign Communist parties to Moscow, and for a Stalinist to surrender Russia's primacy is unthinkable."[11]

Thus, if a Sino-Soviet *rapprochement* is to take place at all, the Chinese must take the initiative. To do this, Peking would have to swallow its pride and accept an inferior status to Moscow—and this is improbable. The Chinese have repeatedly demonstrated that they will be satisfied with nothing less than their recognition as one of the great world powers. Having acquired a nuclear bomb, they are even less likely to curb their aspirations. Moreover, Mao clearly regards himself as the greatest living Communist theoretician and revolutionist and he will take second place to no one. If he refused to bow to Khrushchev, who had served in the Communist movement longer than the Chinese leader, Mao will certainly not take orders from a Russian whom he regards as junior to him. A major reversal of the Chinese position after Mao's demise should not be ruled out, but still seems unlikely.[12] As of now, all Mao's potential heirs appear to share his views, and they are personally implicated in one or another aspect of the Sino-Soviet quarrel. Moreover, the longer the rift continues, the more difficult it will be to heal. With each new round of polemics between Moscow and Peking—with the hardening of their theoretical positions, with the exchange of accusations of betrayal of Communism, and with the agitation of the masses in a spirit of enmity toward the ideological adversary—at each step, the dispute gathers in momentum. In the end, it may no longer be controllable by political leaders on either side.

The factors generating the Sino-Soviet conflict, however, are by no means confined to dogmatism embedded in the Communist doctrine. The ideological dispute between the two parties is a reflection of the power struggle between the two states, rather than vice versa. At the roots of the differences lie the divergent conceptions of national interests. Each side accuses the other of being motivated by nationalism. "The present positions of the Chinese leadership," assert the Russians, "stem from the increasing, openly nationalistic, great-power aspirations."[13] "The leaders of the CPSU," the Chinese declare, "are quite unscrupulous in the pursuit of the policy of great-power chauvinism."[14]

Several grave issues in the conflict represent essentially a continuation of the centuries-old rivalry between the two nations. The territorial claims and counterclaims are advanced in the name of old-fashioned imperialism. On the one hand, Peking's title to the Soviet provinces stems from the fact that at one time they formed a part, or were tributary states, of the ancient "Middle Kingdom." On the other hand, Moscow's right to retain those territories is derived from the military conquest in the nineteenth century by the Czarist Empire. Racial prejudice is also very much a part of the dispute. The Chinese regard the Russians as the hated Occidentals who, taking advantage of China's temporary weakness, humiliated and exploited her. They assert that now "the wind from the East is beginning to prevail over the wind from the West."[15] The Russians, in turn, look down on the Chinese as backward Asiatics, who, while claiming to approach a millennium, walk "in shoes made out of rags" and eat "thin cabbage soup from a common bowl."[16]

The rapid transformation of the Sino-Soviet dispute from what at first appeared to be doctrinal squabbles between Communist parties into an open contest between the great nations certainly does not enhance the chances of its termination. On the contrary, the prospects appear to be for a prolonged and harsh struggle. This creates an unprecedented situation in the Far East. For the first time since Russia became actively involved in the politics of that region in the late nineteenth century, she is faced with an antagonistic and united, although internally still weak, China. Such a drastic political change in the heartland of Asia must produce far-reaching repercussions in other parts of that continent, and, indeed, in the world at large.

The form that the Sino-Soviet conflict has taken so far is that of an ideological and diplomatic rivalry. Each side, in addition to consolidating its internal strength, has tried to improve its position vis-à-vis the other through external alliances. These have been primarily sought in the international Communist movement—among the other Communist states as well as among the parties outside the Communist orbit. The contest between Moscow and Peking for support from foreign Communists in fact got under way at the very outbreak of their ideological debate in the late 1950's. On the one hand, the Russians tried to prevent the spread of the Chinese interpretation of Marxism-Leninism at all costs, aiming at the isolation of Peking in the international Communist movement. On the other hand, the Chinese made every effort to disseminate their own brand of Communist ideology with a view to winning as many adherents in the Communist ranks as possible. The contest between the two centers of Communism—each proclaiming itself to be the only source of the true gospel—rocked the Communist movement all over the world.

Under the impact of the Sino-Soviet clash, the Communist alliance split into two groupings of states centered around Moscow and Peking respectively. The Russians managed to retain the loyalty of seven Communist states—Poland, Hungary, Czechoslovakia, Bulgaria, East Germany, Outer Mongolia, and Cuba—while the Chinese succeeded in winning the support of Albania, North Korea, and North Viet-Nam. The relations between the two sides deteriorated rapidly. The Soviet Union and its allies came out with stern reprisals against the dissidents. They were not only accused of apostasy from Marxism-Leninism but also exposed to economic and political sanctions. All three Communist states siding with China were excluded from the CEMA. North Korea and North Viet-Nam, in contrast to Outer Mongolia, did not join in 1962; while Albania, one of the founding members, left the organization. At the same time, drastic political pressure was applied against Albania. She was banished from the Warsaw Treaty Organization, diplomatic relations with her were broken by the Soviet Union and most of its followers, and, in all likelihood, a plot aimed at overthrowing the regime in Tirana was instigated by Moscow. China and her allies reciprocated in kind. They charged Russia with trying to impose her will upon the other Communist states, thus violating the principles of Marxist proletarian internationalism. Soon the Chinese side, too, went beyond the limits of ideological debate. Peking and Tirana did their best to aggravate the difficulties that arose between the U.S.S.R. and Cuba following the Caribbean crisis of 1962, and exploited the controversies between the Soviet Union and Romania over the policies of the CEMA in 1963. At the same time, they tried hard to encourage the activities of the opposition groups in those East European Communist parties whose leaders remained loyal to Moscow.

Corresponding with the split in the Communist orbit, the Communist movement in the outside world divided into pro-Soviet and pro-Chinese factions. Despite all Moscow's efforts to isolate Peking, by the end of 1963 the Chinese had managed to secure a dominant influence in about fifteen out of some ninety existing Communist parties. The Chinese did particularly well in Asia, where they won the support of the majority of Communist parties (most notably that of the powerful Indonesian Party). They also prevailed in the

New Zealand Party. In Communist parties where they failed to gain the favor of the leaders, they encouraged the opposition elements to leave the ranks and to form separate groups. This tactic affected the pro-Moscow Communist parties in all five continents. It split virtually all the Asian parties (including the influential Indian Party), the Australian Party, a great many of the Latin American parties (including the Brazilian Party), several European parties, and even the American Communist Party. In many countries where the pro-Chinese factions represented only a small segment of the full Communist membership, they engaged in noisy political campaigns. Armed with the belief that they stand for the true version of Marxism-Leninism, they readily pose as spokesmen for the only genuine Communist movement. In addition to the activities in the Communist movement proper, the Chinese and their followers carried the fight into the various "front organizations." Meetings of the World Peace Council, the Women's International Federation, the International Association of Democratic Lawyers, and other organizations were used by the Chinese as forums to denounce the Soviet Union. A particularly bitter quarrel developed at the Afro-Asian Solidarity conferences, where the Chinese resorted to the racial appeal, denouncing the Russians as whites and denying their right to participate in the movement.

The impact of the collision between the Soviet Union and China, however, went beyond merely dividing the international Communist movement into two antagonistic factions. It led to the assertion of greater autonomy by various individual Communist parties from both Moscow and Peking—thus, to the growth of polycentrism. The rivalry enhanced the role of smaller Communist states, and in some cases, at least, awakened their aspirations for emancipation from the influence of both giants. Three Communist states—Cuba, North Viet-Nam, and Romania—tried to maintain a neutral stand in the dispute. When they eventually joined one side or the other, they were rewarded with concessions fitting their specific needs. The Cubans won from the Russians a promise of increased economic assistance. From the Chinese, the Vietnamese probably secured an assurance of support in carrying on the civil war in South Viet-Nam and Laos. The Romanians did even better. They extracted from the Russians approval of their plans to industrialize independently of the CEMA, but they did not change their neutral stand in the Sino-Soviet dispute. In April, 1964, they issued a declaration in which they strongly emphasized their independence of both sides. And in

August, 1964, on the occasion of the twentieth anniversary of Communist rule in Romania, Chinese delegates participated in the Bucharest celebrations alongside the Russians. The Communist states that from the very outset of the dispute sided with either Moscow or Peking also seem to have profited from the existing situation. In exchange for their support, they have obtained greater leeway in their domestic policies. Poland's persistent failure to carry out collectivization of agriculture, Hungary's reluctance to restrict cultural freedom in 1963, and Czechoslovakia's relaxation of governmental controls over the economy in 1964 all testify to the widening scope for autonomy in the different East European Communist regimes. Likewise, the emergence of "Kim-ism" in North Korea, as well as the virtually free hand in domestic affairs that has been obtained by the Albanian Communists, indicates a willingness on the part of Peking to grant to its allies a considerable measure of internal independence.

The trend toward polycentrism, too, affected the Communist ranks in the outside world. Communist parties in various countries took advantage of the relaxation of discipline in the international Communist movement to achieve their independence from Moscow, without coming under the influence of Peking. The Norwegian and Icelandic parties have been able to preserve their neutrality in the ideological dispute. The powerful Italian Party, although clearly on the Soviet side, strongly emphasized that its policies must be home-made. All in all, as a result of the Sino-Soviet rivalry centrifugal forces were released throughout the entire international Communist movement. "The Communist world," as U.S. Secretary of State Dean Rusk put it, "is no longer a single flock of sheep following blindly behind one leader."[17]

Khrushchev's fall, at least initially, stimulated an even further spread of polycentrism. It certainly undermined Soviet prestige among foe and friend alike. The pro-Peking Communist parties were triumphant. They hailed Khrushchev's removal and demanded that his policies be abandoned. The pro-Moscow parties did not conceal their shock and anxiety. They openly praised Khrushchev and expressed the hope that his policies would be maintained. Several Communist parties—including the French (traditionally the most docile toward Moscow)—requested an explanation of the changes in the CPSU leadership. When this was offered to them, some parties—particularly the independent-minded Italians—were not satisfied. And the maverick Romanians seized the opportunity again to stress their internal independence.

Is the trend toward polycentrism irreversible? Or will the split in the international Communist movement remain confined to two centers, with both Moscow and Peking establishing a rigid hierarchy in their respective factions? As long as the Sino-Soviet conflict continues, the odds are that polycentrism, in one form or another, will also persist. Its growth is generated by the messianic nature of Communist ideology. Moscow and Peking alike, precisely because each of them believes it represents the universally true version of Marxism-Leninism, seek to win adherents in the adversary's camp. To entice converts, both sides must present their respective camps in as attractive a light as possible. This involves showing at least some respect for the aspirations of smaller partners. Thus, in the course of their rivalry, both the Soviet and the Chinese, paradoxically, move in the direction of polycentrism.

As long as the Russians retain the dominant influence in the ranks of the international Communist movement, the Chinese will probably advocate greater autonomy for individual Communist states and parties. They seem to be well aware that at this stage they can only profit from the spread of polycentrism, because even if the dissidents fail to join Peking, Moscow is still the loser. Thus, the Chinese have missed few opportunities to denounce the Russians for pursuing "the policy of great power chauvinism and national egoism toward fraternal socialist countries," and for treating the "fraternal parties as pawns on their diplomatic chessboard."[18] This tactic has placed the Russians in a difficult position. Although they obviously have little desire to see a greater autonomy of smaller Communist states and parties, they can ill afford to come out openly against it. Consequently, they try to steer a middle course. As Jaime Perez, Secretary of the pro-Moscow Communist Party of Uruguay, put it, the Soviet stand is that "there are no 'leading' or 'subordinate' parties in the movement, that all Communists are equal and independent," but also that "recognition of the outstanding role of the CPSU . . . is a question of fundamental importance for the revolutionary struggle."[19]

So far, the Soviet attempts to find a working formula, one that combines their leadership with the autonomy of smaller partners, have not been noticeably successful. In the fall of 1963, the Russians tried to convene an international Communist meeting with a view to restoring discipline in their own faction. In carrying out this plan, however, they encountered serious opposition. The Romanian, Polish, and Italian Communists—all of whom as a result of the Sino-Soviet rift had acquired considerable independence and now had no desire to give it up—refused to participate in such a conference. Only after efforts at mediation between Moscow and Peking by the Poles and the Romanians had failed could the Russians revert to their scheme. In the spring of 1964, they called again for a meeting of the Communist parties; and Khrushchev emphasized the need for closer cooperation among the Communist states adhering to the Warsaw Treaty and the CEMA.[20] Yet, the new proposal for an international conference again met with some resentment in various Communist quarters, and in turn brought about renewed assurances on the part of Soviet leaders of their respect for the independence of the smaller Communist states and parties.[21] At the same time, the existence of "autarchic tendencies" slowing down the progress of CEMA was openly admitted.[22]

Even when, by the late summer of 1964, the Russians formally announced that a conference of the Communist parties was to be held in Moscow in December, they did not arouse enthusiasm among foreign Communists. The Italian Communist Party agreed to participate, but continued to voice its reservations. The Romanian Party put off making a decision. And, of course, the Chinese Party and its allies simply refused to attend what they called a "schismatic meeting." Khrushchev's removal from power in October and the subsequent easing of the conflict with the Chinese enabled the Russians to play down the importance of the conference. In a speech presenting the policies of the new Soviet regime, Leonid Brezhnev assured foreign Communists that the Russians did not intend to restrict their autonomy. "It would be wrong," he declared, "to thrust the experience of one party and country on the other parties and countries. The choice of one or another method of socialist construction is the sovereign right of each people."[23]

By taking advantage of their power position—through resort to a combination of military and economic pressures as well as internal subversion—the Russians would be able to reimpose tight control over the recalcitrant Communist states in Eastern Europe. They could do so, however, only at the expense of even further undermining the influence of Moscow in the international Communist movement as a whole. Any return to a policy of open suppression in Eastern Europe would play straight into the hands of Peking, enhancing its appeal among the Communists outside Moscow's reach. This, as William E. Griffith observed, "would continue to inhibit any sharp increase in Soviet control in Eastern Europe."[24]

There exists another important reason why, in trying to stamp out polycentrism in Eastern Europe, the Soviets find their hands are tied. An attempt of this kind would almost certainly impair their present good relations with Yugoslavia. It was with a view to promoting unity among all Communist states that in the mid-1950's Khrushchev went a long way to heal the rift with Tito. At that stage, owing to the complications arising from the Hungarian Revolution of 1956, the Soviet-Yugoslav *rapprochement* was short-lived. By 1958, the Yugoslavs were again denounced as heretics from Marxism-Leninism and excommunicated from the international Communist movement. As long as the Russians had the Chinese on their side, they could well afford to treat the Yugoslavs in this way. The striking discrepancy in authority between the combined forces of Moscow and Peking and that of Belgrade virtually precluded the risk of Titoism's winning many adherents in the ranks of the international Communist movement. The falling out of the two giants changed this situation drastically. The status of the Yugoslav brand of Communism was greatly enhanced. With the emergence of two competing centers of Communism, the development of a third one became a distinct possibility. In order to avoid being caught in an ideological struggle on two fronts—that is, to prevent the emergence of polycentrism—Khrushchev again healed the rift with Tito. In the early 1960's, relations between the Soviet Union and Yugoslavia visibly improved. The Yugoslavs supported the Russians against the Chinese; in return, the Russians recognized the Yugoslavs as faithful followers of Marxism-Leninism. Were Russia to resort to a policy of open suppression in Eastern Europe, it would certainly alienate Yugoslavia again. It could even push Belgrade in the direction of openly advancing her claim to a position as a third center of international Communism which could be particularly attractive to the Communists outside Moscow's reach—such as the Italian Communist Party, whose program comes close to that of the League of Yugoslav Communists; and this is precisely the situation that Moscow wants to avoid. Paradoxically, if the present pattern of Soviet-Yugoslav relations should continue unchanged, it, too, is likely to contribute in the long run to the growth of polycentrism. Yugoslavia's example as a Communist state independent of Russia, both in her internal and foreign policies, might have a far-reaching impact upon the other Communist states in Eastern Europe. It might encourage the Gheorghiu-Dejs and the Gomulkas, and even the Kadars and the Novotnys, to seek similar status for their regimes.

With the passage of time, the spread of polycentrism becomes less dependent on the Sino-Soviet dispute and develops its own dynamics. As Wolfgang Leonhard aptly observed: "The longer the process of divergence goes on, the more Communist parties and Communist-dominated organizations will change from obedient vassals to courted allies, and the greater will be their ability to differ, to disagree, to strike out on their own."[25] In the end, the increasing fragmentation within the Communist ranks may largely be divorced from the Sino-Soviet conflict. Polycentrism will acquire its own momentum and breed still more polycentrism.

Communism's messianism, however, is not the only element contributing to the growth of polycentrism. Nascent nationalism is also to be found in it. In choosing between Moscow and Peking, and especially in attempting to steer a neutral course, various Communist states are motivated not only by a preference for one or the other brand of Communist ideology, but also by their national interests. Albania's siding with China was to a considerable degree influenced by fear of a new Soviet *rapprochement* with her traditional enemy, Yugoslavia. North Viet-Nam's initial hesitance in coming out against the Soviet Union was prompted by anxiety to preserve Moscow's military and diplomatic support in waging war in Viet-Nam and Laos, while its ultimate decision to back up China was induced by recognition of the necessity of continued support from Peking in those same ventures. Conversely, in siding with Russia, Poland was influenced to a large extent by apprehension of her position being weakened in the territorial dispute with the German Federal Republic. Cuba's early reluctance to turn against China was prompted by sympathy with Peking's militant program of spreading unrest in Latin America, while her eventual falling in line with the Soviet Union was induced by the realization that only Moscow could offer Havana effective protection against the United States. The appeal of the Chinese radical and racist Communist ideology among the Asian parties can largely be explained by its relevance to the circumstances of poor, formerly colonial nations. Conversely, the generally favorable response among the West European parties to the Soviet brand of Communism can, to a considerable degree, be attributed to the appeal for those countries of its stress on the peaceful or even parliamentary transition to socialism. The fusion of revolutionary and nationalist goals in the policies of various Communist parties, of course, reduces still further the chances of restoring unity in the international Communist ranks. On the contrary, the prospect for world Communism seems to be growing fragmentation.

The situation brought about in world Communism by the Sino-Soviet conflict is without precedent. Splits in the movement, of course, are not new. In the past, there have been other attempts to question Moscow's position as Communism's sole center: In the late 1920's and the 1930's, the challenge was issued by the followers of Trotsky; in the late 1940's and the 1950's, by the Yugoslav Communists. The Trotskyites, however, were eventually reduced to impotence, and the Titoists were virtually contained to a single country. When, in the late 1950's, a new threat emerged from the Chinese Communists, Moscow was unable either to extinguish or to quarantine it. For the first time since the Bolshevik Revolution, the role of Moscow as the center of the international Communist movement has been effectively challenged. Communism as a unified political force in the world scene has ceased to exist.

In their quest for allies, both the Soviet Union and China have reached beyond the Communist movement. The realities of international politics—the limited extent of the Communist orbit, its entanglement with the non-Communist world, and the relative weakness of Communist parties out of power—have pushed the Russians and the Chinese alike to a search for partners outside the Communist ranks. The Soviets, in their policy to contain China, increasingly have striven for accommodation (if not alignment) with some non-Communist powers. The Chinese, in attempting to overcome political as well as economic isolation (the need to find new outlets for foreign trade being particularly important in their case), have resorted to similar tactics. Thus, the ripples of change caused by the Sino-Soviet conflict have spread into the outside world.

By introducing a novel element, the Sino-Soviet rivalry in itself has affected the existing balance of power in the various parts of the non-Communist orbit. The most striking shift in the pattern of alliances has taken place on the Indian subcontinent. Throughout all the stages of the Sino-Indian conflict, the Russians not only failed to support the Chinese but continued uninterrupted their military and other assistance to the Indians.* Faced with what appeared to them to be an emerging Russo-Indian encirclement, the Chinese countered by courting the favors of India's traditional enemy, Pakistan—notwithstanding its membership in the anti-Communist alliances SEATO and CENTO. By endorsing Pakistan's claims

---

* After the fall of Khrushchev, the new Soviet leaders assured the Indians that relations between the two countries would remain unchanged.

to Kashmir, Peking achieved a visible improvement in its relations with Rawalpindi. At the same time, the Soviet Union and China became engaged in a contest for influence among the other Asian and African countries. The Russians, emphasizing the policy of peaceful coexistence, moved closer to the group of nonaligned states led by Yugoslavia, India, and the United Arab Republic, which held to hold their second meeting in Cairo in the fall of 1964. In response, the Chinese, stressing the bonds among nonwhite, former colonial nations, backed up Indonesia's proposal for a second conference of Afro-Asian countries to take place in the spring of 1965. Significantly, India's initial suggestion of inviting the u.s.s.r. to this conference was rejected. Chinese Foreign Minister Chen Yi explained that such an invitation "was improper . . . because the Soviet Union was not an Asian or African country."[26]

Since the Caribbean crisis in the fall of 1962, as if striving for accommodation with another major power encircling China, the Soviet policy vis-à-vis the United States has shown a good deal of moderation. Russia not only has refrained from aggravating tensions in areas where American interests are at stake—notably in Berlin and Cuba—but also has agreed to some steps that, without striking at the roots of the Cold War, at least have improved the climate of relations between Moscow and Washington. The Russians joined with the United States and Britain in sponsoring the limited nuclear-test-ban treaty; they agreed not to orbit nuclear weapons in outer space, and concurred in cutting back the production of fissionable explosives.* China, in turn, resorted to a softer line vis-à-vis the other Western countries, notably France. Noting with approval France's growing independence of the United States in the field of foreign policy, and especially her refusal to adhere to the nuclear test-ban treaty, the Chinese underlined the advantages of a Sino-French *rapprochement*. After Paris recognition of the Chinese Communist regime early in 1964, Peking went still further and suggested the creation of an "intermediate zone" between the United States and the u.s.s.r. both in Europe and in Asia. "France herself," Mao is reported to have told the group of French parliamentarians visiting China, "Germany, Italy, England, on condition that she

* Khrushchev's fall brought little change in this regard. Immediately after assuming power, the new Soviet leaders declared themselves in favor of a continued *détente* with the West. At the very least, this reflected their need to consolidate their internal position before taking any aggressive foreign-policy measures. However, it also meant that, in all likelihood, the Soviet Union could take no major steps toward accommodation with the West.

ceases to be the courtier of America, Japan, and we, ourselves—there is your third world."[27] In short, in response to what they regarded as a Russian attempt at the encirclement of China, the Chinese were now proposing to encircle the Soviet Union.

The change in the attitude of the Communist states toward the non-Communist world, however, has been prompted not only by the Sino-Soviet conflict but also by its by-product, the growth of polycentrism. As the smaller Communist states were emancipated from the towering shadow of Moscow, they were freer to pursue their national objectives; but at the same time, they have had to adopt to the exigencies of local balances of power. Both these factors have tended to affect their pattern of relations with the non-Communist neighboring states. A shift toward closer bonds with the countries outside the Communist orbit has already been noticeable in the foreign policy of some Communist states. Thus, the Romanians, in advancing the industrialization of their country in defiance of the CEMA, have expanded their economic cooperation with Western Europe and the United States. Symbolically, in the construction of the huge steel works in Galati—which had been a major bone of contention between Bucharest and Moscow—contracts went to French and British firms. After the establishment of economic bonds, Romanian political contacts with the West followed. In May, 1964, a Romanian Government delegation visited the United States; in July, another delegation went to France. While in Paris, Premier Maurer underlined strongly the long tradition of Franco-Romanian unity.

Likewise, the Albanians, after their break with the Soviet Union, established closer economic ties with Western Europe; in particular, trade with Italy increased. Despite her adherence to the Chinese militant version of Communist ideology, Albania stressed her willingness to improve political relations with non-Communist countries. "We want to establish diplomatic relations," asserted the organ of the Albanian Communist Party early in 1962, "and to have good trade, cultural, and other relations with all capitalist countries that want them, especially with our neighbors."[28] Thus, the spread of polycentrism has contributed to at least a partial restoration of the traditionally close bonds between different East European countries and the West, and especially with Western Europe.

The change in attitude toward the non-Communists as a result of the spread of polycentrism also has been manifested among Communist parties out of power. As the Communist parties in various countries have secured greater autonomy from Moscow, they have become more responsive to the exigencies of local politics. Thus, in order to advance their political fortunes, Italian (and more recently also French) Communists have turned to searching for allies among the non-Communist political movements in their country. All in all, under the impact of the Sino-Soviet rift and the subsequent growth of polycentrism, an important change in the position of the Communists vis-à-vis the non-Communists has been under way in various parts of the world.

How do the changes in international Communism affect the global balance of power between East and West? There seems to be little doubt that, as a result of the Sino-Soviet schism and the growth of polycentrism in the Communist ranks, the position of the West as a whole has improved considerably. This is recognized by the Communists themselves. As the *Problems of Peace and Socialism* put it in a somewhat roundabout way: "Differences in the Communist movement are a source of joy to all the enemies of Communism. Indeed, the imperialists openly talk about the differences being 'an obstacle to Communist successes' and advantageous to the 'free world,' i.e. imperialism."[29]

The position of the West is enhanced in both the power and ideological struggles against the East. In terms of power politics, according to the old rule of *divide et impera,* the differences in international Communism strengthen the West. By weakening both contestants, the breakdown of the Sino-Soviet alliance exerts a restraining influence on any aggressive designs against the West by either one of them. On the one hand, in planning any offensive moves against the West, the Russians can no longer count on the immense Chinese manpower resources and extensive territorial base. Nor does the Soviet Union any longer have direct access to several crucial areas in world politics. China and her Asian allies are interposed between Russia and the West throughout almost the entire Asian continent; and by joining with China, Albania deprived the Soviet Union of entry to the Mediterranean. On the other hand, in contemplating any military step against the West, the Chinese must reckon that their armies would be deprived of the Soviet nuclear umbrella as well as of supplies of modern equipment. Since in the place of an alignment there has emerged a conflict between the Soviet Union and China, the moderating impact upon their respective strategies vis-à-vis the West goes still further. Both the Russians and the Chinese cannot rule out the possibility that, in the event of their engaging in major military operations against the West, the other side might exploit the situation by stirring up trouble along the Sino-Soviet border. Thus, the Soviet Union, threatened by China in its Asian "soft underbelly," is less likely to take up aggression in Europe or the Caribbean. Likewise China, menaced by Russia along her entire northern frontier, is less likely to resort to an all-out assault in India, Indochina, Taiwan, or South Korea. The growth of polycentrism also exerts a restraining influence on any aggressive Communist plans against the West. The greater autonomy of the smaller Communist states, by undermining the internal cohesion of both the Soviet bloc and the Chinese bloc, makes it difficult for either of them to follow an aggressive line against the Western powers. As to the Communist parties not in power, their very independence from Moscow and Peking limits their effectiveness as "fifth columns" in subverting the Western countries from within.

The disintegration of the monistic nature of Communism, and the emergence of dualism or even pluralism, breeds incipient pragmatism. This has a sobering effect upon at least some aspects of Communism's universalist and messianic aspirations.[30] Indeed, in the course of the ideological polemics between Moscow and Peking, various statements have been made by both sides that point to the growing confrontation of dogma with reality. On the one hand, there is the Russian recognition of the destructive potential of nuclear weapons; their playing down of the necessity of violent revolution; their denunciation of mass terror; and their emphasis on the people's economic welfare. All these mark a departure from the tenets of the past version of Marxism-Leninism. On the other hand, the Chinese criticism of Soviet domination of East Europe, and their insistence on real independence for all Communist states, represents a revision of one of the essential principles of the old brand of Communist ideology. By joining in the Sino-Soviet ideological debate, the foreign Communists have contributed to the erosion of Communist militancy. Paradoxically, the Yugoslavs, the Romanians, and to a large extent the Italians have endorsed the moderating changes in the Marxist doctrine introduced by both the Russians and the Chinese. Communists in other countries have followed the lead of either one or the other center; but in doing so, at least some of them—notably the Poles and the Hungarians—have elaborated the amendments in the direction of even greater restraint.

Thus, under the combined impact of the Sino-Soviet split and the spread of polycentrism, the position of the West vis-à-vis world Communism has improved. "International Communism," as Zbigniew Brzezinski put it, "has lost its momentum and the rhythm of Communist policy has been disrupted."[31] In international politics, the danger of aggression on the part of Communist states has diminished. In the domestic sphere, the risk of a violent Communist revolutionary outbreak has been reduced. In short, the changes in the Communist world carry with them the prospect of the West's being less troubled by the Communist menace.

The consequences of the changes in world Communism, however, are not confined to the improvement of the position of the West in its global struggle against the East, but are more complex. Paradoxically, as a result of the weakening of the East, the West also tends to be internally weakened. Precisely because the danger of Communist aggression is diminished, the cohesion of the Western alliance is reduced. Centrifugal forces are released in the West. Feeling more secure, the various countries are apt to place their individual objectives over those of the alliance as a whole. The offers of accommodation, or even alignment, from the Communist states only increase the temptation on the part of the Western nations to pursue their own interests. Polycentrism in the East thus tends to breed polycentrism in the West.

There are signs that the trends toward fragmentation are already under way in the Western alliance. They are perhaps most apparent in Asia. Pakistan's warm response to China's overtures for cooperation has virtually amounted to its forsaking the goals of the anti-Communist alliances, SEATO and CENTO. Indeed, President Ayub Khan asserted that "the object of the two alliances has been achieved."[32] Under the impact of the growing Sino-Pakistani *rapprochement,* India has largely abandoned her traditional posture of nonalignment and entered into close cooperation with the United States and the Soviet Union, receiving military assistance from both. The Chinese Nationalist regime in Taiwan has indicated a readiness to assume a position similar to that of India. Generalissimo Chiang K'ai-shek has given up advocating an invasion of the mainland of China in the name of the world-wide anti-Communist crusade. On the contrary, he has assured the Americans that now such a step would be acceptable to the Russians. "It is no longer necessary," he declared, "for the United States to feel that action to remove the source of all trouble in Asia will touch off a global war. I am certain the Russians will not intervene."[33] The changes in Asia, in turn, have had repercussions in relations among the noncommitted states. India's prestige as one of the leaders of the nonaligned nations has been undermined. A rivalry has developed between some of the countries fostering the conference of nonaligned states and those advocating the meeting of Afro-Asian nations. Notably, the past friendly relations between Yugoslavia and Indonesia have deteriorated—as was evidenced by the clash between Tito and Sukarno at the Cairo meeting of the nonaligned countries in October, 1964.

Finally, the impact of the changes in the Communist bloc has also been felt among the members of NATO in Europe. The eastern flank of this alliance has been ruptured by the bitter dispute between Turkey and Greece over Cyprus, while relations between Greece and Communist Bulgaria have shown signs of improvement. Indeed, when the tension reached a climax in mid–1964, the Greek Cypriots hardly concealed their hopes for Russian support against the Turks. The very core of NATO also has been undermined. Often in defiance of its objectives, France has exploited the existing situation to advance her own interests in Europe. She has refused to follow the United States in the various moves aimed at reducing tensions with Russia, and has entered into diplomatic and even political cooperation with China. Peking's plan to create an "intermediate zone" between the United States and the U.S.S.R. on a global scale found a sympathetic ear in Paris. President de Gaulle's own objective, it seems, is to promote a grand disengagement of the two major adversaries in Europe similar to that which was accomplished by China in Asia. He would like to see American and Soviet armies removed from the heart of the European continent and to fill the vacuum with the growing French nuclear forces. In short, General de Gaulle is striving to extract concessions from the Soviet Union in Europe by exploiting China's threat to Russia in Asia. France's recognition of Communist China, as George Liska suggests, has been aimed at giving the Russians "a foretaste of a new kind of diplomatic encirclement of Russia in Euroasia."[34]

The fall of Khrushchev in the Soviet Union not only failed to terminate the disarray in NATO, but in fact coincided with its acute crisis. The U.S.-fostered plan to revitalize the alliance by creating a multinational fleet of nuclear vessels (MLF) was found to be incompatible with the French objective of creating a separate West European nuclear force. To prevent the adoption of the MLF plan, France threatened to withdraw its forces from NATO. Furthermore, since West Germany sided with the United States in the Franco-American conflict (over the relaxation of tensions with the U.S.S.R. and over the establishment of MLF), France retaliated in kind. Following the overthrow of Khrushchev, who had planned to go to Bonn for talks with Chancellor Ludwig Erhard early in 1965,

French relations with the new leaders in Moscow underwent swift improvement. Within a few weeks, amid praise of de Gaulle's policies by the Soviet press, a Franco-Soviet trade agreement was signed. Thus, by giving the West Germans a foretaste of diplomatic encirclement in Europe, France demonstrated that in conducting an independent foreign policy she was not confined to a single road but had other viable alternatives.

The erosion of internal unity, and the growth in its place of fragmentation both in the East and the West, represents a novel situation in the postwar world. The centrifugal forces of nationalism, cutting across the lines of ideological divisions, are on the ascendancy everywhere. Under their impact, the old pattern of international politics—rigidly polarized between Moscow and Washington—is breaking up. For better or for worse, a new world seems to be emerging—one with more than two great powers and two centers.

Notes

Chapter 1. Sino-Soviet Relations in Historical Perspective

1. *Russko-Kitaiskie otnosheniia, 1689–1916, ofitsial'nie dokumenti* (Moscow, 1958), pp. 9–11.

2. Helmut G. Callis, *China, Confucian and Communist* (New York, 1959), p. 189.

3. *Izvestia*, September 21, 1963; *Peking Review*, February 7, 1964.

4. *Sovetsko-Kitaiskie otnosheniia, 1917–1957, sbornik dokumentov* (Moscow, 1959), pp. 43–45.

5. George Paloczi-Horvath, *Mao Tse-tung, Emperor of the Blue Ants* (London and New York, 1962), p. 82.

6. Conrad Brandt, Benjamin Isidore Schwartz, and John K. Fairbank, *A Documentary History of Chinese Communism* (Cambridge, Mass., 1952), p. 80.

7. See L. A. Sikirianskaia, *Velikii Pokhod Kitaiskoi Krasnoi Armii, 1934–1936gg.* (Moscow, 1962).

8. Mao Tse-tung, "On the Tactics of Fighting Japanese Imperialism," *Selected Works* (New York, 1954), I, 162.

9. For the official Communist history of the CCP during the Kiangsi, Long March, and Yenan periods, see Miao Chu-khuan, *Kratkaia Istoriia Kommunisticheskoi Partii Kitaia* (Moscow, 1958), pp. 73–212.

10. An interesting comparison can be made with the Yugoslav Party, which also fought independently of Moscow's control. The CCP and the YCP became the two Communist parties in the postwar world that Stalin could not rule, because they owed him nothing for their success. For further dis-

cussion of this comparison, see Chalmers A. Johnson, *Peasant Nationalism and Communist Power: The Emergence of Revolutionary China, 1937–1945* (Stanford, Calif., 1962).

11. For excerpted versions of Mao's "On the New Democracy," see Dan N. Jacobs and Hans Baerwald (eds.), *Chinese Communism: Selected Documents* (New York, 1963), pp. 60–77; and Robert V. Daniels (ed.), *A Documentary History of Communism* (New York, 1962), II, 307–12.

12. An interesting sidelight in the Sino-Soviet dispute is that, with the exception of Chou En-lai, few of the Chinese Communist leaders have ever traveled widely outside their country. Their entire life and training have been centered inwardly on China, and this has given them a restricted view and understanding of the outside world. This is especially true of their comprehension of the West, and also has relevance to their relations with the Soviet Union. The isolated self-centeredness of Mao and the other Chinese officials is not a healthy condition, and may have serious implications for the future.

13. For texts of the Soviet-Chinese agreements at Moscow, see *Sovetsko-Kitaiskie otnosheniia . . .* , pp. 217–27.

14. Quoted from Jacobs and Baerwald, *op. cit.*, title page; italics added.

15. January 12, 1964.

Chapter 2. The Sino-Soviet Split: A Reconstructed History, 1956–64

1. For a more detailed statement of my views and for documentation, see William E. Griffith, *The Sino-Soviet Rift* (Cambridge, Mass., 1964). Earlier analyses include Zbigniew Brzezinski, *The Soviet Bloc* (2nd ed., New York, 1961), especially the epilogue, "The Impact of the Sino-Soviet Dispute," pp. 409–42; G. F. Hudson, Richard Lowenthal, and Roderick MacFarquhar (eds.), *The Sino-Soviet Dispute* (New York, 1961); Kurt L. London (ed.), *Unity and Contradiction* (New York, 1962); and Donald S. Zagoria, *The Sino-Soviet Conflict 1956–1961* (Princeton, 1962).

2. Griffith, *Albania and the Sino-Soviet Rift* (Cambridge, Mass., 1963).

3. For the Soviet and Chinese views, see the "open letter" of the CPSU Central Committee to "All Party Organizations and All Communists of the Soviet Union," July 14, 1963, and "The Origin and Development of the Differences Between the Leadership of the CPSU and Ourselves: Comment on the Open Letter of the Central Committee of the CPSU," September 6, 1963; complete texts of both documents appear in Griffith, *Sino-Soviet Rift.*

4. "Peaceful Coexistence—Two Diametrically Opposed Policies: Comment on the Open Letter of the Central Committee of the CPSU (6)," *Peking Review,* December 20, 1963, pp. 6–19.

5. In early December, 1963, however, the Soviets began substituting the concept of "revolutionary-democratic" so as to stress the "revolutionary" rather than the "national" elements in the regimes of underdeveloped countries. See "For Unity and Cohesion of the International Communist Movement," *Pravda,* December 6, 1963.

6. "The Proletarian Revolution and Khrushchev's Revisionism—Comment on the Open Letter of the Central Committee of the CPSU (8)," *Peking Review,* April 14, 1964.

7. "Marxism-Leninism, the Basis of the Unity of the Communist Movement," *Kommunist,* No. 15 (October, 1963), pp. 13–47.

8. "Statement by the Spokesman of the Chinese Government—A Comment on the Soviet Government's Statement of August 3–August 15, 1963," *Peking Review,* August 16, 1963, p. 14.

9. *Ibid.*

10. David A. Charles, "The Dismissal of Marshal P'eng Teh-huai," *The China Quarterly,* October–December, 1961, pp. 63–76.

11. "How the Leaders of the CPSU Have Allied Themselves with India Against China," *Jen Min Jih Pao (People's Daily),* November 2, 1963, and *Peking Review,* November 8, 1963, pp. 18–27.

12. See Enver Hoxha, "Speech Delivered at the Celebration of the 20th Anniversary of the Albanian Party of Labor and the 44th Anniversary of the Great October Socialist Revolution," *Zeri i Popullit,* November 8, 1961; complete text in Griffith, *Albania and the Sino-Soviet Rift,* pp. 242–70.

13. *Pravda,* October 18 and 29, 1961.

14. *Peking Review,* October 27, 1961, p. 9.

15. Ernst Halperin, "Letter from Cuba," *Encounter,* February, 1964, pp. 57–66.

16. See East Berlin dispatches in *Pravda, l'Unità, and Borba,* January 19, 1963; and "Let Us Unite on the Basis of the Moscow Declaration and the Moscow Statement," *Peking Review,* February 1, 1963, p. 5.

17. "Apologists of Neo-Colonialism—Comment on the Open Letter of the Central Committee of the CPSU (4)," *Peking Review,* October 25, 1963, pp. 6–15.

18. "A Proposal Concerning the General Line of the International Communist Movement—The Letter of the Central Committee of the Communist Party of China in Reply to the Letter of the Central Committee of the Communist Party of the Soviet Union of March 30, 1963," complete text in Griffith, *Sino-Soviet Rift.*

19. "The Proletarian Revolution and Khrushchev's Revisionism—Comment on the Open Letter of the Central Committee of the CPSU (8)," *Peking Review,* April 14, 1964.

20. The text of Mao's interview with the Japanese socialists appears in *Pravda,* September 2, 1964.

21. *Pravda,* April 3, 1964.

22. Editorial on Mao's interview, *Pravda,* September 2, 1964.

Chapter 3. Poland

1. Anthony Sylvester, "Poland Observed," *East Europe,* October, 1963; Richard Hiscocks, *Poland—A Bridge for the Abyss?* (London, 1963).

2. A Polish economist, who had participated in negotiations with the Soviet leaders in 1960, admitted to this author that they repeatedly accepted "the Polish way" in agrarian matters. One of them said to the Poles: "Do whatever serves your purposes best, provided you do not bother us with requests for help. We have our hands full with our own problems." This concession may be a price Khrushchev has paid to Gomulka for his support in the Sino-Soviet dispute.

3. Sylvester, *op. cit.,* p. 13.

4. The East German and Czechoslovak farmers use twice as much mineral fertilizers as their Polish counterparts.

5. Marshall D. Shulman, "The Communist States and Western Integration," *International Organization,* XVII, No. 3 (1963), 659. In March, 1963, the Poles signed a separate bilateral trade agreement with West Germany despite the fact that they do not have diplomatic relations with Bonn.

6. *Trybuna Ludu,* December 29, 1963.

7. See Zawieyski's parliamentary speech published in *Tygodnik Powszechny* (Kraków), May 20, 1963. Apparently during the audience the Pope said some friendly words about Gomulka.

8. *Trybuna Ludu,* June 13, 1962.

9. For a typical example of this sort of planted story see Henry Raymont, "U.S. Favors Efforts to End Sino-Soviet Rift," *New York Times,* December 1, 1963.

10. Paul E. Zinner, (ed.), *National Communism and Popular Revolt in Eastern Europe* (New York, 1957), pp. 493–94. See also an interesting article by John Gittling, "Cooperation and Conflict in Sino-Soviet Relations," *International Affairs* (London), XL, No. 1 (January, 1964).

11. *New York Times,* January 15, 1957. For a brilliant discussion of the early phases of Sino-Polish relations, see Zbigniew Brzezinski, *The Soviet Bloc: Unity and Conflict* (Cambridge, Mass., 1960; rev. ed., New York, 1961), pp. 290–300.

12. For the stenographic record of the Plenum, see Radio Free Europe, *News and Information Service* (Munich), December 9, 1958. For an attempt at a "calm evaluation" of the historic importance of the Chinese from a Polish point of view, see M. Rakowski, "The Historical Background," *Polityka,* December 29, 1962. The article preached the standard Gomulka doctrine of separate, national roads toward Communism: "The Communist doctrine and movement unites more than 90 parties numbering 42 million members. . . . Since each party grows in its own soil, it is understandable that when we speak of forms we must take into consideration the different economic, cultural and political levels on which each party is active."

13. *Trybuna Ludu,* June 8, 1960.

14. *Trybuna Ludu,* July 8, 1960.

15. For much inside information and an interesting discussion of the official Polish Party attitude toward the Moscow-Peking controversy, see H. Stehle, "Polish Communism and the Sino-Soviet Rift" in William E. Griffith, (ed.), *Communism in Europe* (Cambridge, Mass., 1964).

16. *Trybuna Ludu,* February 18, 1961. See also Griffith, *Albania and the Sino-Soviet Rift* (Cambridge, Mass., 1963, pp. 68–77.

17. *Trybuna Ludu,* November 24, 1961, in Alexander Dallin (ed.), *Diversity in International Communism* (New York and London, 1963), pp. 318–19.

18. *Ibid.,* p. 329.

19. "The Direction of Renewal and the March Toward Communism," *Nowe Drogi,* December, 1961, in Dallin, *op. cit.,* p. 345.

20. "Content and Forms of Unity," *Nowe Drogi,* January, 1962, in Dallin, *op. cit.,* p. 347.

21. *Nowe Drogi,* January, 1962. See also the editorial "The Peaceful Co-existence of Two Systems and the Ideological Struggle," *ibid.,* February, 1963.

22. Quoted in *East Europe,* October, 1963, p. 37.

23. *Ibid.*

24. *East Europe,* February, 1964. For a belated attempt of the Polish Party to pour oil on the troubled waters, see the already mentioned editorial in its main theoretical organ, "The Peaceful Coexistence of the Two Systems and the Ideological Struggle," *Nowe Drogi,* February, 1963. The article takes a middle position between the two positions: Coexistence means neither ideological armistice nor sharpening of "the ideological struggle against everything that the capitalistic world" can offer, because "many ideological opponents can be our allies in the struggle for peace."

25. *Swiat powojenny a Polska* (*The Postwar World and Poland*) (Warsaw, 1931), p. 186.

26. For an early and penetrating evaluation of the Sino-Soviet conflict and its impact on Poland, see Adam Bromke, "Poland: A Matter of Timing," *Problems of Communism,* May–June, 1962.

27. Philip E. Mosely, "The Chinese-Soviet Rift: Origins and Portents," *Foreign Affairs,* October, 1963, p. 20.

28. In a letter to the Editor, *New York Times,* January 22, 1964.

Chapter 4. Hungary

1. Ministerial Decree No. 3/1963 of May 19, 1963. In the past, educational standards had, especially in the universities, greatly deteriorated, because the best qualified students were mostly those whose class origin was defective, or who were contaminated otherwise by "counter-revolutionary parentage."

2. See "Communist Gamble in Hungary," *The Times* (London), March 8, 1963.

3. See Kadar's address to the workers of the Icarus-plant on March 3, 1962: "We must bear in mind that different people, with different pasts and views live together with us in our people's system. . . . They don't rise against us—and we only want to fight those who try to overthrow the people's power. . . . The people of this category—and they are the majority —are on our side. . . . But they are not Marxists. We must never forget that the trained Marxists are not in the majority." *Nepszabadsag,* March 4, 1962.

4. *Nepszabadsag,* January 20, 1963.

5. *Jen Min Jih Pao* (*People's Daily*), September 5, 1963. That some members of the Soviet Presidium voiced doubts concerning the expediency or correctness of the second Soviet armed intervention was admitted by Khrushchev in a speech before the Hungarian Party Congress on December 2, 1959. See Ferenc A. Vali, *Rift and Revolt in Hungary* (Cambridge, Mass., 1961), pp. 344, 356, 555.

6. *Nepszabadsag,* December 24, 1963.

7. The original version of Khrushchev's speech was by some indiscretion distributed to the non-Communist press. *New York Times,* April 5, 1964.

8. For this point of view, see "Interview with Isaac Deutscher," *Review* (Brussels), No. 3, 1963, p. 26.

9. For instance, on April 1, 1964, Khrushchev told workers in Budapest that it is incorrect to believe "only one thing is important—revolution." Instead, "The important thing is that we should have more to eat—good goulash —schools, housing, and ballet . . ." *New York Times,* April 2, 1964.

10. See Vali, *op. cit.,* pp. 384–99.

11. See Kadar's statement, *Nepszabadsag,* December 24, 1963.

12. See William E. Griffith, "European Communism and the Sino-Soviet Schism," *The Annals,* September, 1963, p. 146. For Hungarian-Yugoslav relations in 1956 and 1958, see Vali, *op. cit.,* pp. 350–52, 472–78.

13. See "The Hungarian Minority Problem in Rumania," *Bulletin of the International Commission of Jurists* (Geneva), No. 17 (December, 1963), pp. 34–41.

14. "Khvostism" (tailing, following behind popular trends like a tail) was strongly condemned by Lenin. The Party should, by all means, set itself at the head and direct and channel popular movements, and not let itself be dragged or pushed by them.

15. The speech was pronounced before the Twentieth Congress of Hungarian Trade Unions in Budapest; see *Hungary Under Soviet Rule VII* (New York, 1964), p. 14. On March 19, 1964, Kadar, in an address to the Patriotic People's Front, expressly stated that withdrawal of Soviet forces from Hungary depended upon withdrawal of NATO forces from West Germany; *New York Times,* March 20, 1964.

Chapter 5. Czechoslovakia

1. The history of the Communist Party of Czechoslovakia has been dealt with by this author in a series of articles in the *American Slavic and East European Review* (new title, *Slavic Review*), October, 1955; April, 1960; and December, 1961.

2. See Bruno Kohler, *Zivot strany,* No. 6, 1957; and the speech of J. Hendrych, *Rude pravo,* June 19, 1957.

3. See, for instance, J. Horak, "Revisionism—The Main Danger," *Rude pravo,* January 9, 1958.

4. *Ibid.,* May 8, 1958.

5. Not without significance, as an indication of Czechoslovakia's reliability, was the fact that in the fall of 1958 Prague became the location of the editorial board of the new international Communist journal, *Problemy mira i sotsialisma* (*Problems of Peace and Socialism*).

6. See, for instance, the speech by Karol Bacilek, at the Slovak Central Committee, January 9–10, 1958, *Praca,* January 12, 1958. Vladimir Koucky, at a seminar devoted to contemporary revisionism in October, 1958, warned of the vestiges of the traditions of social democratism, Masarykism, and nationalism among Czech intellectuals (*Rude pravo,* November 1, 1958).

7. As early as July, 1957, a joint Soviet-Czechoslovak statement had made an attack on dogmatism, the first time in which dogmatism had been classed with revisionism as a danger. See Donald S. Zagoria, *The Sino-Soviet Conflict, 1956–1961* (Princeton, N.J., 1962), p. 53.

8. See the defense of peaceful coexistence and competition by C. Cisar, in *Rude pravo,* July 2, 1960. "To reject all negotiation and every compromise with the bourgeoisie means to drive matters to an inevitable armed conflict," he wrote. "There is a difference between a capitalist who wants to compete with us in peace and one who wants only to compete in atomic destruction. Therefore, we negotiate with the supporters of peaceful competition within the bourgeois class; therefore, we separate them from the aggressive circles."

9. Novotny, *Rude pravo,* November 21, 1961.

10. See D. Rozehnal, "Peaceful Coexistence or a Nuclear Holocaust," *Nova mysl,* No. 3, March, 1962; Jan Fojtik, "Peaceful Coexistence, the Fight for Peace, and the Revolutionary Movement," *Rude pravo,* January 24, 1962.

11. *Rude pravo,* November 24, 1961.

12. *Ibid.,* December 12, 1961.

13. "The Leninist Way," *Nova mysl,* No. 12, December, 1961.

14. See unsigned article in *Zivot strany,* No. 9, May, 1962.

15. *Rude pravo,* December 8 and 9, 1962.

16. See an article by Jan Fojtik, in *Rude pravo,* December 30, 1962, in which dogmatism was now termed "the main danger."

17. See the editorial in *Rude pravo,* January 15, 1963. Julius Fucik was a Czech journalist who died in a German prison and has been treated as a national hero.

18. See in particular the article by C. Cisar, "The Pure Shield of Communism," *Nova mysl,* No. 4, April, 1963, pp. 385–97.

19. See especially the speech by Novotny, in Ostrava, at the end of March, in *Rude pravo,* March 24, 1963.

20. This is fully dealt with in my article, "Ferment Among Czechs and Slovaks," *International Journal* (Toronto) XIX, No. 4 (Autumn, 1964); also included in the author's *Communism National and International: Eastern Europe After Stalin* (Toronto, 1964).

21. *Pravda* (Bratislava), June 3, 1963.

22. *Rude pravo,* June 13, 1963.

23. *Rude pravo,* August 22, 1963.

24. See *Nova mysl,* Nos. 9, 10, 11, and 12, 1963. In the first article, the similarity of the Chinese views with Trotsky's position was stressed.

25. Jan Fojtik, *Rude pravo,* July 11, 1963.

26. *Rude pravo,* December 21, 1963.

27. *Kulturny zivot,* December 21, 1963.

Chapter 6. Romania and Hungary

1. For example, it supported the Soviet Union's claims to Bessarabia and was implicated in the Soviet-inspired Tatar Bunar rising of 1924.

2. The present Romanian leadership, though dominated by the Gheorghiu-Dej group, is not composed entirely of "home" Communists. The Soviet-trained Emil Bodnaras is still a full member of the Politburo and enjoys considerable influence. The Soviet-trained Petre Borilla is also still a full member of the Politburo. Such men as these, however, must now be considered more as individuals than as forming a "Muscovite" faction. The only Jew remaining in the Politburo is the candidate-member Leonte Rautu, the regime's agit-prop chief.

3. All three are now vice-premiers and may, with considerable justification, be described as the men behind the current "boom."

4. Khrushchev himself attended this Congress and heartily endorsed the Romanian program. *Scanteia,* June 22, 1960.

5. For a summary of the Romanian-Soviet conflict on CEMA and the Romanians' subsequent "flirtation" with China in order to gain their point,

see my article, "Rumania Steps Out of Line," *Survey,* October, 1963. Some of the following description and analysis is based on that article, which supplies the necessary documentation for most of the events that are enumerated in the Romanian section of this chapter.

6. For example, under the terms of the five-year trade agreement signed between the two countries in November, 1960, the Soviet Union promised to supply Romania with 7 million tons of iron ore by 1965 and with certain complete installations for the Galati combine. *Tass,* November 11, 1960.

7. *Scanteia,* June 26, 1963.

8. Romania has made important purchases of industrial equipment (including installations for the Galati plant) in Great Britain, France, Germany, and Italy, and has shown interest in purchasing equipment and processes from Sweden and Austria. It should also be noted that in October, 1963, an unspecified American company was authorized by the U.S. Government to sell to Romania technical documentation for an oxygen steel mill, also believed to be Galati. In 1963 also, some 600 Western technicians were working in Romania. To prove her "good will" toward the West, and hence to induce the Western governments to adopt a more liberal trading policy with her, Romania has made other gestures, such as increasing cultural contacts and the cessation of all jamming of Western broadcasts.

9. At a Romanian Central Committee plenum held at the beginning of March, 1963, the CEMA delegate, Barladeanu, reported on the Moscow proceedings and was given a vote of confidence. Afterward, according to Yugoslav sources, the basic Party organizations were informed of the leadership's stand.

10. Gheorghiu-Dej gave this impressive performance at the November-December, 1961, Central Committee, which met to hear his report on the Twenty-second Congress of the CPSU.

11. The chief example of this occurred at the United Nations General Assembly session in November, 1963, when the Romanian delegate supported the proposal for a denuclearized zone in Latin America while the other Soviet-bloc countries abstained.

12. Kostov was legally rehabilitated in 1956 and politically rehabilitated in 1962. Many decorations were posthumously bestowed on him. One of his closest followers, Petko Kunin, who was imprisoned when Kostov was executed, was re-elected to the Central Committee at the Eighth Party Congress in November, 1962, and is a foremost proponent of a new system of economic planning for Bulgaria.

13. Chervenkov himself finally put an end to any Bulgarian doubts about the ideological pretensions of the Chinese communes in an article in *Rabotnichesko Delo* of January 15, 1959. He may have been forced to do this because he was suspected of being the man who had inspired the Bulgarian fascination with the concept.

14. For a detailed study of the Bulgarian "great leap forward," see John Kalo, "The Bulgarian Economy," *Survey,* December, 1961.

15. For example, during Khrushchev's visit to Bulgaria in May, 1962, the Soviet leader's references to Yugov were considerably less cordial than those to Zhivkov. Also, when the agenda for the Eighth Congress was published, it was announced that the economic plan at the Congress would be presented by Zhivkov and not, as had been the case at the Seventh Congress, by Yugov.

16. Georgi Tsankov was, like Yugov, disgraced at the Congress itself when

he was removed from his Politburo position and his post as Vice-Premier. As a faithful supporter of Chervenkov and former Minister of the Interior, he was an obvious target for the de-Stalinizers.

17. The trial of the "CIA spy" Assen Georgiev in December, 1963, is another example of this repressive policy caused by insecurity. While Zhivkov was obviously responsible for the trial of Georgiev, he was probably not privy to the demonstration outside the American Legation. This may have been inspired by lower-level "Stalinists" anxious to embarrass him in his relations with the United States.

18. Kremikovtsi, the large metallurgical combine near Sofia, is the biggest single project in the Bulgarian industrialization drive and has become the symbol of it.

Chapter 7. East Germany

1. East Berlin Domestic Television Service, January 15, 1963.
2. See *Einheit,* October, 1963, and O. F., "Die SED im sowjetisch-chinesischen Konflikt," *Neue Zürcher Zeitung,* November 1, 1963.
3. *Neues Deutschland,* November 2, 1963.
4. *Neues Deutschland,* December 2, 1961. See also my article "East Germany: Lesson in Survival," *Problems of Communism,* May-June, 1962.
5. The relevant excerpts from the Peking *Jen Min Jih Pao (People's Daily)* have been taken from the *Frankfurter Allgemeine Zeitung,* August 24, 1963.
6. *Ibid.*
7. Donald S. Zagoria, *The Sino-Soviet Conflict, 1956–1961* (Princeton, N.J., 1962), p. 396.
8. *New York Times,* December 6, 1962.
9. *Süddeutsche Zeitung,* January 17, 1963.
10. Speech of N. S. Khrushchev, in *Protokoll des VI. Parteitages der Sozialistischen Einheitspartei,* I, 295.
11. See Fradkin's "Vor neuen Aufgaben," in *Sowjetwissenschaft—Kunst und Literatur,* January, 1962, and Kurella's rebuttal, "Den Blick nach vorn, auf das Neue gerichtet," *ibid.,* February, 1962.
12. *Neues Deutschland,* April 4, 1963.
13. *Neues Deutschland,* February 13, 1964.
14. "Leserbrief," *Einheit,* September, 1963, pp. 115–16.

Chapter 8. Outer Mongolia, North Korea, and North Viet-Nam

For the reader who must rely on English translations of original documentation on the three Communist states examined in this chapter, there exist various useful source materials.

Soviet materials on Outer Mongolia, North Korea, and North Viet-Nam will be found in English translation in the *Current Digest of the Soviet Press,* issued weekly in New York. The Soviet journals *International Affairs* and *New Times* are published in the English language in Moscow.

Chinese articles on the three Communist states appear in English translation in the daily *Survey of China Mainland Press,* issued by the American

Consulate General in Hong Kong, as well as in Peking's very comprehensive *Hsinhua News Agency* (NCNA) daily bulletins and in the weekly *Peking Review*.

The most convenient English-language source on developments in Outer Mongolia, North Korea, and North Viet-Nam are the several series of translations issued by the *Joint Publications Research Service* (JPRS) in the Office of Technical Services of the U.S. Department of Commerce. Of special interest is the series entitled *Translations on International Communist Developments* and the serial publications *Translations on Mongolia, Translations of Political and Sociological Information on North Korea, Economic Report on North Korea,* and *Translations of Political and Sociological Information on North Vietnam.*

For additional bibliographic information, see the pertinent sections in the multi-author *Soviet Foreign Relations and World Communism since 1917: A Selected Annotated Bibliography of Books in 25 Languages,* edited by T. T. Hammond (Princeton, N.J., in press).

1. *Pravda,* May 17, 1957.

2. The demarcation of the Sino-Mongolian border on the basis of the 1962 agreement is apparently going on as scheduled. *Hsinhua News Agency,* April 2, 1964.

3. For details of Soviet and Chinese grants to the M.P.R. after World War II, see the table in the excellent essay by Robert A. Rupen, an American authority on Outer Mongolia, "The Mongolian People's Republic and Sino-Soviet Competition," in A. Doak Barnett (ed.), *Communist Strategies in Asia—A Comparative Analysis of Governments and Parties* (New York and London, 1963).

4. *Unen,* November 5, 1963, reported extensively on the foundation-laying ceremony at the Darkhan thermal power plant at which N. G. Ignatov, Deputy Chairman of the Presidium of the Supreme Soviet of the U.S.S.R., addressed the audience. See also Tsedenbal's speech of the previous day. Translation in *Joint Publications Research Service* (JPRS) 22,680 (January 10, 1964), and *New Times,* September 23, 1964.

5. Several statements made by the Chinese Communists in April, 1964, suggest that the withdrawal of Chinese workers was undertaken in response to a Mongolian request. See the *New York Times,* April 26, 1964.

6. For details on some of these activities, see "Mongolians Celebrate Mongolia-Soviet Friendship Month and Bolshevik Revolution Anniversary," JPRS 22,813 (January 20, 1964).

7. For example, in November, 1963, *Namyn Am'dral,* the theoretical organ of the Central Committee of the Mongolian People's Revolutionary Party, attacked the CCP leaders as having "completely lost their shame," and spoke of "the erroneous and improper policies of the Chinese communist party leaders which are intended to create rifts . . . in the ranks of the world Communist movement." Translation in JPRS 23,579 (March 9, 1964).

8. Significantly, *Namyn Am'dral,* April, 1963, asserted in an editorial that "some of the new and young nations are learning from our experience." Translation in JPRS 19,802 (June 24, 1963).

9. However, Robert A. Rupen, "Recent Trends in the Mongolian People's Republic," *Asian Survey,* April, 1964, concludes that Tsend's downfall may have been due to his attempt to undercut Tsedenbal.

10. For additional details, see Chong-sik Lee, "Politics in North Korea:

Pre-Korean War Stage," and Glenn D. Paige and Dong Jun Lee, "The Post-War Politics of Communist Korea," in the special North Korea issue of *The China Quarterly,* April-June, 1963.

11. Glenn D. Paige points out that "although Kim Il-sung is portrayed as having been a guerrilla in China for at least a decade, there is absolutely no acknowledgment of Mao Tse-tung as a font of revolutionary wisdom and guerrilla strategy." See his significant contribution to our understanding of Kim's policies, in "North Korea and the Emulation of Russian and Chinese Behavior," in Barnett, *op. cit.*

12. See, for example, *Nodong Sinmun,* December 12, 1963. Translation in JPRS 23,675 (March 13, 1964).

13. *Kulloja,* a Korean Party monthly, September 20, 1963. Translation in JPRS 22,740 (January 15, 1964).

14. See *Nodong Sinmun,* September 20, 1963. Translation in JPRS 22,179 (December 6, 1963).

15. Pyongyang *Minju Choson,* October 25, 1963. Translation in JPRS 22,277 (December 13, 1963). On February 21, 1964, the same paper, in an editorial, referred to the Chinese people as "our near and dear neighbor and reliable comrade-in-arms."

16. See documents 53 and 54 and commentary in Alexander Dallin (ed.), *Diversity in International Communism—A Documentary Record, 1961–1963* (New York, 1963).

17. In 1964, the North Korean press made it a point to state its support for the Albanians by referring to the "correct leadership of the Albanian Workers Party headed by Comrade Enver Hoxha" and to the "clear-sighted guidance of the Albanian Workers Party." See, for example, *Nodong Sinmun,* February 17, 1964.

18. The warmth of Chinese-Korean relations after Liu's visit is also attested to by the tone of Kim's greetings to Mao's seventieth birthday (broadcast by Pyongyang International Service in English on December 25, 1963). This message contained such phrases as "leader of the great Chinese people, outstanding figure of the international Communist and working class movement and close friend of the Korean people" and "creatively applying the universal truth of Marxism-Leninism," and ended on this rousing theme: "You have made a great contribution to the defense of the purity of Marxism-Leninism against imperialism and revisionism. . . ."

19. On December 6, 1963, *Nodong Sinmun,* in an editorial which was broadcast also in English by Radio Pyongyang, summed up the Korean position on the test ban as follows: "The partial nuclear test-ban treaty cooked up under the manipulation of U.S. imperialism is a good specimen showing what 'obedience' to the policy of imperialism brings. In fact, the signing of the Moscow treaty was by no means a 'victory of the peaceful foreign policy.' It legalized the nuclear blackmail of U.S. imperialism and offered it a chance to achieve its aggressive design at will." Another Pyongyang broadcast of the same day referred to the late President Kennedy as "a principal war criminal."

20. As quoted in Glenn D. Paige, "Korea," in Cyril E. Black and Thomas P. Thornton (eds.), *Communism and Revolution—The Strategic Uses of Political Violence* (Princeton, N.J., 1964).

21. For an example, see a D.R.V. ministerial statement in *Nhan Dan,* September 17, 1963. Translation in JPRS 22,039 (November 26, 1963).

22. See, for example, "Statement of the South Viet-Nam National Front of Liberation," *New Times* (Moscow), March 4, 1964.

23. He was then known as Nguyen Ai Quoc.

24. From an editorial in *Nhan Dan,* May 19, 1963, the seventy-third birthday of Ho. Translation in JPRS 19,961 (July 1, 1963).

25. See George Modelski, "The Viet Minh Complex," in Black and Thornton, *op. cit.*

26. For a discussion of the Vietnamese Workers Party leadership, see P. J. Honey, *Communism in North Vietnam—Its Role in the Sino-Soviet Dispute* (Cambridge, Mass., 1963). This fine study constitutes the most detailed and reliable examination of the zigzags of North Vietnamese policy during the past several years.

27. Honey, *op. cit.,* in an appendix, has contrasted the joint statements made on the occasion of the visits of Novotny and Liu, demonstrating the Vietnamese concessions made to the viewpoints of these visitors, who represented strongly conflicting strategies. The portions presented include reference to the world situation, disarmament, Cuba, India, peaceful coexistence, revisionism, Yugoslavia, and peaceful evolution.

28. Document 57 of Dallin, *op. cit.,* gives the text of the communiqué issued by the Vietnamese Workers Party after hearing the report of its delegation to the Soviet Congress, and indicates those passages which *Pravda,* in reproducing the communiqué, preferred to suppress.

29. For a discussion of the D.R.V.'s domestic programs, see Bernard B. Fall, "The Road to Socialism in North Viet-Nam," in Barnett, *op. cit.*

30. *Thong Nhat* (Hanoi), December 27, 1963. Translation in JPRS 23,338 (February 20, 1963).

Chapter 9. Cuba

1. *New Republic,* December 14, 1963, p. 16. The quotation is attributed to the late President Kennedy by the French journalist Jean Daniel. M. Daniel subsequently revealed that, before his tragic death, the President had not actually approved the content of the articles for publication. See *New Republic,* December 21, 1963, p. 6.

2. *New York Times,* January 3, 1961.

3. The thesis of Theodore Draper, *Castro's Revolution: Myths and Realities* (New York, 1962), is that Castro betrayed the original revolution. William Appleman Williams, *The United States, Cuba and Castro* (New York, 1962), contends that the United States by default, and by active opposition to the revolution, forced it into an alliance with the Soviet bloc. See also Hugh Thomas, "The Origins of the Cuban Revolution," *World Today,* October, 1963, pp. 448–60.

4. Public attention was first drawn to the CIA base in Retalhuleu, Guatemala, by Ronald Hilton, editor of *Hispanic American Report,* November, 1960, p. 583. Richard Nixon, former Vice-President of the United States, revealed at a later date (*Six Crises,* New York, 1962, pp. 351–56) that he had advocated counterrevolutionary measures as early as April, 1959.

5. *New York Times,* July 10, 1960.

6. *Hoy,* December 2, 1961.

7. Herbert L. Matthews, *Return to Cuba* (Stanford, Calif., 1964), p. 16.

Matthews, an editor of the *New York Times,* interviewed Castro on October 29, 1963, and again by long-distance telephone on January 7, 1964. Castro asserted, contrary to the report of Jean Daniel in the *New Republic,* December 14, 1963, that it was the Cubans "who put forward the idea of the missiles."

8. *Hoy,* August 11, 1963. By 1963, the harvest had fallen to 3,883,000 tons.

9. Whether or not they have good cause, the fact remains that throughout the five years of the revolution, the Cubans have been obsessed by the fear of American intervention. See Fernando Alvarez Tabio, "El Pretenso Derecho de Intervencion y la Autodefensa Simulada," *Politica Internacional,* April, 1963, pp. 7–26.

10. *New York Times,* August 30, 1962.

11. Ricardo Alarcon, "La 11 Declaracion de la Habana," *Politica Internacional,* July, 1963, p. 109.

12. The "differences" were admitted by Castro on November 1, 1963, over the Cuban TV network. *Politica Internacional,* January, 1963, p. 31.

13. *Peking Review,* November 2, 1962, p. 6.

14. *Fidel Castro Calls for Unity,* Political Documents No. 5, Ministry of Foreign Relations (Havana, 1963), p. 26.

15. *Ibid.,* p. 47.

16. *Politica Internacional,* April, 1963, pp. 156–67.

17. *Hoy,* July 27, 1963.

18. Ernesto "Che" Guevara, "Guerrilla Warfare: A Means," *Peking Review,* January 10, 1964, pp. 14–21.

19. *Hoy,* December 22, 1963.

20. *Hoy,* January 23, 1964.

21. *World Marxist Review* (English Edition), May, 1963, p. 51–52. Too much authority, however, should not be given to spokesmen for Latin American Communist parties, for a historical phenomenon of the movement in Latin America has been the existence of more than one party within the various countries. The Communist Party of Brazil, as opposed to Prestes' Brazilian Communist Party, accuses Khrushchev of revisionism and of disrupting "the unity of the world Communist movement." *Peking Review,* September 13, 1963, p. 42.

22. *World Marxist Review* (English Edition), May, 1963, p. 88; *World Marxist Review* (Canadian Edition), January, 1964, p. 14; and *World Marxist Review* (English Edition), December, 1963, p. 72. The case of Colombia is of great interest since "objective conditions" in that country are particularly favorable to a Cuban-style guerrilla movement; see E. J. Hobsbawm, "The Revolutionary Situation in Colombia," *World Today,* June, 1963, pp. 248–58.

23. *World Marxist Review* (Canadian Edition), December, 1962, p. 30.

24. Luis Corvalan, "The Peaceful Way—a Form of Revolution," *World Marxist Review* (English Edition), December, 1963, pp. 2–9. *World Marxist Review* (Canadian Edition), December, 1962, pp. 22.

25. Antonio Nunez Jimenez, *Geografía de Cuba* (Havana, 1959), p. 309.

26. Fidel Castro, *Hoy,* October 1, 1963.

27. Jose Figueres, former President of Costa Rica, *Christian Science Monitor,* April 28, 1961.

28. *Hispanic America Report,* October, 1963, p. 827.

Chapter 10. Yugoslavia

1. Reporting about his conversation with Edvard Kardelj on June 5, 1945, Sadchikov, Soviet Ambassador in Yugoslavia, wrote: ". . . Kardelj said he would like the Soviet Union to regard them [the Yugoslav Communists] not as representatives of another country, capable of solving questions independently, but as representatives of one of the future Soviet Republics, and the CPY as a part of the All-Union Communist Party, that is, that our relations should be based on the prospect of Yugoslavia becoming in the future a constituent part of the U.S.S.R." Quoted in *The Soviet-Yugoslav Dispute* (London, 1948), p. 37.

2. Vlado Teslic, *Kineska revolucija i Moskva* (Beograd, 1953), pp. 316 and 342.

3. This sentence is taken from the so-called Belgrade Declaration signed between Khrushchev and Tito on June 2, 1955. It was reaffirmed a year later, in Moscow, in the "Declaration on Relations between the League of Communists of Yugoslavia and the Communist Party of the Soviet Union," and again in the official communiqué following the Khrushchev-Tito meeting in Romania early in August, 1957.

4. *Govori i članci (Speeches and Articles)* (Zagreb, 1959), XI, 16–17.

5. *Report of the Central Committee of the Communist Party of the Soviet Union to the 20th Party Congress* (Moscow, 1956), p. 44.

6. *Govori i članci,* XI, 111.

7. *Eighth National Congress of the Communist Party of China* (Peking, 1956), I, 85.

8. *Jen Min Jih Pao (People's Daily)*, December 29, 1956.

9. *Pravda,* November 23, 1956.

10. September 12, 1957.

11. "An Historical Meeting," *Review of International Affairs,* VIII (September 16, 1957), p. 11.

12. In his television interview with Edward R. Murrow, Tito declared that his views on the different national paths to Communism were "to a great extent identical to those of Mao Tse-tung." *New York Times,* July 1, 1957.

13. "At the time of the fortieth anniversary celebration in Moscow, Mao's insistence on strengthening the declaration of the Communist countries by the reaffirmation of subordination to Moscow prevented Yugoslavia from signing, although Tito's Party had agreed to an earlier milder statement proposed by Moscow. Mao was reported enraged almost to the point of hysteria, insisting that the Yugoslav comrades had to sign the declaration." Richard L. Walker, "Chairman Mao and the Cult of Personality," *Encounter,* June, 1960, p. 41.

14. See Adam Bromke and Milorad M. Drachkovitch, "Poland and Yugoslavia: The Abortive Alliance," *Problems of Communism,* March-April, 1961, pp. 26–33.

15. An editorial in *Jen Min Jih Pao,* May 5, 1958.

16. *Kommunist* (Moscow), quoted in Robert Bass and Elizabeth Marbury (eds.), *The Soviet-Yugoslav Controversy, 1948–58: A Documentary Record* (New York, 1959), p. 166.

17. *Pravda,* May 9, 1958.

18. Bass and Marbury (eds.), *op. cit.,* pp. 191–200.

19. *Ibid.*, pp. 202–14.

20. A typical example of this directive was the following sentence from Khrushchev's speech at the Congress of the East German Communist Party on July 11, 1958: ". . . in our struggle for the Communist cause, we should not devote greater attention to the Yugoslav revisionists than they actually deserve."

21. In a speech in Zagreb, December 12, 1959, Tito petulantly complained about relations with other Communist countries: ". . . recently these attacks have been reduced. But there is another system of keeping quiet about and ignoring any of our important statements, declarations, and even the national holiday which we had. The press did not take any notice. This is not very nice. This should not be done."

22. Klaus Mehnert, *Peking and Moscow* (New York, 1963), p. 371.

23. "My Marathon Talk with Russia's Boss," *Life,* January 12, 1959, p. 86.

24. *Control Figures for the Economic Development of the* U.S.S.R. *for 1959–1965,* Report Delivered at the 21st Extraordinary Congress of the Communist Party of the Soviet Union, January 27, 1959 (Moscow, 1959), p. 135.

25. April 16, 1960.

26. February 27, 1963.

27. The prevailing consensus among Western experts is that the April 16, 1960, *Red Flag* article marked the beginning of the ideological phase of the Sino-Soviet conflict. See David Floyd, *Mao Against Khrushchev* (New York, 1963), p. 266; Roderick MacFarquhar and others, *The Sino-Soviet Dispute* (New York, 1961); special edition of the *China Quarterly,* 1961, p. 78; Donald S. Zagoria, *The Sino-Soviet Conflict* (Princeton, N.J., 1962), p. 299.

28. "Listening to Tito [that is, to his September 22 speech before the General Assembly of the United Nations] nobody could doubt that he is positively pro-Soviet and icily neutral toward us." Max Ascoli, "Khrushchev's Blunder at the U.N.," *The Reporter,* October 13, 1960, p. 21.

29. *A Step Backward* (Beograd, 1961), pp. 23 and 81.

30. The degree of Khrushchev's furor against Enver Hoxha and his regime is reflected in his speech on foreign policy, delivered December 12, 1962, before the Supreme Soviet. In that speech, while highly praising Tito and "Socialist Yugoslavia," he assailed "a bestial morality that the Albanian sectarians and splitters want us to adopt in relations with Yugoslavia."

31. Paul Underwood, "Tito's Neutral Road—Toward Moscow," *New York Times Magazine,* November 26, 1961, p. 32.

32. "Some people contend that Yugoslavia is not a socialist country. In that case, allow me to ask, what kind of a country is it? . . . It is known that in Yugoslavia there have for a long time been no landlords and capitalists, no private capital, no private enterprises or private estates and no private banks. We see also that the Yugoslav Communists and their leaders are directing their efforts to the development of the economy, the consolidation of the conquests of socialism. Therefore, if one is to proceed from objective laws, from the teaching of Marxism-Leninism, it is impossible to deny that Yugoslavia is a socialist country."

33. This official tendency of the Titoist regime to reorient toward the East the sympathies and interests of Yugoslav Communists and of intellectuals at large was the dominant feature of a speech made in September, 1961, at the Congress of the Association of Yugoslav Writers, by Dobrica

Cosic, a prominent Yugoslav Communist writer who is very close to Tito: "Whatever the conceptions we cannot adopt, whatever spirit officially dominates cultural life in the Soviet Union and in the countries of the socialist camp, these countries are creating values of universal world importance; they are offering comprehensive knowledge and experience, and carrying a tremendous potential of energy, which will be turned into undreamt-of creative intensity in culture and the arts in the near future. If we do not show more curiosity and more critical interest in cultural, social, and ideological trends in the countries with socialist systems, I am afraid that our humanist horizon will be narrowed and we shall, without reason, renounce many valuable impulses for our structure and in this way show the lack of historical perspective and far-sightedness."

34. This problem is discussed in detail in my recent study, *United States Aid to Yugoslavia and Poland: Analysis of a Controversy* (Washington, D.C., 1963).

35. *New York Times,* March 18, 1964.

36. These sentences are taken from a pronouncement addressed to "the leading organs and members of the League of Yugoslav Communists" by the LYC's Executive Committee (Politburo) and printed in the Belgrade *Komunist* of June 14, 1962. The document is a major text of the LYC's supreme organ and an important source for the study of contradictions in Titoism.

37. This problem is discussed in my article "Succession and Charismatic Leader in Yugoslavia," *Journal of International Affairs* (New York), January, 1964, pp. 54–66.

Chapter 11. Economic Relations Among the Communist States

1. *Pravda,* June 17, 1962.

2. *Peking Review,* February 7, 1964.

3. Statistics on Sino-Soviet trade are taken from the appropriate annual editions of *Foreign Trade in the* U.S.S.R. (Moscow).

4. The statistics given here are taken from Penelope Hartland Thunberg, "The Soviet Union in the World Economy," *Dimensions of Soviet Economic Power: Materials Prepared for the Joint Economic Committee, Congress of the United States* (Washington, 1962), p. 429.

5. The figure of $2.0 billion (1.816 billion rubles) was given by Suslov in his February 14, 1964, report to the Central Committee of the CPSU; *Pravda,* April 3, 1964. Previous Western estimates had been $1.7 billion.

6. George C. Carnett and Morris H. Crawford, "The Scope and Distribution of Soviet Economic Aid," in *Dimensions of Soviet Economic Power,* p. 462.

7. *Pravda,* April 3, 1964.

8. J. F. Brown, "Albania, Mirror of Conflict," *Survey,* January, 1962, p. 27.

9. N. S. Khrushchev, "Vital Questions of the Development of the Socialist World System," *Kommunist,* August, 1962, p. 19.

10. The present status of Soviet economic aid to North Viet-Nam is not clear. However, there have been reports that, following the failure of the North Vietnamese to sign the test-ban treaty in August, 1963, the Soviet

Union recalled its technicians and cut back economic aid. See Ernst Kux, "Ho Chi Minh Between Moscow and Peking," *Swiss Review of World Affairs,* April, 1964, p. 13.

11. *Pravda,* April 3, 1964.

12. Stanislav Kuzinski, Chairman of the Sejm Commission for Foreign Trade, in the Polish-language weekly publication *Zycie Gospodarcze (Economic Life),* Warsaw, November, 1963. (JPRS Translation on East European Trade No. 141.)

13. Imre Vajda, in the Hungarian-language periodical *Tarsadalmi Szemle (Social Life),* December, 1963, pp. 12–24. (JPRS Translation on East European Trade No. 147.)

14. *Rude pravo,* April 10, 1963. Quoted in the *New York Times,* April 12, 1963.

15. Vajda, *op. cit.*

16. M. Gamarnikov, "Comecon Today," *East Europe,* March, 1964, p. 5.

17. For a detailed account of the Romanian move, see J. F. Brown, "Rumania Out of Line," *Survey,* October, 1963.

18. This has been a frequent theme of Chinese statements in recent years. For example, the report on 1962 in *Peking Review,* January 4, 1963, states: "We must rely on our own efforts to build the country into a powerful socialist state."

19. *Jen Min Jih Pao (People's Daily),* June 17, 1963.

20. For example, *Peking Review,* May 17 and July 12, 1963.

21. For a more detailed analysis, see Robert S. Jaster, "The Defeat of Khrushchev's Plan to Integrate Eastern Europe," *The World Today,* December, 1963.

22. Quoted in Jaster, *op. cit.*

23. *Pravda,* July 28, 1963.

24. *Pravda,* November 20, 1962.

25. N. Suta, in the Romanian-language periodical *Revista de Statistica (Statistical Review)* October, 1963, pp. 46–57. (JPRS Translations on East European Trade No. 142.)

26. On April 3, 1964, Moscow Radio explained the delay in the publication of Suslov's February 14 report by saying, "one fraternal party expressed the wish that the CPSU Central Committee should postpone the publication of reports on the plenum for a time, since they had decided to make another effort to put an end to open polemics."

27. M. Horovitz, in the Romanian-language publication *Probleme Economice (Economic Problems),* December, 1963, pp. 94–103. (JPRS Translations in East European Trade No. 150.)

28. Zbigniew Brzezinski, "Russia and Europe," *Foreign Affairs,* April, 1964, pp. 428–44.

29. Marshall D. Shulman, "The Communist States and Western Integration," *Problems of Communism,* September-October, 1963, p. 48.

30. N. S. Khrushchev, "Vital Questions," *op. cit.,* p. 10.

31. *Pravda,* June 8, 1962.

32. Brzezinski, *op. cit.,* pp. 443–44.

33. Frederic L. Pryor, *The Communist Foreign Trade System* (Cambridge, Mass., 1963). This is an excellent study on which I have depended heavily.

34. Academy of Sciences of the U.S.S.R., *Politische Oekonomie Lehrbuch*

(trans. from the first Russian edition; East Berlin: Dietz, 1955), p. 584; quoted in Pryor, *op. cit.*

35. Frederic L. Pryor, "Foreign Trade Theory in the Communist Bloc," *Soviet Studies,* July, 1961, p. 41.

36. Vajda, *op. cit.*

37. *Ibid.*

38. *Pravda,* June 17, 1962.

39. Pryor, *The Communist Foreign Trade Systems,* p. 131.

40. Pryor, "Foreign Trade Theory in the Communist Bloc," *op. cit.,* p. 57.

41. Vajda states that "in recent years the share of CEMA countries in world trade did not increase, while the share of . . . the Common Market . . . grew at a fast rate. We must conclude that market integration . . . progressed there at a faster rate." Vajda, *op. cit.*

42. *Ibid.*

43. Piotr Jarosiewicz, "The Council for Mutual Economic Aid—An Instrument of Cooperation Between Socialist Countries," *World Marxist Review,* Canadian Edition, March, 1964, p. 8. See also Zygmunt Karpinski, in the Polish-language periodical *Wiadomosci Narodowego Banku Polskiego* (*News of the Polish National Bank*), April, 1963, pp. 167–69. (JPRS Translations on East European Trade No. 115.)

Chapter 12. The Communist States and the West

1. George F. Kennan, "Polycentrism and Western Policy," *Foreign Affairs,* January, 1964, p. 171.

2. *Jen Min Jih Pao* (*People's Daily*), September 6, 1963.

3. *Pravda,* April 3, 1964.

4. *Izvestia,* September 21, 1963.

5. *Peking Review,* February 7, 1964, p. 19.

6. *Ibid.,* March 20, 1964, p. 21.

7. For a penetrating discussion of the "generic peculiarities" of Communist ideology aggravating the conflict, see Zbigniew Brzezinski, "Threat and Opportunity in the Communist Schism," *Foreign Affairs,* April, 1963, pp. 513–14; also Donald S. Zagoria, "The Sino-Soviet Conflict and the West," *Foreign Affairs,* October, 1963, pp. 172–73.

8. V. Slavik, N. Freed, and M. Kouvati, "Unity Is the Guarantee of Success," *World Marxist Review, Problems of Peace and Socialism,* Canadian edition. January, 1964, p. 6.

9. "Cementing the Unity of the Communist Movement Is Our Internationalist Duty," *ibid.,* February, 1963, p. 5.

10. For an interesting discussion of the possible impact of changes in the leadership of the Soviet or Chinese Communist Party upon the Sino-Soviet dispute, see John R. Thomas, "Sino-Soviet Relations after Khrushchev and Mao," *Orbis,* Fall, 1963.

11. Philip E. Mosely, "The Chinese-Soviet Rift: Origins and Portents," *Foreign Affairs,* October, 1963, p. 22.

12. The Soviet-Yugoslav *rapprochement* in the mid-1950's indicates that a change in the leadership might have far-reaching effects in bridging the gap between the two quarreling Communist states. However, the subsequent course of Soviet-Yugoslav relations also suggests that the complete healing of a schism and a return to the *status quo ante* would be extremely difficult.

13. *Pravda,* April 3, 1964.

14. *Peking Review,* February 7, 1964, p. 9.

15. The statement was originally used by Mao, at the meeting of the Communist leaders in Moscow in 1957, to describe the preponderance of socialist over capitalist systems; after the eruption of the Sino-Soviet dispute, however, it also acquired strong anti-Russian overtones, which were explicitly noted by the Soviets. See *Pravda,* April 3, 1964.

16. *Pravda,* July 14, 1963.

17. Dean Rusk, "Why We Treat Different Communist Countries Differently," USIS *Text,* February 26, 1964.

18. *The Peking Review,* February 7, 1964, pp. 9–10.

19. Jaime Perez, "The CPSU in the Vanguard of the World Communist Movement," *World Marxist Review, Problems of Peace and Socialism* (Canadian edition), January, 1964, p. 11.

20. *New York Times,* April 4, 1964.

21. For instance in Khrushchev's televised speech of April 12, 1964, *The New York Times,* April 13, 1964.

22. Piotr Jarosiewicz, "The Council for Mutual Economic Aid—An Instrument of Cooperation Between Socialist Countries," *World Marxist Review, Problems of Peace and Socialism* (Canadian edition), June, 1964, p. 3.

23. *Soviet News Bulletin* (Ottawa), November 11–12, 1964.

24. William E. Griffith, "Eastern Europe and World Communism," in Stephen Fisher-Galati (ed.), *Eastern Europe in the Sixties* (New York, 1963), p. 208.

25. Wolfgang Leonhard, "A World in Disarray," *Problems of Communism,* March-April, 1964, p. 26.

26. Chung Ho, "Triumph of the Bandung Spirit," *Peking Review,* April 16, 1964, p. 6.

27. *New York Times,* February 21, 1964. The Chinese plans to create an "intermediate zone" were explicitly acknowledged by the Russians. See *Pravda,* April 3, 1964.

28. *Zeri i Popullit,* January 9, 1962.

29. "Cementing Unity . . . ," *op. cit.*

30. For a penetrating discussion of the decay of Communism's universalism under the impact of Sino-Soviet schism, see Denis Healey, "Ideology and Foreign Policy," *Survey,* January, 1964, pp. 17–18.

31. Brzezinski, *op. cit.,* p. 525.

32. *New York Times,* February 22, 1964.

33. *Ibid.,* April 5, 1964.

34. Letter to the Editor, *New York Times,* January 24, 1964. For a stimulating discussion of French foreign policy in Europe, see George Liska, *Europe Ascendant: The International Politics of Unification* (Baltimore, Md., 1964); and Zbigniew Brzezinski, "Russia and Europe," *Foreign Affairs,* April, 1964; Al. Kawalkowski, "Pour une Europe indépendante et réunifée," *Politique étrangère,* No. 3, 1963.

Notes on the Contributors

ADAM BROMKE is Associate Professor of Political Science and Chairman of the Soviet Studies Programme at Carleton University.

J. F. BROWN, history graduate of Manchester University and former Research Fellow at the University of Michigan, is preparing a book on Eastern Europe.

MELVIN CROAN, Assistant Professor of Government and Director of the Regional Studies Program on the Soviet Union at Harvard University, contributed to the volumes on *Revisionism* and *Polycentrism* and is the author of a forthcoming study of the East German regime.

MILORAD M. DRACHKOVITCH is a Senior Researcher at the Hoover Institution, Stanford University.

M. K. DZIEWANOWSKI, Professor of History at Boston College, is the author of *The Communist Party of Poland*.

WILLIAM E. GRIFFITH, Professor at the Fletcher School of Law and Diplomacy at Tufts University and Director of the International Communism Project at the Center for International Studies, Massachusetts Institute of Technology, is the author of *The Sino-Soviet Rift*.

PAUL F. LANGER, of the Social Science Department of the Rand Corporation, is the author of several books on Communism in Asia, including *The Red Flag in Japan*.

C. IAN LUMSDEN specialized in Hispanic studies at Stanford University; at present he is a Teaching Fellow in the Department of Political Economy at the University of Toronto.

PHILIP E. MOSELY is Director of the European Institute and Associate Dean of the Faculty of International Affairs at Columbia University.

Among his published works are *The Kremlin in World Politics,* and *The Soviet Union, 1922–1962* of which he was the editor.

H. GORDON SKILLING is Professor of Political Economy and Director of the Centre for Russian and East European Studies at the University of Toronto.

JOHN W. STRONG is Assistant Professor of History at Carleton University.

PHILIP E. UREN is a member of the Defence Research Board staff in Ottawa and a lecturer in Geography at Carleton University.

FERENC A. VALI, Professor of Government at the University of Massachusetts, is the author of *Rift and Revolt in Hungary*.

Index

Ackermann, Anton, 133
Africa, 12, 80, 93, 197, 234
Albania, 44, 50–51, 53, 64, 91–93, 94, 97, 104, 107, 111, 127, 128, 145, 152, 159, 160, 178, 189, 204, 205, 226, 232, 235, 236
Albanian Communist Party, 63, 74, 92, 183, 190, 192, 228, 235; Fourth Congress of, 62, 63
Albanian Workers' Party, *see* Albanian Communist Party
Alliance for Progress, 177
American Communist Party, 227
Amur River, 46
Amur Valley, 23
Anti-Comintern Pact, 34
Argentina, 167
Argentine Communist Party, 175
Australian Communist Party, 227
Austria, 148
Autumn Harvest Rebellion, 30
Axen, Hermann, 129
Ayub Khan, Muhammad, 238

Bacilek, Karol, 90, 95, 96, 100
Barak, Rudolf, 95–96

Barladeanu, Alexandra, 109
Batista, Fulgencio, 165, 166
Batu Khan, 22, 41
Bay of Pigs, 169
Belgium, 110
Belgrade, 82, 88, 181, 191, 192, 193
Benes, Eduard, 88, 103
Beria, Lavrenti P., 134
Berlin, 18, 37, 93, 104, 234; East, 111, 129; West, 15, 63
Berlin Wall, 126, 131, 136, 138
Bessarabia, 107
Bierut, Boleslaw, 66, 119
Biszku, Bela, 79
Blagoev, Dimitar, 118
Bolívar, Simón, 172
Bolivia, 177
Bolshevik Revolution, 22, 25, 144, 161, 184, 222–23, 233
Borodin, Mikhail, 28, 29
Boxer Rebellion, 24
Bratislava, 99, 101
Brazilian Communist Party, 175, 227
Brezhnev, Leonid I., 191, 230
British Commonwealth, 116
Brown, J. F., 208

Brzezinski, Zbigniew, 209, 211, 237–38

Bucharest, 49, 50, 60, 61, 88, 113, 119, 127, 150, 228

Budapest, 76, 81, 82, 88, 97

Bukovina, Northern, 107

Bulganin, Nikolai A., 39, 142

Bulgaria, 94, 96, 98, 106, 117–25, 191, 208, 215, 226, 239

Bulgarian Communist Party, 117–25 *passim*, 183; Seventh Congress of, 120, 185–86; Eighth Congress of, 122, 123, 124

Burma, 158

Buryat A.S.S.R., 141, 143

Cambodia, 158

Canton, 26, 30

Canton Commune Government, 30

Castro, Fidel, 53, 54, 154, 160, 164–78

Castro, Raúl, 169

CCP, *see* Chinese Communist Party

CEMA, *see* Council for Economic Mutual Assistance

CENTO, *see* Central Treaty Organization

Central Dispatch Administration, 215

Central Intelligence Agency, U.S., 167

Central Treaty Organization (CENTO), 221, 238

Chang Hsueh-liang, 32, 34

Changsha, 31

Ch'en Tu-hsui, 29

Chen Yi, 234

Chervenkov, Vulko, 96, 119–20, 122, 123

Chiang K'ai-shek, 27–29, 32–34, 35, 36, 37, 238

Chilean Communist Party, 175–76

China, People's Republic of, *passim*

China, Republic of, 25, 27–33, 34, 35–36, 37, 41, 46, 220, 237, 238; *see also* Taiwan

Chinese Communist Party (CCP), 22, 25, 26–36, 37, 41, 61, 76, 127, 161, 181, 182, 188, 190, 192, 222, 230, and *passim;* Third Congress of, 26; Eighth Congress of, 182

Ch'ing Dynasty, 23

Chisinevschi, Josif, 114

Choi Yong-kun, 153

Choibalsan, Khorloin, 144, 145

Chollima movement, *see* "Flying Horse" movement

Chou En-lai, 34, 46, 50, 61, 159, 183, 222–23

Ch'u Chi'iu-pai, 29

Chu Teh, 31, 33

Chung Kuo, 42

Clementis, Vladimir, 89, 96

Codovilla, Victorio, 175

Colombia, 174, 175

Colombian Communist Party, 175

COMECON, *see* Council for Economic Mutual Assistance

Cominform, 179–80, 182, 185, 186

Comintern, 26, 34, 35, 45, 50, 88, 97, 118, 119, 157, 179, 225, 229, 231, and *passim*

Common Market (European), 52, 58–59, 196–97, 207, 209–10, 211–12, 216

Communist Party of the Soviet Union (CPSU), 8–9, 15, 22, 25, 29, 34, 40, 41, 87, 89, 91, 94, 128, 129, 134–35, 147, 161, 174, 181, 183, 184, 186, 188, 190, 191, 192, 222, 224, 228, 229, and *passim;* Nineteenth Congress of, 180–81; Twentieth Congress of, 40, 47, 99, 120, 134, 145, 146, 168, 175, 181–82, 193; Twenty-first Congress of, 145, 146, 187, 188; Twenty-second Congress of, 9, 50, 64, 71–72, 92, 94, 96, 97, 98, 110, 113–14, 122–23, 124, 128, 129, 130, 134, 137, 145, 152, 159, 190

Congress of Women of America, 173

Constantinescu, Miron, 114

Corvalan, Luis, 175–76

Council for Economic Mutual Assistance (CEMA), 14, 52, 54, 59, 109–11, 115, 116, 117, 148, 153, 177, 196, 204, 206, 207–8, 209, 210, 211, 212, 213, 214–16, 221, 226, 227, 230, 235

CPC, *see* Czechoslovak Communist Party

CPSU, *see* Communist Party of the Soviet Union

CPY, *see* League of Yugoslav Communists
Cracow, 61
Cuba, 17, 41, 53, 55, 154, 164–78, 200, 221, 226, 227, 232, 234
Cuban Communist Party, *see* Partido Socialista Popular
Cuban crisis, 4, 12–13, 18, 52–53, 131, 146, 153, 190, 221, 234
Cyprus, 234
Cyrankiewicz, Jozef, 61
Czechoslovak Communist Party (CPC), 14, 88, 92; Twelfth Congress of, 96–97, 101–2
Czechoslovakia, 59, 68, 78, 87–105, 108, 110, 114, 115, 137, 143, 204, 206, 215, 226, 228

Dahlem, Franz, 133
Damba, D., 142
Danube Valley, 83
Darkhan industrial complex, 143
De Gaulle, Charles, 68–69, 197, 239–40
Dien Bien Phu, 159
Dimitrov, Georgi, 118–19
Djilas, Milovan, 179–80
Dmowski, Roman, 66
Dobrogeanu-Gherea, Constantine, 107
Dolansky, Jaromir, 95
Dominican Republic, 174
Double Ten Revolution, 25

East Berlin, *see* Berlin
East Germany, *see* German Democratic Republic
Egypt, *see* United Arab Republic
Eisenhower, Dwight D., 168, 221
Erhard, Ludwig, 239
Escalante, Anibal, 170

Federal Republic of Germany, 5, 68–69, 93, 197, 221, 232, 239–40
Fierlinger, Zdenek, 95
"Flying Horse" movement, 151
Fojtik, Jan, 93
Formosa, *see* China, Republic of; Taiwan
Fradkin, Ilya, 137
France, 5, 23, 93, 197, 221, 234, 239–40

French Communist Party, 180, 197, 228, 236
Friendship Oil Pipeline, 59, 215

Galati steel complex, 110, 125, 206, 235
Gaston-Marin, Gheorghe, 109, 117
Genghis Khan, 23, 140, 148
German Communist Party (KPD), 134
German Democratic Republic, 15, 68–69, 78, 94, 110, 114, 115, 126–39, 204, 215, 226
German Socialist Unity Party, *see* Socialist Unity Party
Germany: Nazi, 14, 23, 34; Weimar Republic, 134; *see also* Federal Republic of Germany, German Democratic Republic
Gero, Erno, 73, 75
Gheorghiu-Dej, Gheorghe, 108–17, 119, 125, 206
Goldwater, Barry, 45
Gomulka, Wladyslaw, 14, 56, 57, 58, 59, 61, 62–63, 64–65, 66, 67–68, 77, 85, 89, 90, 95, 108, 183–84
Gosnjak, Ivan, 183
Gottwald, Klement, 88–90, 95, 96, 100, 104
Great Britain, 4, 23, 93, 146, 148, 234, 235
"Great Leap Forward," the, 13, 41, 46, 48, 61, 151, 160, 185
Greece, 37, 239
Griffith, William E., 230
Gromyko, Andrei, 191
Guantanamo, 171
Guatemala, 174
Guevara, Ernesto "Che," 169, 172, 174

Hager, Kurt, 128
Harding, Warren G., 4
Hassan II, King, 46
Havana, Second Declaration of, 172, 173
Havemann, Robert, 136, 137, 138
Hendrych, Jiri, 95
Hitler, Adolf, 33, 180
Ho Chi Minh, 157–60, 161–62
Honduras, 174
Hoxha, Enver, 50, 63–64, 92, 130

Humphrey, Hubert H., 187–88
Hunan Province, 26, 30, 31
"Hundred Flowers," the, 41, 47, 151, 160, 183, 185
Hungarian Communist Party, *see* Hungarian Socialist Workers' Party
Hungarian Revolution, 71, 73, 74, 80–81, 90, 134, 182, 231
Hungarian Socialist Workers' Party, 71–79, 82–85; Eighth Congress of, 71–72, 76
Hungary, 14–15, 40, 47, 56, 61, 71–86, 90, 94, 96, 98, 104, 105, 107, 113–14, 119, 124, 137, 213–14, 215, 226, 228, 237
Husak, Gustav, 90, 100
Hysko, Miro, 99

Icelandic Communist Party, 228
Ignat'ev, Nicholas, 23
Ili Valley, 24
Ilychev, Leonid S., 123
India, 5, 17, 41, 46, 47, 49, 52, 145, 160, 173, 190, 220, 233–34, 237, 238
Indian Communist Party, 52, 227
Indochina, 237
Indochinese Communist Party, 158
Indonesia, 5, 17, 197, 234, 239
Indonesian Communist Party, 226
International Association of Democratic Lawyers, 227
International Bank of Economic Cooperation, 213, 214–15, 217
International Communist movement, *see* Comintern
Iraq, 41
Italian Communist Party, 13, 46, 55, 129, 180, 193, 197, 228, 229–30, 231, 236
Italy, 5, 197, 234

Japan, 28, 31–32, 34, 35, 37, 55, 148, 149, 154, 202, 203, 221, 235
John XXIII, Pope, 59–60
Julião, Francisco, 175

Kadar, Janos, 14–15, 67, 72, 74–86, 114, 124
Kaganovich, Lazar M., 91
Kallai, Gyula, 79

K'ang-hsi, Emperor, 23
Karadjordjevo, 82
Karakhan Manifesto, 25, 38
Kardelj, Edvard, 179–80, 183, 188–89
Kashmir, 234
Katowice, 61
Katz, Nathan, 107
Kazakh S.S.R., 24
Kennan, George F., 220
Kennedy, John F., 45, 165, 171, 177
Khvostism, 85
Kiangsi Province, 30, 31, 33
Kim Il-sung, 149, 151, 152, 153, 154–55, 162, 228
Kirilenko, Andrei, 123
Koenig, Franz, Cardinal, 81
Kohler, Bruno, 100
Kolarov, Vassil, 118–19
Kolder, Drahomir, 95
Kopecky, Vaclav, 90, 99
Korea, North, 5, 149–55, 156, 158, 204–5, 207, 226, 228
Korea, South, 152, 154, 155, 237
Korean War, 38–39, 150, 155, 156
Korean Workers' Party, 149–55 *passim*
Kostov, Traicho, 108, 119, 120, 122, 133
Koucky, Vladimir, 93, 97, 100–101
KPD, *see* German Communist Party
Kremikovtsi metallurgical combine, 125
Khrushchev, Nikita S., 9, 10, 11–20, 21, 36, 39, 40–41, 45, 46, 48–50, 51, 52–53, 54, 55, 65, 66, 67, 75, 77, 78, 82, 87–88, 91–92, 94, 97–98, 100, 103, 104, 108, 111, 113, 114, 115–16, 122–23, 124, 127–29, 130–31, 132, 134, 135–36, 139, 142, 145, 146, 150, 151, 152, 153, 154, 159, 160, 161–62, 168–71, 175, 176, 181–96, 204, 206, 207, 208, 209, 210–11, 212, 213, 220–21, 222, 224, 228, 230, 231, 239
Kuomintang, 25, 26–28, 32, 35–36
Kurella, Alfred, 137

Ladakh, 49, 52
Laos, 158, 227, 232

League of Yugoslav Communists (LYC; formerly known as Communist Party of Yugoslavia [CPY]), 14, 82, 152, 179–80, 182, 183, 185, 186–87, 188, 189, 190, 191, 192, 193, 194, 196, 197, 231; Seventh Congress of, 91, 185, 193
Le Duan, 161, 162
Lenart, 95
Lenin, Vladimir I., 6, 18, 19, 25, 26, 36, 41, 42, 44, 60, 72, 117, 146, 188, 195, 209
Leninism, 5–6, 27, 34, 35, 36, 38, 39, 41, 45, 75, 76, 77, 83, 92, 101, 110, 134, 146, 153–54, 164, 170, 172, 180, 185, 186, 188, 189, 191, 192, 194, 195, 208–9, 211, 212, 223, 225, 226, 227, 229, 231, 237
Leonhard, Wolfgang, 232
Li Li-san, 31
Li Ta-chao, 29
Liberman, Evsei, 135
Liska, George, 68–69, 239
Liu Shao-chi, 33, 153, 159, 160–61, 182
Loga-Sowinski, Ignacy, 61
Long March, the, 33–34
Luca, Vasile, 108
Lushan Plenum, 49
LYC, *see* League of Yugoslav Communists

Macedonia, 123
Machado, Gerardo, 166
Malenkov, Georgi M., 39, 91, 180–81
Manchu Dynasty, 23
Manchuria, 24, 31–32, 34, 36–37, 38, 149
Mao Tse-tung, 13, 21, 26–27, 30–31, 32, 33, 34–35, 36, 37, 38, 39–41, 45, 47, 49, 51, 53, 55, 61, 65, 82, 111, 115–16, 127, 142, 146, 150, 151, 153, 154–55, 159, 161, 181, 182, 183–85, 195, 222, 224, 234–35
Marshall Plan, 89
Martí, José, 172
Marx, Karl, 5, 41, 42, 72, 117, 188
Marxism, 5–6, 16, 18, 25, 26, 27, 29, 31, 34, 35, 36, 38, 39, 41, 45, 75, 76, 77, 94, 103, 110, 118, 128,

Marxism (*Cont.*)
134, 146, 153–54, 164, 170, 172, 185, 186, 188, 189, 191, 194, 195, 211, 212, 218, 223, 225, 226, 227, 229, 231, 237
Maurer, Ion Gheorghe, 116, 235
Maxim Gorky Institute, 113
May Fourth Movement, 25
Michael, King, of Romania, 113
Mikoyan, Anastas I., 150, 169
Mindszenty, Jozsef, Cardinal, 73, 81–82
MLF (Multilateral Force), 239
Mnacko, Ladislav, 102
Molotov, Vyacheslav M., 39, 91
Mongolia, Inner, 141, 144, 148
Mongolian People's Republic, 23, 52, 55, 140–48, 150, 155–56, 158, 162, 204, 221, 226
Mongolian People's Revolutionary Party, 141–48 *passim*
Monroe Doctrine, 166
Mosely, Philip E., 224

Nagy, Imre, 74, 75, 77, 79, 85, 90
Nanking Government, 29
Naszkowski, Marian, 59
NATO, *see* North Atlantic Treaty Organization
Nazism, 32; *see also* Germany
Nehru, Jawaharlal, 46, 52, 145–46
Nerchinsk, Treaty of, 23, 24
New Zealand Communist Party, 222, 227
Nicaragua, 174
Nicholas II, Czar, 24
Norden, Albert, 129
Norodom Sihanouk, Prince, 46
North Atlantic Treaty Organization (NATO), 170, 209, 239
Norwegian Communist Party, 228
Novomesky, Ladislav, 90, 96, 100, 105
Novotny, Antonin, 90, 91, 92, 94–95, 96, 97, 99–100, 104, 114, 159
Nowak, Zenon, 62
Nuclear-test-ban treaty, *see* Test-ban treaty

Ochab, Edward, 61
October Revolution, *see* Bolshevik Revolution

Organizaciones Revolucionarias Integradas (Integrated Revolutionary Organizations, Cuba), 170
Outer Mongolia, *see* Mongolian People's Republic

Pakistan, 221, 233–34, 238
Panama Canal Zone, 175
Paraguay, 174
Paris, 168, 221, 235
Park Chung-hee, 152
Partido Socialista Popular (Popular Socialist Party, Cuba), 164–78 *passim*
Pauker, Ana, 108, 114
P'eng Ch'en, 50
P'eng Teh-huai, 33, 49, 150
Perez, Jaime, 229
Peruvian Communist Party, 175
Peter I, the Great, 23
Petofi Circle, 85
Piasecki, Boleslaw, 62
Platt Amendment, 166
Poland, 14, 47, 56–70, 78, 90, 94, 98, 105, 107, 113–14, 119, 134, 137, 143, 183–84, 185, 205, 210, 215–16, 226, 228, 232, 237
Polish Communist Party, *see* Polish United Workers' Party
Polish National Democratic Party, 66
Polish United Workers' Party, 13, 55, 56, 61, 65, 67–68, 85, 129, 229–30; Twelfth Plenum of, 61, 62
Polycentrism, 15, 21, 41, 42, 78, 93, 129, 135, 227, 228, 229, 231–32, 235–36, 237–38
Popovic, Koca, 191
Port Arthur, 24, 38
Prague, 95, 99, 215
Prestes, Luiz Carlos, 175
Pryor, Frederic L., 212, 214

Radulescu, Gogu, 109
Rajk, Laszlo, 108, 133
Rakosi, Matyas, 72–73, 75, 79, 80, 85, 96, 104, 119
Rakovski, Christian G., 118
Rakowski, Mieczyslaw, 63, 64
Rankovic, Aleksandar, 82, 183
Rapacki Plan, 59

Revisionism, 14, 36, 45, 51, 93–94, 123, 136, 152, 153, 160, 176, 185, 186, 187, 188, 189, 190, 192, 195
Roca, Blas, 170
Rodriguez, Carlos Rafael, 170
Roman Catholic Church: in Hungary, 81–82; in Poland, 57, 60, 62
Romania, 14, 54, 56, 70, 83, 94, 97, 104, 106–17, 183, 206–9, 210, 215, 226, 227–28, 235, 237
Romanian Communist Party, 14, 55, 83, 107–17 *passim*, 127, 207–8, 228, 229–30; 1960 Congress of, 60, 61, 110
Rusk, Dean, 228

St. Petersburg, 118
San Martín, José de, 172
Schirdewan-Wollweber-Oelssner group, 133
School Reform Law (Poland), 57
SEATO, *see* Southeast Asia Treaty Organization
SED, *see* Socialist Unity Party
Shanghai, 25, 26, 28, 32
Shehu, Mehmet, 63–64
Shensi Province, 33, 34
Sian, 34, 35
Siberia, 23, 24, 32, 35, 200
Simunek, Oto, 95
Sindermann, Horst, 129
Sinkiang, 24, 46, 52, 222
Siroky, Viliam, 90, 95, 96, 99
Slansky, Rudolf, 89, 90, 94–95, 96, 100
Slovak Journalists, Congress of, 99
Socialist Unity Party (SED), 126–39 *passim;* Sixth Congress of, 128, 129, 131, 134, 135–36
Sofia, 88, 97, 125, 185, 186
Solzhenitsyn, Alexander, 10, 137
Southeast Asia Treaty Organization (SEATO), 221, 238
Soviet Academy of Sciences, 151–52
Soviet Union, *passim*
Soviet Union, Communist Party of the, *see* Communist Party of the Soviet Union
Soviet-Mongolian Friendship Association, 194
Sovroms, 107, 109

Spain, 166
Spanish-American War, 166
Stalin, Josef V., 4, 7, 8, 10, 13, 15, 17, 19, 20, 25, 27–28, 29, 30–31, 32, 34–35, 37, 38, 39, 40, 47, 50–51, 54, 56, 63, 65, 66, 78, 81, 89, 90, 91, 94, 95, 96, 103, 104, 108–9, 114, 119, 132–33, 134, 135, 141, 145, 149, 150, 151, 152, 165, 167, 179–81, 182, 186, 187, 193, 195, 196, 212
Stalingrad, 182
Stalinism, 10, 11, 14, 15, 39, 40, 66, 69, 71, 72, 73, 75, 78, 79, 84, 87, 89, 90, 91–92, 94, 96, 98–100, 103–4, 115, 119, 122–23, 126–27, 132, 133, 134, 136–37, 138, 145, 150, 152, 180, 182, 184, 193, 196, 206, 217, 224
Stambolic, Peter, 183
Stehle, Hansjakob, 62
Stevcek, Pavol, 101–2
Sukarno, 239
Sun Yat-sen, 25, 26, 27
Suslov, Mikhail A., 205
Switzerland, 148

Taiwan, 37, 46, 220, 237, 238
Taskov, Boris, 121–22
Test-ban treaty, 44, 47, 54, 130, 146, 153, 160, 221
Thailand, 158
Thant, U, 81
Tirana, 50, 63, 226
Tito (Josip Broz), 14, 51, 53, 54, 82–83, 89, 122, 145, 158, 160, 162, 180–87, 188, 189, 191, 192–98, 212, 231, 239
Togliatti, Palmiro, 193–94
Tomor-Ochir, 148
Transylvania, 83
Trotsky, Leon, 27–28, 233
Trotskyism, 27, 29, 128, 175, 176, 233
Truong Chinh, 159, 160
Tsankov, Georgi, 123
Tsedenbal, Yumjagiin, 142, 143, 144, 145, 146
Tsend, Laibuzyn, 148
Turkestan, Chinese, 24
Turkey, 239

Ulan Bator, 140, 141, 142, 143, 145, 146, 147, 148
Ulbricht, Walter, 126–28, 129, 130, 131, 132–36, 137–39, 183
Unified Electrical Power System, 215
United Arab Republic, 17, 234
United Nations, 39, 80–81, 148, 150, 189
United States, 4, 47, 52, 69, 74, 81, 82, 86, 93, 117, 146, 149–50, 152, 153–54, 155, 156, 160, 161, 164–78, 181, 185, 186, 194–95, 196, 220–21, 232, 234–35, 238, 239
Uruguayan Communist Party, 175, 229
Ushakov, V. B., 112–13

Vajda, Imre, 205, 206, 213, 217
Vatican, 81–82
Venezuela, 174, 176
Versailles Peace Conference, 25
Veselinov, Jovan, 182
Vienna, 73, 81
Viet-Cong, 156
Viet-Nam, North, 5, 54, 149–50, 154, 155–63, 204, 226, 227, 232
Viet-Nam, South, 156, 157, 161, 227
Vietnamese Workers' Party, 155–63
Vladivostok, 24
Vlahovic Veljko, 189–90
Vo Nguyên Giap, 159
Vukmanovic, Svetozar, 183

Wang Ching-wei, 28–29
Warsaw, 88, 183
Warsaw Treaty Organization, 196, 226, 230
West Berlin, *see* Berlin
West Germany, *see* Federal Republic of Germany
Wilcox, Victor G., 222
Women's International Federation, 227
World Federation of Trade Unions, Congress of the, 60, 61
World Peace Council, 227
Wuhan, 26, 28
Wuhan Government, 28–29

Yangtze Valley, 28
Yenan, 33, 34, 149

Yevtushenko, Yevgeny, 10–11
Yugoslav Communist Party, *see* League of Yugoslav Communists
Yugoslavia, 14, 37, 47–48, 50, 51–52, 53, 57, 59, 61, 62, 63, 82, 88–89, 91, 93, 97, 98, 107, 123, 179–98, 212, 231, 232, 234, 237, 239

Yugov, Anton, 120, 122, 123

Zaisser-Herrnstadt group, 133
Zapotocky, Antonin, 90
Zawieyski, Jerzy, 59
Zhivkov, Todor, 119–20, 122–24, 125